IN WORLD ART THE EGG OF CAULDRON

The Restored Lost Core of Kabbalah and Its Scientific Implications

by

Gary Kent Spain

Restored with the indispensable assistance of Celtic bardic tradition, runes and other ancient alphabets, and the Tarot of Marseilles, which, contrary to current scholarly opinion, is the original and most profoundly esoteric version of tarot.

To
All
Seekers of Knowledge

Preface

Once before I attempted to forge into words an account of this momentous discovery that took decades to fully surface and quite clearly proves we moderns were not the first ever to grasp such things as chemistry and particle physics, nor do we evidently yet possess as coherent a view of matter as did the last civilization (destroyed around the eleventh millennium BCE?), judging by how its remnant—this relic?—fits its physics and chemistry into a model that integrates most other chief areas of human interest: phonetics, physiology, psychology, epistemology, ontology, ethics, alchemy, metallurgy, poetic symbolism, a verifiable view of man's origin, the intricacies of number, and indeed a complete cosmology in both its physical and metaphysical aspects. My apologies for starting with such an involved sentence, but we must cut to the chase.

As I said, I attempted once before to describe this discovery but in so doing used up so much space on scholarly justification for the close kinship between the ancient Celtic and Judaic traditions that I fear readers would have yawned before ever getting to the meat of the matter. It is now clear to me that the end result is so *very* striking (and certainly beyond any ability on my part to fabricate) that it will 'sell itself'. Better to just tell the story of how I pieced back together this ancient model of reality by bringing together artifacts of the ancient traditions surrounding letters in two very striking cultures that valued highly their poet-prophets. And I was fortunate in having stumbled on the meaning of the *Ofanim* (Ezekiel's Wheels) and in being endowed with a wide diversity of interests coupled with a tendency to learn by obsession.

This last was why I left school: I dropped out of college to get an education, something not really possible while having to buy into professors' fixation on the current standard model in every field. To fully grasp the new-old model explained herein requires jettisoning much that is generally accepted yet unsubstantiated. Two examples: (1) the popular but poorly supported theory (albeit taught as fact) that humans evolved from a lower creature, rather than devolved from a higher one; and (2) the ubiquitous and frankly *ridiculous* theory (albeit taught as fact) called the 'big bang'. It is helpful also to seriously consider certain maverick theories that are *not* generally accepted even *though* well substantiated, the classic example being EU or electric universe theory: that electromagnetic forces are what generate stars and galaxies, not gravity, a conclusion necessitated by advances in recent decades in understanding how plasma (a gas of charged particles, meaning 99.999% of all visible matter in the heavens) behaves on large scale and small, as explained in Eric J. Lerner's *The Big Bang Never Happened* (see bibliography).

Currently the forces of peer review keep almost any new way of looking at things from gaining a foothold for consideration in academia. Were we to limit ourselves to what is deemed correct by those who dominate human understanding today, we would miss most of the picture, as indeed most do.

Without further ado, then, let us proceed.

G.K.Spain, 1300 Thurs 11 June 2020

Table of Contents

List of Illustrations

INTRODUCTION

I am the black sheep. I love not the flowers.
I love the green of grass and forest firs.
Take back your pillars and your mighty towers.
Give me a tree, that bends when a breeze stirs.

If you attempt to piece together the ancient Hebrew esoteric teachings just from what has survived of them, or the core of Irish and Welsh letter-tradition from its relics alone, you will not glimpse one tenth of the original scope of either. Only by superimposing what has survived of each *on* one another do we find that they are two branches of a single awesome tree: decayed in different ways, they *fill each other's holes*. And that original tree they branched from is firmly rooted in a more uncanny familiarity with, and deeper perspective concerning, disciplines such as chemistry and particle physics than any modern school of thought I am aware of. It is less mathematically detailed perhaps, the physical technology on which it was based having been destroyed ages ago. But it is conceptually more sophisticated, which is what counts.

What technology was this, you ask? We certainly have had little or no word of it from the professors. Nor have we had much even from mavericks: Graham Hancock's writings—most especially *Fingerprints of the Gods*—and a few other sources—to include Giorgio de Santillana and Hertha von Dechend, *Hamlet's Mill*, and Andrew Tomas, *We Are Not the First* (see bibliography)—offer hints that something more was afoot in *very* ancient times than is generally supposed, but essentially whatever civilization's last gasps took place near the end of the last ice age, ninety-nine percent of its traces have vanished from the face of the earth, vast land masses wiped clean by glacial meltings held back at times by ice dams till grown immense. Practically all that remain are Tiahuanaco, the Great Pyramid, and the Sphinx.

There are indications that Tiahuanaco, Bolivia, may be a site of great antiquity, judging by its current distance from the lake it originally sat beside (see Hancock's *Fingerprints of the Gods*, pp. 70*f*), though the imposing modern god Radiocarbon appears to claim otherwise.

The immense age of the Sphinx is obvious just from looking at it: geologists confirm this from the high degree of water erosion, which can only have occurred millennia before the area's current dry climate. The only thing done in Kephren's day, I assure you, was to re-carve the unrecognizable lion's head into that of Pharaoh.

The Great Pyramid is too finely machined to be a mere tomb. One author cautiously reverse engineered it and concluded it was probably a *maser* power plant: Christopher Dunn, *The Giza Power Plant: Technologies of Ancient Egypt* (see bibliography). One inescapable fact is that the 'sarcophagus' (originally a standard of volume measure?) has a place where the saw bit too deep and was backed off: Flinders Petrie noted it had bitten into the quartz of the granite more deeply than into the surrounding feldspar. The only tool we know of that would do that is a sonic drill (Dunn, p. 84).

One artifact of scientific knowhow that predates the modern era is clear referencing of chemical 'elements' (by atomic number) in the trumps of the Tarot of Marseilles (the only true tarot). Two examples should give a clear idea of what I mean. Card XVII L'Etoile (The Star) bears the atomic number of chlorine and shows a nude woman pouring some in her pool. Even more strikingly, it is patently obvious (though it took *me* decades to notice it) that II La Papesse (The Female Pope), whom no-one seems to have ever quite explained, is a Pope who has sucked in some helium (atomic number 2) and it has raised his voice's pitch. All but a few are just that straightforward. Carbon is VI The Lover, since it joins together to form the molecular chains on which organic matter is built; nitrogen, four-fifths of the air, is VII The Chariot, whose driver is the only character among the trumps with wind in his face; neon is X The Wheel of Fortune.

I cannot rule out this referencing of atom-types originating in some kind of clairvoyance. Uncanny reports of long-sightedness in some shamans anthropologists have worked with suggest this possibility. Then there is Harold W. Percival, someone I believe experienced *gnosis* (a great flash of knowledge) nearly a century ago, described at length in his book *Thinking and Destiny* (see bibliography). If one with similar knowledge lived and taught in the medieval or ancient world (within historic times), that might be a possibility: perhaps that Jesus fellow. And yet it is clear that bardic numbering is at least as old as the name Apollōn, as it makes a calendar: A = 1 extra day; P = 7-day week; O = 4-week month of L = 14 x 2 = 28 days; N = 13 of them. To me, Kabbalah's deeper implications seem most likely an artifact of the previous civilization, one that was probably much older and more advanced than us (and note that I did not say *than ours*).

A quick note before we proceed. I do not capitalize zodiac signs, because I treat them as terms, as distinguished from constellations named after them (which are names). That signs are first and foremost parts of the human form is clear from the symbols themselves: rams (aries) butt heads; bulls (taurus) have strong necks; shoulders are twins (gemini); crabs walk sideways (cancer is at right angles to aries); lions (leo) symbolize strong hearts; a virgin (virgo) signifies the womb; and so on. Thus aries the head stands for spring, when things spring up; cancer the breasts blossom out like summer; libra is down, direction leaves and fruit fall; capricorn the mid-spine is winter, nature at her most held back. This round is then projected onto the heavens to mark the sun's positions at equinox and solstice. The constellations are merely the relic of an attempt to stamp this round onto the heavens permanently. (In fact it would appear to have been done incorrectly, since the aries of the moveable zodiac of the stellar heavens is most likely in the direction of constellation Virgo, towards the center of the local galactic cluster.)

Anyway, I do not wish to eat up the reader's time with preliminaries. This book is far from being a rehash of what has already been published on the subject, excepting of course *Sefer Yetzirah* and the *Bahir*. The reason I am the one writing it is an 'accident' of synchronicity that bestowed upon me a peculiar set of varied interests—physics, basic chemistry, history, poetry, mythology, metaphysics, and a focus on ancient alphabets—plus stubbornness born of obsession. I sincerely hope you will find what you learn herein rewarding. My reward is to at last elucidate for others the results of a long, arduous, and utterly exhilarating journey of discovery.

PART

ONE

:

THE

LETTERS

Language

Wind, why do you carry
the pompous chatter of mankind
upon your great highway?
These words that furless mammals
cough into the air
are like some chemist's artificial brew
devised to give false sense of majesty.
We think ourselves worthy of laziness
because we have our tongues
with which to make excuses for ourselves.
Why, wind, must you play
a part in this conspiracy?
Methinks you have no love of laziness,
so why do you blow men's words to me?
You who touch all things,
why do you aid the cause of untouching
and help men send illusions of themselves
across the air?

(circa 1970)

ONE
Tree-Letters and a Bright Yellow Cover

It was the spring (I think) of 1972 and I was in a rather substantial little bookshop in Venice Beach (where Mao's Kitchen now stands). As was then my wont, I was browsing the occult section, my interest being what constituted magic (as opposed to sleight of hand). I have since determined its roots must lie in shamanism: a learned ability to distinguish ordinary reality from non-ordinary reality. But at that time I had not yet established this to my satisfaction. A book with a bright yellow cover caught my attention from the next section to my right, which was the mythology section: it was Robert Graves's *The White Goddess*.[1]

I looked at the table of contents and discovered it had two chapters entitled 'The Tree Alphabet (1)' and 'The Tree Alphabet (2)' (chapters X and XI). This piqued my interest and I purchased the book forthwith. It proved to be an exposition of many specifics of Irish and Welsh bardic (poetico-mythological) lore and how this is linked to traditions of other regions: northern European, Mediterranean, Mesopotamian, Mesoamerican.

At the time, I had already studied what survives of the Jewish Kabbalah enough to notice that the twelve 'simple' letters of the Hebrew *alef-beyt*, assigned—by the very important *Sefer Yetzirah* or 'Book of Formation'—to the zodiac signs in alef-beyt order, bore no resemblance to the parts of the human form their assigned signs symbolized. Also, in that order they showed no coherent phonetic pattern that I could discern. I strongly sensed the order was 'skewed' in this ancient source, and thus in the alef-beyt itself. Nor was there any phonetic sense to how various versions of *Sefer Yetzirah* distributed the seven 'double' letters—beyt-gimel-dalet-kaf-peh-reysh-tav (the six main stops, plus rolled R, a repeated stop)—to the six directions, up-down-east-west-south-north and the 'holy center', where the three axes meet. So in the back of my mind I was on the lookout for clues to rectifying such obvious jumbling of an original correct pattern, no doubt one of those essential bits of ancient lore lost through too much secrecy.

The Tree Alphabet turned out to be a set of thirteen consonants associated with thirteen trees representing *months* of a calendar, plus two *doubled* consonants, Cc (Q) and Ss (St), which shared the months of the consonants they doubled, capped off by a set of five vowels associated with five trees standing for *seasons*, theoretically augmented also by a pair of doubled vowels, Aa and Ii, making twenty-two letters altogether. Examples of vowels as seasons: Ii, mistletoe, dark of the moon, or advent of Yule (winter solstice); A, fir, new moon, a setting forth towards spring with upturned spirits; U, heather, full moon, or summer. Examples of tree-months: the month that includes the sign or point virgo, shared by C (K) hazel and Cc (Q) apple because their harvests coincide in late summer; followed by M, month of vine harvest and celebration ("mm"); then G ivy, fall's Dionysian revels, the month that includes Samhain (Halloween). The vine and ivy here symbolize yoga's *kundalini* or 'serpent power' coiled up at the base of the spine, where their signs libra (loins) and scorpio ('privates') are.

In those two chapters alone I acquired more than I had until then ever hoped to find by way of clues. Admittedly I am a slow and methodical piecer-together of things, so it took still a dozen years or so for me to fully solve to my satisfaction the mystery of the twelve 'simples', the bulk of it making sure which Hebrew letter corresponded to which tree-letter. Then there was the problem of assigning *Sefer Yetzirah*'s seven 'double' letters to their respective extremities, and the remaining three, the 'mothers', to their correct axes, tasks that took much longer. The correct order of the twelve simples on the wheel of the year, coupled with correct placement of the rest in relation to them, each letter assigned its proper *bardic*, rather than Hebrew, number— five of which were secret, yet quite easily surmised—is the key to the whole mystery. Without this key, Kabbalah's core as regards letters remains utterly hidden.

Several things became clear to me immediately. In *Sefer Yetzirah*,[2] the letters shin (our S) and mem (our M), two of what it calls the three 'mothers', were stationed at 'head' and 'belly' respectively, with alef (our A), the remaining 'mother', standing for the torso bridging the two; and in the tree-calendar Graves postulates based on the letter-order of the *bethluisnion* or tree alphabet, S, saille ('SAL-yuh') the willow, is early spring, near aries the head, M, muin the vine, is libra (autumnal equinox), *straight down* from aries (meaning the loins), A, ailm (pronounced 'alev') the silver fir—our 'Christmas tree'—is at capricorn (winter solstice), the spine opposite the heart in the closed or circular zodiac (knees in the broken-and-extended zodiac of astrology), midway between aries and libra.[3] And in *ogham* ('OH-um'), the notched lettering used by Irish Gaels in the Dark Ages, S is even shifted back one in the sequence, placing it *at* aries the head.

Furthermore, *Sefer Yetzirah*'s seven 'double' letters[4] (supposedly so-called because each has a hard and a soft pronunciation)—stops B-P-D-T-G-K and rolled stop R, which Celts roll on the tongue's tip but Hebrew rolls in the throat—the tree-calendar places across the bottom half of the year, from cancer, summer solstice, to capricorn, winter solstice, interrupted only by 'mother' letter M at libra (the autumn equinox). This makes eight letters spread across seven signs, you say: well, there are thirteen tree-months, so R, the last of them, is 'left over', and we relegate it to the center of the circle until it becomes clear what to do with it. The ancient Numidian or Libyan alphabet (table 5), when put in tree-calendar order, starts at B with our sign for the sun— a circle with a dot in the center—but ends at R with an empty circle, awaiting its renewal (a new dot). Clarity on this matter is swift in coming: R's original, proper position is where M is now.

So it was clear from the start that there is a profound link between the Hebrew and Celtic traditions, just as Graves postulated in *The White Goddess* (hereafter referred to as *tWG*). He based this on a host of reasons *other* than the several that strike *me* as most telling. I found no sign Graves had ever even read *Sefer Yetzirah* (hereafter referred to as *SY*). He did not always reveal his sources (unfortunately) or all that he knew. Most odd, I find, was his failure to note that Hebrew yod is suspended above ground, like mistletoe! (Graves mistakenly identifies yod with idho the yew.)[5] This is one of the more telling bits of evidence the two traditions are linked.

Astrologers, I believe, like to place their first 'house' on the eastern horizon when they cast horoscopes (or think of the zodiac). But actually the signs are twelve equidistant spokes of a circle symbolizing the torso when seated in meditation: aries the head points up, the direction spring springs; libra the loins points down, the direction leaves and fruit fall in the fall; cancer the breasts blossom outward, like summer; capricorn, mid-spine, 'held back' like winter, (what builds backbone), or 'weak in the knees', if we take winter as old age, the signs from scorpio on having a secondary aspect wherein they proceed down the legs to the feet—one's privates (called 'secrets' in old almanacs), thighs, knees, ankles, and feet respectively.

The full tree-calendar runs: B-L-N-F-S-H-D-T-C-M-G-P-R. I will refer to C from now on as K, since that is its equivalent in our alphabet. These are: birch-rowan-ash-alder-willow-hawthorn-oak-holly-hazel-vine-ivy-whitten-elder. They tell the story of the Spirit of the Year in symbolic terms (*tWG*, chapter 10). Birch, a birth tree (white bark), declares the Year new-born (at winter solstice). Rowan, which shelters young of other species, shows it being sheltered and schooled. Ash, wood of spear shafts and tool handles, says he is readying for war or toil. Alder surmounts the mire, resistant to moisture as ferry or bridge piling, tree that fixes nitrogen in the soil—the spirit of vegetation (spring equinox). Willow's weeping form symbolizes the fount of spring gushing forth. Hawthorn, also called may, is the flowering hedge of late spring, Maytime. Oak is the tree of the King of the Waxing Year, the oak king, who dies at summer solstice: wood of doors and tree that attracts lightning (sacred to Thor and Zeus).

Holly inaugurates the reign of the King of the Waning Year, the holly king, and with its prickly leaves symbolizes the law of the phalanx, how a multitude of little pricks can equal one big one: through discipline. Hazel is concentrated wisdom, what is 'in a nutshell'. Vine and its successor, ivy, represent the harvest celebration and, in a deeper sense (as the signs libra-scorpio, where the zodiac decides whether to go up the spine to the head or down the legs to the feet), the *kundalini* or serpent power 'coiled at the base of the spine'. Whitten or guelder rose is obscure but apparently an ink-maker's tree (from its dried berries), meaning perhaps the recording of the exploits of the Spirit of the Year. But ogham lettering has in its place Ng, reed, which stands for writing (papyrus) but also for freshly thatched roofs and the arrows of the hunt (late autumn). R, elder, is medicinal, a tree of death (Year's end) guarded by the Elder Mother (a powerful spirit). This is an overview; the meanings go much deeper (briefly summarized in table zero).

In addition to the thirteen consonant-months of the tree-calendar, there are five vowels in both ogham and *bethluisnion* (*tWG*, chapter 11): A, ailm, silver fir, standing for the Yule season and new moon; O, onn, furze, symbol of spring and the waxing moon; U, ura, heather, symbol of summer and the full moon; E, eadhe, aspen, symbol of autumn and the waning moon; I, idho, the yew, symbol of old moon winter—which for Celts began at Samhain (Halloween), that is, *prior* to the Yule season. Graves also postulates two secret doubled vowels—Aa the palm and Ii the mistletoe or loranthus—making a total of twenty-two letters, as in Hebrew.

The first problem was this: if, based on *SY*, we assign whatever turn out to be the tree-letter equivalents of the twelve 'simples' to the twelve signs of the *zodiac of the seated torso*, what do we do with the seven 'doubles', which ostensibly occupy the bottom half of that same round? The key to this rather simple problem is to be found in the nature of Ezekiel's Wheels.

TWO
The *Ofanim* (Ezekiel's Wheels)

Both the earliest specifically Kabbalistic writings (starting in the twelfth century) and those of its more ancient root, *Ma'aseh Merkavah* or Work of the Chariot, take care to make clear they are *not* revealing the inner or secret understanding that makes all intelligible.[6] Today this fact is glossed over, and what *was* put in writing—much of it in later centuries—is presented *as* that understanding. In other words, the inner teachings' loss is not commonly realized. This shipwreck might have begun as early as the transfer-of-focus from Languedoc to Spain in the thirteenth century, no doubt fleeing the Albigensian Crusade and Inquisition. But in the main it must have occurred during the turmoil surrounding Jews' expulsion *from* Spain in 1492.

The vision described in the first chapter of Ezekiel was the conceptual basis of *Ma'aseh Merkavah*. The text describes the *Ofanim* of this vision as 'as it were a wheel within a wheel', there being four in all. Each is described as having four faces: bull, lion, eagle, man. These stand for the four signs astrology incorrectly calls 'fixed': taurus (bull), leo (lion), scorpio (a scorpion, serpent, or eagle, depending on context), and aquarius (water bearer, water pourer). What this means is that each wheel is a zodiac—as opposed to a flying saucer, crop circle, or other geo-electric phenomenon. [That UFOs are geo-electric was empirically demonstrated on ABC's news magazine *20/20* decades ago: the technical term is *luminous display*, generated by seismic pressure on quartz-bearing rock, basically ball lightning endowed by spin with a saucer-like shape, dome on top and bottom, exhibiting erratic patterns of motion, and if approached it grounds off through you with what looks like a ray, whose effect on humans is known to entail time loss and hallucinations, part of every 'abduction' event; crop circles are often accompanied by luminous displays, so they are also obviously geo-electric in character.]

Briefly, before we continue, have you ever wondered why there are *twelve* signs, not, say, ten, or sixteen, or some other number? It is a simple construction on any circle: put a diameter through its center, bisect this, then swing the compass in both directions from each of the four crossing points. But on a symbolic level, the direction the circumference is *heading* at any point is at right angles to where it is from the center, and to actually *get* where it is heading, the round has to *depart* its current position and *approach* the new one. So the signs between each cardinal sign and the next symbolize departing the one and approaching the other.

The only four zodiacal wheels relating to man that I know of that present the aspect of 'as it were a wheel within a wheel' are as follows. Imagine Upright Sentience Itself: what enables a two-legged being of either sex (or no sex) to stand upright. It is sexless, being present in all, and it is drawn by, or to, the point atop the head of the standing form. Taking this point as the hub of the first wheel and the axis of that upright form as its downward-pointing spoke, there turns out to be a second wheel within it, half its height, one that is also centered atop the head, but when seated in meditation. *Being* seated in meditation brings all four wheels into proper alignment; for mortals do not quite embody *in the flesh* that pure Upright Sentience, which is what Kabbalah calls *Adam Qadmon* ('primordial Adam'), to whose Being we aspire and atop Whom the first wheel is centered. Forward on this second wheel is the horizon without (what is before us), and straight back from this is the horizon within (what is behind us).

We already know there is a third wheel inside this second wheel that is precisely half *its* height: the zodiac of the seated torso, symbolizing the yearly cycle (atop which is the center of the second wheel). Finally, within that, and half *its* height, is a fourth, symbolizing the womb; and when a baby rotates from *head up* to *head down* in that wheel, it is about to be born. Each of the wheels has twelve stations or signs, hence faces of bull-lion-eagle-and-man.

This sequence of four symbolic wheels (figure 2) is the only such sequence common to all humankind and is indeed associated with the human form—'the likeness of a man' (Ezekiel 1:5). Why the above has been so difficult for commentators to figure out, I do not know. I did not come across it in any book on Jewish esoteric thought but deduced it from an arrangement of four zodiacs (symbolizing the four worlds) in a book called *Thinking and Destiny*,[7] by Harold W. Percival, to which I am indebted for much else besides. Indeed however strange some of what he stipulates may appear, much, including what seemed very unorthodox at first, has since been verified, at least to my satisfaction, else I would not bring it up. More of Percival later.

You will notice that each of these wheels *except the last* has at least one other wheel in its belly: these are what are meant by the 'three mothers'. Two we can identify with certainty. The mother letter shin, atop the head of the seated torso and shaped like a crown (שׁ), sits at the hub of the second wheel, which it represents. And mother letter alef, perched at half shin's height and shaped (א) like a whirlwind, represents the third wheel, that of the seated torso.

The remaining mother letter (see figure 4, top), whose place in the tree-calendar is the month containing sign libra and whose position according to *SY* might be construed to indicate the fourth wheel or womb, would *seem* to be out of place. Yet there are two forms of mem: the intermediate mem, shaped like a person making obeisance (מ), and mem sofit, shaped more or less like the box containing the Ark of the Covenant (ם). And this final form stands for the first wheel, its place at that wheel's hub, atop the head of Adam Qadmon. Strapping *tefillin* atop the head in prayer is surely in reverent mimicry of this. In the tree-alphabet, mem is muin the vine: Æsop's fable of the sour grapes confirms them being about human height (out of fox's reach).

These four wheels cannot be other than the four worlds of Kabbalah: Atzilut, that of 'emanation(s)' or 'nearness' (to Adam Qadmon); Beri'ah, that of 'creation'; Yetzirah, that of 'formation'; and Asiah, that of 'action' or 'deed'. The first is (to us) the Monad, the whole that contains the rest. The second is our immediate surroundings (creation); the third is one's seated form in those surroundings; the fourth is where physical bodies are made by an *act* of creation.

Let us take a closer look at the second of these wheels, that representing our immediate surroundings (figure 3). Straight ahead from the crown of one's head when seated in meditation is the horizon without. Straight back from that must mean the horizon within, since the horizon *behind* is no longer behind us if we have turned to look at it. (Even in a mirror, what is seen is ahead not behind.) So the wheel straddles inner and outer, ahead (without) being nature matter, behind (within) being intelligent matter, 'matter' that is aware it exists. So the horizon without, meaning the sign cancer on this second wheel, is not one point *on* that horizon but that whole horizon, our focus being one point on it only with the eye; from the mind's viewpoint the outer horizon includes its whole sweep, reflected (on) by an inner horizon as well (its inner analogue), symbolized by, or located at, the second wheel's capricorn, opposite cancer. Our four wheels are symbolic wheels (being permanent), not physical ones. Straight back from the horizon without means back towards *self*, so capricorn ultimately signifies self-knowledge.

The next sign down from cancer, the leo of the second wheel, obviously symbolizes that which approaches within easy earshot. You will notice here also the approach it signifies can be from any direction, which here is true for the ear as well, albeit perhaps slightly more acute when from ahead. Its inner counterpart, sagittary—what approaches within earshot *within*—is thought.

The next sign, virgo, points to what is within reach: what can be reached for and tasted, whose inner counterpart scorpio must mean desire, that which *chooses* what to have within reach (one's 'taste'). Finally, libra, straight down, indicates physical location, that with which one is in surface contact. It stands for *two* of what are normally thought of as 'five' senses, namely touch and smell: smell is really just touch at its most focused, wherein it senses surfaces of individual molecules. From a more discerning viewpoint than that of ordinary science today (which is not difficult, believe me), there are only *four* senses, which correspond to the four 'philosophical' elements: sight is attuned to fire or light; hearing to air or life; taste to water, since things must be in solution to be tasted; and smell or touch is surface contact, alchemical earth, the 'here and now'. On the second wheel, they arrive in their natural order: fire-air-water-earth.

Note that on this wheel of the immediate surroundings the upper half is not manifest to us. We see the bottom halves of things that are *in* the sky, but sky itself is unmanifested. So this second wheel, to *human* perception, resembles a great bowl, not just from horizon to horizon but two complete bowls so to speak, with two rims, outer and inner. This, I strongly suspect, is what was meant by the Holy Grail (or just plain Grail). It has seven stations on it, seven *hekhalot* or palaces, to use the term from Judaic tradition. For the *Beri'ah* world is also called the Throne world,[8] thus confirming its being centered atop the divine Form when *seated* and wearing shin, a crown. This bowl corresponds to the *lower half of the year* (the 'waning' year, of decreasing day length), where the tree-calendar places the seven 'double letters' of *SY*. So the problem of what to do with these once the simples are allotted the third wheel solves itself: they can occupy their calendar stations, but on the Grail or Cauldron. As stated above, placement of R is easily solved, its solution being an important clue to how we mortals ended up in this mess called mortality.

It is the relation between the third and second wheels, between the round of the seated torso and this double 'bowl' of its surroundings inner and outer, that I have affectionately termed the World Egg (us, the human form) in the Cauldron of Art (creation). The Orphic Mysteries, whence comes the World Egg symbol, were most likely privy to much of what is propounded herein. But what will be even more surprising to most is that the fashioners of the Elder Futhark of Germanic runes were as well, which I shall effortlessly prove in chapter 13.

THREE
Mouth (Cauldron) and Tongue (Egg)

A coherent phonetic pattern begins to emerge. The order of letter-months on the bottom side of the year is D-T-K-M-G-P-R-B. But R is the *thirteenth* month, by which time all twelve *signs* have been spoken for; B, next to it, is the first month, at capricorn's winter solstice, where the year begins. So we banish R for the moment to the center of the round, from which, it being obvious the seven doubles occupy the seven stations of the Cauldron, R drops down to libra to replace calendar's M once mem sofit is raised to its proper station as hub of the first wheel. The resulting Cauldron reads: D-T-K-R-G-P-B (figure 4).

Notice R's being down between K and G suggests the Hebrew or French guttural R, not the more flamboyant Scots, Spanish, or Arabic R rolled on tongue's tip, meaning the R of the calendar (on a level with D phonetically). What jumped out at me at this point was the obvious original sequence representing how sounds are arranged in the mouth: P-T-K-R-G-D-B—voiced within, unvoiced without, with P and B up on the *lip* or rim, K-R-G down in the throat, T and D in between. This requires only that D and P trade places. This reversal happens to be a key part of the map the sages who crafted this model left of the Fall, that descent from a higher being or state referenced in both Bible and Kabbalah (and glimpsed by many a shaman[9]). R's desertion of its more proper or humble *original* station, libra (guttural R), to usurp a station higher up in the Cauldron (farther forward in the mouth, i.e. the R rolled on tongue's tip), left a vacancy at libra, the loins. This vacancy was filled by M ("mm")—representing Light, creative power (the ultimate sweetness, so to speak)—from its center atop the head of Adam Qadmon. For as the Monad, the all-containing first wheel, M, sound of the closed mouth (enclosing the apparatus for producing all the other sounds), symbolizes the omnipresent, already present at every station, now evident at libra by default because of R's absence. This is accompanied by the reversal of D and P, the meaning of which will shortly become clear.

The above is buttressed by the five consonants the calendar put on top of the Egg: they are placed as if on the tongue lodged in the mouth formed by the Cauldron and oriented as if incanting towards the sky. That sequence is L-N-F-S-H: they shift *towards*—and in F *beyond*—tongue's tip *voiced* (F can be voiced or unvoiced), then back *unvoiced*. Now F is a fascinating nexus of lore in itself and will serve as our entryway into (1) the finer points of phonetics, (2) how they interface with what is being symbolized, (3) appropriateness of the number symbolism, (4) the tree lore behind it, and (5) apparent schism or division between two disparate traditions.

For F is fearn, the alder, tree of Vran the raven or crow, Bran, god of vegetation—the Corn Spirit, Sir James Frazer would call him. An old common root *vron* would appear to link him to Fro,[10] Scandinavian god of fertility whose totem was the boar (from man's having learned to plow from watching the boar root up the ground with his snout?). Ancient reverence for the alder is well deserved: more than any other tree, it fixes nitrogen in the soil, thus enriching it.

Nitrogen's atomic number is 7, but vegetation itself is our source of oxygen, atomic number 8, the number 8 being assigned by bardic tradition to F, the number 7 to F's 'alter ego' P. And the exquisite appropriateness of this is that F occupies the direction *up* on the zodiac of the human form, oxygen being the only atom-type without which there *is* no up (for us).

I maintain, with solid phonetic footing (or rather heading), that fearn's placement at the top of the Egg symbolizes the Corn Spirit sprouting out *beyond* or *above* the top of the seed or Egg, just as phonetically F is out (up) beyond the tongue's or Egg's tip. The Welsh *Cad Goddeu* or 'Battle of the Trees' references a struggle deposing Bran from some local British shrine,[11] so disagreements must have existed between different branches of letter tradition (and currents of religious lore) that otherwise had much in common. It happens that the Hebrew letter at aries the head—because technically *on*, not *beyond*, tongue's tip—sounded *s*, not *f*, namely samekh. How this conclusion was arrived at I will elucidate below, in the context of how the original order of the simples was determined. Suffice it here to point out that the *bethluisnion* contains *two* letters corresponding to Hebrew peh: peith the whitten, and fearn the alder. Indeed peith was given the very atomic number (7) of the nitrogen which alder as Corn Spirit fixes in the soil.

The letter directly linked to samekh is ngetal the reed, which replaced peith the whitten in that other main branch of Celtic lore, the tree-letters linked to ogham. Ngetal was omitted from the *bethluisnion*, allowing room for it to have two peh-equivalents; and where they were placed shows P's track as it was withdrawn from the Cauldron's outer rim to be replaced there by D: it first went straight back from that outer rim to Egg's aries, where it left its residue in the form of F; then as P it continued on over to the Cauldron's sagittary (to replace ogham Ng).

Consider the two main branches of the tradition we are dealing with that do *not* have two peh-equivalents. In ogham, peh-equivalent F remained at its aries station—out of deference to Vran or Bran, the Corn Spirit—while for Cauldron's sagittary it instead has Ng (sound indicated in Greek by doubled gamma), where it follows G (Cauldron's scorpio). In the Hebrew alef-beyt, on the other hand, it was pegged as phonetically inappropriate (hence heretical?) for F's sound to reside at aries, on the tongue's tip, so they kept the other peh, the one at Cauldron's sagittary, and replaced the one at aries (F, Greek digamma) with a sound that *is* on the tongue's tip, samekh.

Now the actual order of things would more likely have been (and in fact probably was) that Hebrew samekh was replaced by F at aries to express some people's reverence for the Corn Spirit, then later, perhaps in transmission from P-Celts to Q-Celts (Gaels), who had little need for P, replaced the harder peh-equivalent at sagittary with Ng. They may have been allied to users of the Lycian alphabet of southern Asia Minor (see table 10), who also had this letter Ng (ñ)—in its earliest ogham shape (even though not an ogham alphabet). An important consideration here is that ogham *itself* is a much older method of writing than either Graves *or* today's powers-that-be in academia think they have to account for. For *ogam consaine*, the consonants-only form of ogham from which the Lycian form of consonant Ng (ñ) derives, was in use by Scandinavians evidently as far back as the first half of the second millennium BCE, alongside another alphabet called Tifinag.[12] (See tables 5, 6, and 10 [inset].)

FOUR
The Four Actual Elements

Isaac Newton was a practicing alchemist.[13] I would bet most readers are unaware of this. It was in the ensuing century (the eighteenth) that *chemists* gained the upper hand (not entirely a bad thing), but *since* then they, and the physicists, have (without any rational basis) been pooh-poohing the idea of four 'philosophical' elements, an idea so fundamental that without it there is no geometry—and without geometry, no physics. What chemists ended up calling 'elements' are not so by either of the term's accepted (at one time or another) definitions: being indivisible, or being point-like. The fact is by the mid-twentieth century, with the discovery of the pi-meson, whose mass had been predicted (albeit underestimated) by applying the Heisenberg uncertainty principle to the range of the strong nuclear force (of which it is the exchange particle), particle physics had firmly established that there are four types of elementary particle: photons (or *spin one* bosons, if you prefer), leptons (electrons and neutrinos), mesons (*spin zero* bosons), and baryons (the nucleons, meaning protons and neutrons).

So embarrassed were physicists by this (though I doubt any would have admitted it in public) that they rushed to create a kind of smokescreen to hide the fact, called quark theory. This grouped baryons and mesons together as *hadrons* via the claim that they are both made up of lesser particles called *quarks*. Photons (quanta of energy) are now considered just one of a larger classification called *spin one bosons*, which includes the hypothetical *gluons* supposed to hold quarks together, as well as the supposedly empirically demonstrated W^+, W^-, and Z bosons, those *very* massive 'exchange particles' (nearly a hundred times the proton's mass) needed (they theorize) to explain the weak force, cause of nuclear decay. This last strikes me as just the form turbulence takes at the subatomic scale, their half-lives being quite short (about 3×10^{-25} second). I am not really qualified to pass judgment on 'electroweak' theory (unifying the electromagnetic and weak forces), but it makes little difference, as spin one bosons are one of the four *original* particle types. I *can* say with certainty that *gluons* are a fiction (see below).

It is ironic physicists ended up having to postulate a fourth type of elementary particle anyway, the so-called spin zero *Higgs* boson (H^0)—just to be able to 'explain' why the W and Z bosons themselves were not massless! This too makes little difference, belonging as it does to another of the original four types. Still, despite the physicists' claim to have discovered all these various bosons, I am skeptical, not of the phenomena they claim to have observed, but of their status as 'particles' rather than mere turbulence phenomena as observed at the incredibly small scale of nuclear decay. For it is *quite* clear the other group of 'particles' they speak of, the six varieties of quark, are not particles at all but what they were originally thought to be, *partons*: articulations *within* (or *of*) mesons and baryons. For there are at least three *extremely* serious problems with quark theory and the tale it tries to tell.

First, it is highly misleading to lump mesons and baryons together as 'hadrons', since they fall into opposite categories of the much more fundamental division between *bosons*, or 'exchange particles' (quanta of force)—which love to gather together in the same energy state (what makes lasers possible)—and *fermions*, or actual particles of matter—which by the Pauli exclusion principle refuse to occupy any energy state already occupied in a given system (such as an atom). Mesons are bosons. Baryons are fermions.

Second, 'quarks' not only *have never been* but *can never be* separated from the baryon or meson of which they are part—which is why they were originally called *partons*. They are mere point-like articulations *within* particles, demonstrated in scattering experiments that show charge is clumped together at more than one location within a meson or baryon. Current thought seems to value *point-like* over *indivisible* in defining 'elementary': I do not.

Third, in order to 'explain' this inability to separate out a quark from its fellows—the phenomenon called 'quark confinement' (or color confinement)—quark theory postulates a force (binding quarks together) that *cannot be overcome by a greater force*. It also is not attenuated by distance, that is, remains constant as distance increases. I am sorry, but a force that cannot be overcome by a greater force—and is not attenuated by distance—is not a force but something of quite a different order. Yes, energy can be extracted from an individual 'quark' (parton); but then where else is energy to come from? Physicists need to return to the concept of *parton*, a discrete location of motion or matter *within* a particle, a *part* of it.

In the physics of the *very ancients* (my term for those who devised this symbol system we are unpeeling) a much more understandable and *logical* model has been set forth. I will explain it and show how I discovered it in chapter 16; but let me here describe it at least briefly. It is a wheel, our Egg, on which the cardinal signs (points) denote the four particle types: the vertical axis is that on which *spin* (quantized angular momentum) is measured and bosons are perched, the horizontal axis that on which *charge* is measured and fermions are perched (see figure 10). By charge is meant the overall electric charge of the aggregate of that type of particle in the cosmos. So the spin one boson is on top, the spin zero boson on the bottom, and spin one-half lepton and baryon halfway up on the right (active) and left (passive) sides, respectively.

Here, I need to convince the average reader how utterly fundamental the four elements are to any understanding of nature. Yes, matter as we observe it occurs in four states: a plasma state (where electro-magnetic forces trump those of turbulence), a gaseous state (where the laws of thermodynamics take over), a liquid state, and a solid state. The four particle types tend to imitate these states: photons are quanta (units) of light or energy; electrons are the atmospheres of atoms; pi mesons (pions) cause cohesion of atomic nuclei (like moisture causing cohesion of dirt into clods); and nucleons are the mass or bulk of atoms and molecules (the dirt itself).

But it goes way deeper. Take geometry—Euclidean please, as we are *not* nineteenth-century madmen who, failing to note Euclid had already *proven* parallel lines, ended up making such constructions as eventually led to belief in 'curved space-time'. Geometry involves four kinds of objects: 'zero dimensional' points; 'one dimensional' lines; 'two dimensional' angles or plane figures; and 'three dimensional' surfaces or solid figures. Beyond 'three dimensions' (in single quotes because Percival suggests a different take on the term *dimensions*, see below), we encroach on higher mathematics, which despite any useful applications is a bit suspect, since it often treats *infinity* as a 'number' even though *infinite* means 'numberless' (the same fallacy as trying to 'divide by zero', albeit not recognized as such).

I believe Percival's concept of *dimensions* more logical than the current scientific one, so I shall briefly expound it then explain why I consider it superior. He says that matter is actually *made up of* point matter, line matter, angle matter, and solid matter[14] (what else *could* it be made up of), making four dimensions[15] (in parentheses are added my possibly flawed interpretations): *presence* (of a point or location); *through-ness* (of a line through space); *in-ness* (capacity of an angle or plane figure to contain); and *on-ness* (capacity of a solid surface to have something *on* it). These are the *elements* as they exist in geometry. Our human perception is limited to *on-ness*: we see only surfaces of things. Even in doing something like using sound waves to probe earth's interior, all that is achieved is some suggestion of where refractive or reflective *surfaces* might possibly explain the results. I consider Percival's take on dimensions much more logical because they are distinct and cannot be mixed together, whereas distinguishing between one axis and another (length versus depth say) is purely arbitrary and can be rotated about at will.

To address the objection (as stated later on) that motion cannot actually be 'smeared out' over a volume (or along a 'string') because then there would be motion at an 'infinite number' of locations—an impossibility, since *infinite* means 'numberless'—I should point out that by 'line matter' I mean an *axis* determined by *direction of motion* (all motions being point-like), not an actual line or line segment; and by 'angle matter' I mean the *radius of curvature* of a direction of motion; and by 'solid matter' I mean the *twisting* of said curvature beyond containment in one plane. Motion's continuity in time thus accounts for matter's fourfold structure and avoids the paradox of motion existing at an 'infinite number' of locations.

The fundamental reason there are four elements is that given the division of things into what determines and what is determined—between active and passive, if you will—there is the purely determinative fire, the predominately determinative air, the predominately determined water, and the purely determined earth. The balanced state would be what alchemists called the *quintessence*, which corresponds to the *soul*, what Thomas Aquinas termed the *substantial form*, for which I will offer (later on) a rigorous definition. The soul is not to be confused, as it usually is, with the conscious self, which is on the intelligent or inner side of things. The soul is of the nature side: it is what binds the four elements together into a single upright living form in which a conscious self can dwell (ultimately balanced, but in our case still seeking that state).

Let us apply this fundamental definition of elements to the circle or round. At aries, the direction from center to circumference is vertical: straight up. At taurus, it is more vertical than horizontal: more up than out. At gemini, it is more horizontal than vertical: more out than up. And at cancer, it is horizontal: straight out. These generate the four elementary triads stipulated in the *Zohar*:[16] fire points north or up, water points south or down, air points east (to our right as we look at the Egg), earth points west (to our left as we look at the Egg). You will notice though that in the astrological arrangement, air-water-earth have been rotated forward one sign (skipping fire). The probable reason for this, plus some intricate coding involving yet a third arrangement of triads, will be dealt with in the context of the twelve simples and their alef-beyt letter order (chapter 19). Here, let us examine this primordial, geometry-dictated arrangement of triads.

Remember how the senses correlate with the first four stations on the Cauldron? The horizon straight out is linked to us by fire's sense, sight; leo by air's sense, hearing; virgo by water's sense, taste (more or less by default, yet correctly, as we shall see); and libra by earth's sense, surface contact (smell-touch). These are the four signs on the Cauldron's outer half, all manifested signs. Hence it seems clear that each element's triad must manifest in the element following: fire's in leo or manifested air; air's in virgo or manifested water; water's in libra or manifested earth; and earth's in cancer or manifested fire. Here the difference between triads and manifested elements is that the degree of activity or passivity determining them is: in the case of each triad, the slope of the radius at its first or determining sign; in the case of manifested elements, the slope of the *circumference* there. The determining radii are in the unmanifested half of the round, while the determining points on the circumference are in the manifested half, all on the nature side. The intelligent side operates by a different (though related) dynamic.

By applying our fundamental definition of elements to geometry, it becomes clear that the balanced state is not itself an element but rather requires the combining of elements. A point is obviously determinative of location along *all three* of any set of three perpendicular axes passing through it. A line is determinative along two—any two but itself. An angle or plane figure is determinative of location only along the axis normal to it (perpendicular to its plane). And a solid surface does not determine one location along *any* three axes passing through it. Passing *through* an angle or solid surface does not of course mean *skimming* it (at one of its vortices or edges), as that would be passing through a point or line, not an angle or solid surface.

To *make* a solid surface requires the *use* of points, lines, and angles. A solid surface, not *itself* determinative along any axis passing through it, contains elements that *are*. A solid surface cannot *exist* without cooperation from the other three elements. If there is to *be* any balanced state between determinative and determined, it must involve this cooperation. Is it clear now why Euclid's treatise on geometry is called the *Elements*?

According to Percival, the cancer radius of the round indicates a line of point matter; the cancer-leo angle an angle of line matter; the leo-virgo angle an angle of angle matter; and the virgo-libra angle an angle of surface matter. This probably explains partons (alias quarks): the line of point matter that is a photon is not discernible as a 'particle' (despite its momentum and quantized nature); an angle of line matter *is*, which accounts for the lepton (electron, neutrino); when an angle of angle matter is added to one of line matter, they manifest as two articulations, the two that make up a meson (called a quark-antiquark pair in today's physics); and when an angle of surface matter is added to one of angle matter and one of line matter, they manifest as three articulations, the three partons (alias quarks) that make up a baryon.

FIVE
A Sequence of Differences

It is time now to delve more deeply into the numbers bardic lore assigned the tree-letters. They are not the same as the numbers assigned letters in *Hebrew*, arguably a later development and certainly not nearly as vital to the first and most important layer of symbolism. Today's literature on the Kabbalah seems to be obsessed with *Gematria* and other techniques that use Hebrew numeration to equate various terms. There is a work by Aryeh Kaplan that claims to reveal secrets for which special approval was given by "the great living masters of Kabbalah,"[17] yet it deals largely with such techniques, including permutations of divine names whose import remains obscure because basic understanding of the letters composing them is no longer extant. A book called *The Greek Qabalah*[18] claims that since Jews may have gotten their numbering of letters from the Greeks (a possibility), Kabbalah is more of a Greek thing: perhaps it would be if that were what Kabbalah actually is. But Gershom Scholem, the greatest scholar of Kabbalah in the twentieth century, said: "As a matter of historical fact, none of these techniques of mystical exegesis [referring to *Gematria*, *Notarikon*, and *Temurah*] can be called Kabbalistic in the strict sense of the word."[19] What use there was of such techniques in the writings of thirteenth- and fourteenth-century Kabbalists he ascribes mainly to the influence of German Hasidim.[20]

We are concerned here with numbers assigned letters in Irish and Welsh poetic tradition. The numerical values assigned tree-letters in medieval Irish literature are given on page 295 of *tWG* and discussed on that and the following page. Confirmation that the same numeration was present also in Wales can be found on page 79 of *Barddas*,[21] a controversial source that will be discussed in greater detail below. These numbers had deep symbolic connection to each letter. For example, beth the birch is 5, standing for our counting the digits of each limb when a child is born; coll the hazel is 9, based on the Nine Hazels of Poetic Art. A sequence of three numbers marking spring's increase—onn the furze, fearn the alder, saille the willow—are 4, 8, and 16. As mentioned earlier, in the god-name Apollōn, the *bardic* numbers (1-7-4-14-14-x-13) formed the tree-calendar: 1 extra day (winter solstice), 7-day weeks, 4-week months of 2 x 14 (28) days, and a 13-month year. And there are *much* deeper layers to this number symbolism.

We will start with the seven doubles and the mother letter mem, none of whose numbers were kept secret (as were those of five of the simples). The tree-calendar sequence of the bottom half of the year (cancer to capricorn), skipping, that is, the month of the sun's death, R, which we banished to the center, is D-T-K-M-G-P-B. Their numbers: 12-11-9-6-10-7-5. Notice anything interesting about this sequence? Their *differences* run: 1-2-3-4-3-2. Progressing on to the only other letter *on* the Cauldron's round, the M at the top of it (mem sofit), takes us to 6 again, and the entire sequence of differences reads: 1-2-3-4-3-2-1.

First, let me make clear the correspondence between the numbers 1 through 4 and the four elements. Obviously it is *signs* 1 through 4 that generate their triads on the round, and signs

1 through 4 of the manifested half (the Cauldron) that are the manifested elements themselves. But also look at geometry: one point is a point, whereof it takes two to determine a line, three not on a line to determine an angle, and at least four not on a plane to determine a solid surface.

Next, consider the intimate interplay between the number of digits (10), and the number of elements: 10 is the sum of 1 through 4 (as immortalized in the *tetraktys* of the Pythagoreans). And, obviously, it is built into the human form: each hand has four fingers (elements) opposed by one thumb (soul or quintessence). In our state before the Fall (an event discussed further in part two, in the context of the Tree of Forms), we perhaps acted on elements and souls through digits of the right hand and received input from them through those of the left. Furthermore, number, when considered in 'base ten', has a structure that is very interesting and *absolutely essential* to the dynamics of this symbol system, and to a more profound understanding of the structure of the periodic table (of atom-types, the chemical 'elements').

In the process of digital summation (reducing any number to a single digit by adding the digits till you get there), 1 through 4 always *add* their value to the end result, 5 through 8 always *subtract* 4 through 1 (respectively) from the end result, and 9 always leaves the result unaltered, always assuming 1 follows 9 (zero or no-thing), that is, circularity. Hence the pattern +1, +2, +3, +4, -4, -3, -2, -1, ±0 is endlessly repeated as an 'undercurrent' in number. Setting aside positive versus negative, the only discrepancy between this and our sequence of differences is that here 4 is repeated. This is also its only discrepancy with valence in the periodic table (hint, hint).

We note that the difference upon departing each level of the Cauldron's manifested half connects it with the element manifested at that level on the nature side. Moreover it suggests that this identification of each *level* with its respective element extends somehow to the intelligent side as well. In other words, whatever is happening (in the manifested half) *within* is acting on a level linked in some way to its (manifested) element *without*. This connects to the idea that fire or light *symbolizes* (self-)knowledge; that air or life (sound) *expresses* thought; and so on.

I should point out that when R—numbered 15—drops down into libra's 'slot' to replace mother letter M at the lowest station of the Cauldron, its digital sum is the same as the number it replaces. I am reminded when I say this just how *non-arbitrary* this numbering system is; but that must wait a bit. I can illustrate it here to a considerable degree just by these tree-letters on the Cauldron, that is, by how number and tree symbolism interact.

Duir the oak is 12, atomic number of magnesium, which burns with highly actinic light used in signal lamps to penetrate heavy fog. Oak's symbolic import centers around its spread: it is royal because it compasses a wide domain and attracts lightning—largely because lightning has a tendency to veer away from its target as it nears the ground and oak has enough spread to still catch it with one of its outer limbs. The link between this outer rim of the Cauldron (the horizon before) and one's sense of sight is illustrated by its trump in the Tarot of Marseilles, XII Le Pendu (The Hanged Man), which shows him ostensibly hanging by one foot, arms akimbo, the other leg crossed behind the one by which he hangs. The inescapable impression is of a man not hanging at all but dancing a jig upside down, which is right on the mark: he is *not* hanging, he is *the inverted image on the back of the eye* (of a man dancing a jig).

Oak is the wood of doors: its Hebrew name, dalet, *means* 'door', and D in the Tifinag writing of bronze age Scandinavia (and later Libya) pictured a doorway (see table 5) and was probably originally named *dyrr* ('door'). It is the first (manifested) sign of the Cauldron and thus is the doorway into manifestation. The line connecting its station to Egg's aries (the head) is roughly the line of sight linking us to the horizon without, our ultimate reach; the D of Egyptian hieroglyphs was a hand gesturing (table 1). And aries, if you recall, is 8, oxygen. Since photons of light are usually generated by combustion or oxidation, and straight forward from it we find the magnesium used in signal lamps, you can see how the *very ancients* managed to encode the association of aries with the photon so that a dullard like me might eventually take note of it.

Next is tinne the holly: 11, sodium. It follows oak to mark the fact that traditionally the oak king, symbolizing the waxing year, is sacrificed or deposed at summer solstice (which his month encompasses), whereupon begins the reign of the holly king or waning year. The reason *sodium* is here is a tale involving simple letters, but it should be noted that oaths are traditionally sealed with salt, and T in ancient Hebrew was an X, signifying one's *mark* (its name in Hebrew): one's obligation. Holly's prickly leaves represent the law of the phalanx: the many little pricks (individual spearmen), by doing their *duty* to each other (maintaining cohesion), add up to one big one. Its trump depicts one's oath: XI Force, a woman manipulating the jaws (roar) of a lion.

Next comes coll the hazel. (Celtic C is always hard, but as our C comes from gamma not kappa, I replace it with K.) Lore surrounding this letter concerns 'Nine Hazels of Poetic Art' and the nine nuts that fell from them into a spring, where an ordinary salmon ate them and gained all knowledge. It was finally caught by the poet Finn Eces (Finn the Seer), who entrusted cooking it to Fionn Mac Cumhail, who was instructed not to partake; but it splattered and burnt his thumb, and inserting thumb in mouth he became a recipient of its knowledge (poetic inspiration), able to access it at any time by inserting thumb in mouth (being reborn as child?). A salmon also figures in the tale of Gwion Bach (the 'proto-Taliesin), being the second shape he transforms into. The nine hazels and the salmon who fed on them also figure in the myth of the origin of the river Boyne. The lore of hazel usually involves a river or spring, hence coll's connection to water.

Its atom-type, fluorine, is one of the more enigmatic on some levels, though ultimately its properties and number symbolism are breathtaking: the electro-chemical reaction between it and hydrogen (alef) is the strongest one known. Its trump, VIIII The Hermit, warns us that fluorine (at least when combined with hydrogen) needs to be kept away from people (dangerous stuff). He carries a lamp: knowledge gotten from the 'salmon of knowledge'. The number of months of human gestation is quite at home here near the womb (what is gathered close).

Mem sofit, that mother of all mothers who is also the bowing supplicant *intermediate* mem here at the foot of the round at libra, is that greatest (in a sense) of all atom-types, carbon. I remember taking biology at my high school (I was reading Thucydides at the time) the summer before I entered tenth grade, my main goal being to learn what distinguished living matter from mere stuff. The answer was clear: it is built upon carbon chains. Carbon loves to combine with *other* carbon atoms to build the elaborate structures that form the basis of all organic molecules.

Its love of others of its kind is shown by its trump, VI The Lover (L'Amoureux). This is muin the vine (whose grapes also form clusters), harvested around the autumn equinox.

Continuing this serpent-like theme, being near the base of the spine where the *kundalini* or 'serpent power' is coiled up waiting to be raised up the spine to the head, the next tree is gort the ivy, symbol of the Dionysian revels.[22] Being desire, from ivy's clinging nature, its atom-type should come as no shock: neon. Being neon, its trump should come as no shock: X The Wheel of Fortune (La Roue de Fortune). Its number signifies the grasping fingers.

Next is peith the whitten or guelder rose, the basis of whose symbolism is that ink can be made from its dried berries (got from *healthbenefitstimes.com* under *guelder rose*): this fits its being the Cauldron's sign standing for thought, as does its square-Hebrew shape, the opened mouth and tongue (כ), suggesting speech. Moreover, Wikipedia says, "[This tree's] symbolic roots can be traced to the Slavic paganism of millennia ago. According to a legend, *kalyna* [viburnum opulus] was associated with the birth of the Universe, the so-called *Fire Trinity*: the Sun, the Moon, and the Star." (It gives a couple of Ukrainian sources for this, one of which is *Lady of Prykarpattia*, in Ukrainian.) This suits P's original station being at Cauldron's cancer (manifested fire), while P trading places with D calls to mind that while the letter and tree of the Germanic thunder god (Thor or Donar) is D the oak (rune *þurisaz*, 'giant', Thor being the giant-slayer), his Slavic and Baltic counterparts, Perun and Perkunas, both start with P. At sagittary, its atom-type is nitrogen (four-fifths of the air), or what conveys the *sound* of thunder or speech, and its trump is VII Le Chariot—thunder as the rumbling of the sky god's chariot.

The last tree—actually the beginning of the calendar, at winter solstice—is beth the birch, which stands for birth, whiteness (light), innocence (what is lily-white); its atom-type is boron, whose ore is borax, a cleanser. This cleansing aspect correlates with the fact that capricorn or self-knowledge is *straight back*, that is, *completely cleansed* of all that is without, all that is of nature. Its number reminds us that the first thing we do when a child is born is count the digits of each limb to make sure there are five. Strangely, with regard to its trump, V The Pope, no-one but I (in discussions at length on a website devoted to the tarot) seemed to see the mother's arm extending into the picture from the right *presenting* her two young twins (the waxing and waning year) to be blessed by the pope, though it really is quite obvious (I suspect there were fixed ideas getting in the way). Most interpretations of this card treat it as a very masculine symbol, when in reality this is B, whose shape is a pregnant torso in profile and which stands (as we shall see) for the female pillar Boaz (of the two doorposts of Solomon's Temple, the other being Jachin, the male pillar or spine). Its Hebrew name (*beyt*) means 'house', as in 'house of' or 'temple of' and as in children being 'about the house'. It does raise the question why exactly this letter standing for the female pillar is way over on the extreme inner or spinal side of the Cauldron. The answer is somewhat involved and relates to the seven pillars of wisdom; but we are not there yet, so the reader will have to be left in suspense a little while longer.

SIX
Enlistment of Allies: The Tarot

Let us now tackle the ticklish problem of the twelve simples. Most of the preceding was clear to me long before I had finished solving the problem of the arrangement of simples in their correct order on the zodiac of the seated torso. This problem was indeed a sticky one.

First of all, the only way to find a one-to-one correspondence between Hebrew letters and tree-letters was to accept Graves's hypothesis of two extra letters that were kept hidden even in the twenty-letter ogham version of the Celtic alphabet, which itself contained two letters which were not part of the eighteen-letter *bethluisnion*. And in the end his hypothesis turned out to be so uncannily correct as to make me suspect Graves was somehow privy to an unbroken line of (oral?) tradition that he did not confess being privy to. This is quite possible, since his father was very learned in the field and for several years president of the Irish Literary Society.

Much skepticism surrounds *tWG*. Much in it I myself disapprove of: too much space is allotted to consideration of numberings *not* used by the bards themselves; and he failed to name his source(s) for the numbering that *was* used by them, which I have had to take on his word alone except for one oblique reference in another controversial source (*Barddas*)[23] to that same numbering having been used also in Wales. Still, the conclusions herein will make more than clear not only the correctness of the numbering he passed on to us but the incalculable value of Graves's revelations, however flawed the instrument: bless his quirky soul! (If you would like to see just how quirky, read his short stories, as they reveal an utterly unique and charming sense of humor; one relates the tale of when he was visited by his friend actress Ava Gardner.)

A second problem is the fact that this now-augmented-to-*twenty-two*-letter version of the tree alphabet contains seven vowels ostensibly, while the Hebrew alef-beyt is said to consist of twenty-two *consonants*. This however turns out to not be a huge problem, for as we know Greek and other versions of essentially the same alphabet identify a set of vowel equivalents and thus pave the way to our not being too shy about postulating the rest. Alef-heh-yod-ayin-vav are, in Greek, alpha-epsilon-iota-omicron-upsilon: that gives us five already. To be clear, vav is also blamed for the letter vau-digamma—our F—indicating once again the presence of that shall-we-say *heresy* wherein the Corn Spirit was invoked by stationing F at aries to represent sprouting of the grain up (out) beyond the seed or tongue: samekh's equivalent was dropped in the western Greek alphabet, where digamma stuck around and became F. Eastern Greek's two other vowels, eta and omega, demand special treatment and do not fulfill the role of completing our tally of seven bardic vowels: eta because it was *not* a vowel in western Greek (where it became our H), and omega because it appears to play a different role altogether, one which indicates that it *was* in a sense (as most scholars believe) a late addition to the Greek alphabet and that even *if* (as Martin Bernal thinks)[24] it was an archaic holdover in its *shape*, it at least was one serving a purpose somewhat transcending the main line of letter-tradition (see chapter on Logos below).

A third problem involved our heretical letter F: where to locate the Hebrew equivalent of ogham letter Ng, which stands in place of the P of the *bethluisnion*. This is actually the simplest to fix, given familiarity with the much earlier Scandinavian form of ogham—*ogam consaine*—in which the vowels were omitted and the third group of five consonants, M-G-Ng-Ss-R, had the lines go *straight* across the central staff, instead of slanted (so that vowels could have them go straight across). This Ng (three lines straight across) is exactly the form of the ancient Hebrew or Canaanite letter samekh, which in the ancient Lycian alphabet (from southern Asia Minor) actually had the phonetic value of ñ (see table 10). Problem solved, though it turns out samekh takes a different place in the sequence than ogham Ng, namely at aries; the ogham-letter that follows it, Ss, is similarly displaced: it doubles S and thus shares S's calendar position, taurus, whereas ogham places it between Ng and R. In the Hebrew scheme, which I take as primary in every sense *except* the fact that its vowels hide behind consonants, samekh replaces peh's softer offshoot F at aries, rather than its harder offshoot P at sagittary, as Ng does.

In order to complete the solving of this puzzle, we must enlist two allies: the Tarot of Marseilles, and the Elder Futhark, the earliest version of Germanic runes. The former of these I have already referenced (mainly in the preceding chapter), and I saw early on that I was digging into what would prove to be the origin of these enigmatic cards: when tree-letters are applied to trumps by their *bardic* numeration, rather than by some permutation of their order in the Hebrew alef-beyt, they fit snugly, in an unforced way (table 11). Just how uncritical are the occultists' attempts to justify their respective approaches is illustrated by the fact that the two main accepted methods of applying Hebrew letters to tarot trumps are to apply them in Hebrew order starting with *The Fool* (Le Mat), the one unnumbered trump, or to apply them in Hebrew order starting with *I The Magician* (Le Bateleur) then choose some arbitrary place along the way to insert The Fool: both schools of 'thought' appear to be quite happy with their results.

With bardic numbering, we already have a letter *specifically assigned* by tradition to 'no number' (The Fool), namely H, huath the hawthorn, which, since it is a *hedge* and is shaped in most alphabets like a section of *fence* correlates naturally with the 'no-thing' or empty space that separates all things. Thus spake (h)eta.

The initial value of this easy fit between tree-letters and Tarot of Marseilles is to give us invaluable help in confirming the numbering of those tree-letters whose numbers have *not* been handed down by tradition, which means all those above 16. Other considerations will determine them for us initially, but it is nice to have them confirmed by their corresponding trumps.

The Tarot of Marseilles is the only version of tarot with any real claim to actually *being* tarot—hence *hands down* the only candidate to be seriously considered as the original version— for many reasons, the main one being that there are details in some trumps that are absolutely essential to their interpretation as symbols (and to their correspondence with tree-letters) that are missing in all other versions. Scholars will try to make you believe that a northern Italian set of paintings closely related to tarot trumps are the original version, or at least that the cards got their start in Italy, simply because we do not have any surviving examples of Tarot of Marseilles that date back as far as that set of paintings or as the early *tarocchi* deck fragments found discarded in wells and cisterns in northern Italy (which would of course be the region of Italy first to acquire them, if they, as I maintain, originated north of the Alps).

To dismiss the paintings first. The Visconti-Sforza version of XI Force shows Hercules *beating the poor lion to death* with a club: it is eminently obvious, to me anyway, that this is a much less sophisticated poetic symbol than that of a woman manipulating the lion's jaws; for the importance of T (tav) as a symbol has to do with limits placed *on* force by duty or responsibility, by one's *oath*, by conscience, not brute force per se. Very important details are missing from the other paintings as well, but I shall leave it at this and not belabor it. As for other early versions, cards which are *block-printed* like the Marseille deck (albeit without color), the Cary sheet of uncut cards, dated possibly to Milan around 1500, shows the *influence* of the Tarot of Marseille but again lacks important details; for instance trump V The Pope contains no reference to twins or mother but merely shows the pontiff and one altar boy.

One variation *is* worth looking at in the Cary sheet: the Magician's table is shaped like a bridge, and A (alef) definitely has the connotation of 'bridge builder' from its bridging shin and mem in *SY*, and from its ultimate identification with the middle of three pillars in the Masonic lodge, representing, according to Percival, "Hiram Abiff, the bridge or bridge builder, between the [other] two."[25] And there is a recurring version of XXI The World in other early finds (from the 1500s) which suggests to me modification by someone or ones *in the know* as to its symbolic significance (location, location, location): it shows a small hamlet viewed as through the round porthole of a jet flying very low (I invented the 'jet' part). So there is some wiggle room in all this, and I do not consider it *completely* settled. Reports of tarot-like decks occur as early as the mid-fifteenth century in Italy, which would force any Provençal origin for tarot back at least that far. Ordinary playing cards were present from the late *fourteenth*, having seemingly come from the Mamelukes originally, from block-printing methods originally brought west by the Mongols.

One key consideration buttresses my belief in a north-of-the-Alps origin, and that is that the various cities of Italy could not even agree on the *order* or *ranking* of the trumps! whereas a lengthy consideration of extant early versions of Tarot of Marseilles on a tarot chat site I once frequented (Eclectic Tarot) came to the conclusion the original trumps were *not even numbered!* (or *titled*), meaning their ranking was so ingrained in players' minds that they did not need to be reminded by having it (or even the titles) printed on the cards themselves. We all came to this conclusion based on the obscuring of parts of the pictures themselves by the numbered titles.

I can much more easily explain a Provençal origin than an Italian one. Though signs of early influx of Arthurian lore *is* found in northern Italy (in the form of wall engravings), it is via the land of the Troubadours that British bardic tradition breached the Continent, riding on the coattails of the 'Matter of Britain'. Tristan's story, for instance, was popular with Troubadours, and earlier affinity between Britain and that region can be discerned in biographies of various 'saints'. Absence of earlier examples of Tarot of Marseilles can be explained on the one hand by block-printed cards being so common that old worn-out decks were just discarded and replaced. And on the other hand, by the strife and oppression that plagued Provence-Languedoc: violent suppression of the Cathar 'heresy'—and collaterally the courtly Troubadour 'scene' flourishing beside it—by the *Albigensian Crusade*, when Pope Innocent III called on the barons of France to crush the heresy, resulting in French annexation. As cards would not have dated clear back to the early thirteenth century, I mainly refer to continued repression by the early Inquisition, which was originally formed for the extermination of the Cathar heresy.[26]

To my untrained eye, the art on the Tarot of Marseilles appears late medieval, rather than Renaissance. The version I personally believe closest to the original in coloration is the Grimaud version (acquired around 1851 from Eugène Martineau), as it is in three-color images and has, for instance, a yellow headdress and throne-back for VIII La Justice, which is fitting for the Corn Spirit. This yellow fully outlines and emphasizes her head, which is this trump's station on the zodiac of the seated torso. The Jodorowsky version, on the other hand, which adds green into the mix, has her yellow crown obscured by other colors, the designer evidently unaware of its deeper (symbolic) significance. Even the earliest extant (mid seventeenth-century) versions of Tarot of Marseilles (Jean Noblet, Jacques Vieville, especially Vieville) appear to be *already* degenerated from the original. I think the original cards were like the Grimaud of today, possibly without the rounded corners and probably without the trumps' names and numbers printed on them.

While scholars do not believe the cards had any esoteric implications to begin with, the very titles of the trumps belie that; I know for a fact that they did. My picture of their origination is as a game, yes, but one embodying symbols evocative to players in a region where Gnostic heresy, and its concomitant wisdom not yet fully eradicated by the Church, still flourished in secret and needed a way to keep the symbols of their faith alive but 'under the radar', to avoid being burned at the stake or tortured by the Inquisition. (It fooled modern scholars, did it not?)

Provence-Languedoc was the region in which Jewish esoteric schools flourished and the Kabbalah originally sprang up to differentiate itself from the earlier Ma'aseh Merkavah or 'Work of the Chariot'. This flowering can only have occurred as a result of the meeting of this Jewish esotericism (already there) with British bardic tradition; they filled each other's holes (having decayed by different routes) to reveal the original, greater teaching, as in my case eight centuries later. The 78-card Tarot of Marseilles embodies the entire world-model of the Kabbalah (from when it was still intact) but couched in Christian Gnostic terms, such as one might expect from the transplantation of early British bardic lore to the Continent. Early British *and* Irish (pre-St. Patrick) Churches were, many agree, rather Gnostic in character, with both direct and indirect (through Gaul) ties to the eastern Mediterranean, and to the Desert Fathers.

At any rate, these cards are an invaluable ally in confirming the structure of the Kabbalah in its twelfth-century inception—its rebirth, if you will, from the remains of Ma'aseh Merkavah.

SEVEN
Enlistment of Allies: The Elder Futhark

The second ally whose help we are enlisting is the oldest version of Germanic runes. This is the alphabet that is closest kin of any to the bardic tree alphabet. Two runes even bore the names of their respective trees, the two that correspond, in fact, to the twin doorposts of Solomon's Temple, Boaz and Jachin: B the birch—named **bairkana* or 'birch twig'—and I the yew—named **eihwaz* or 'yew tree'. Runes' names are scholarly reconstructions based on the names of corresponding letters in the Gothic alphabet of Ulfilas. It is the latter of the above two runes that was the most useful of any of them in unraveling the puzzle of the twelve simples.

Let me begin by specifying the two letters Graves adds to the twenty of ogham. Setting aside his detailed justification (which you can read for yourself in *tWG* and actually *is* somewhat compelling), they are: doubled A (Aa) and doubled I (Ii). Now A is ailm (pronounced 'alev') the silver fir, and its 'double' he also calls ailm, claiming this can also refer to the palm.[27] Now whether this is true or is just one of his mischievous shortcuts (cutting of corners) I know not; but identification with the palm fits the letter's symbolism as pointed to by all the other evidence, so palm it will be. Admittedly he treats all letter-names of the *bethluisnion* as names of trees (based on O'Flaherty's *Ogygia*), whereas modern scholars insist many of the names actually are not tree names, though there is still ample evidence from antiquity *connecting* them to their trees (e.g. the *Book of Ballymote*). This need not trouble us overmuch: the non-tree meanings tend to reinforce the tree meanings, as for example 'earth' for ura the heather (similar to *heath* in English).

The proposed letter Ii he associates with mistletoe[28]—of paramount importance to the *Gallic* druids—and cites the name *ixias* in Greek, which refers to the loranthus, a mistletoe-like 'tree' of the eastern Mediterranean which, it turns out, grows naturally on oaks, unlike mistletoe itself, which presumably the druids *grafted onto* oak (oak-mistletoe being what they preferred). Now mistletoe and loranthus both grow on other trees, not directly out of the soil. Just so—and oddly enough Graves does not seem to have noticed this—there is one Hebrew letter which also is not rooted in the 'soil' (the line on which one writes) but rather in midair, and that is yod (ʾ). Graves claims the name of bardic I, idho (yew), is pronounced 'iodh', pointing to the similarity this bears to the name of Hebrew yod.[29] But idho is *not* yod, as you can see! hence we are faced with the problem of finding its Hebrew equivalent from amongst a group of letters that appear (stubbornly) to be consonants.

Ogham Ss is often labeled Z instead, which is what Graves calls it: he identifies it with Greek zeta—though oddly enough with Hebrew tzaddi,[30] as do I. Its ogham name, however, is straif, the blackthorn, seemingly akin to our word *strife*, and it is traditionally identified as St, not Z. Old English strong stress alliterative verse—*rowing meter* I call it—distinguished St from S. Hebrew has three unvoiced sibilants: samekh, tzaddi, shin. Shin, S, is one of the three mothers, which leaves samekh and tzaddi. Samekh (Greek xi) is most likely the equivalent of ogham Ng, since in ancient Hebrew it had Ng's *ogam consaine* form, and that same form is the sound ñ in Lycian. This leaves tzaddi free to represent ogham Ss or St, it being close to St in sound, an unvoiced whistling *tz* sound—fitting in shape, as it originally depicted a banner seen waving in battle. Once zayin is thus freed, consider the following.

The Elder Futhark has *both* I the yew *and* another front vowel, an Ii if you will, that can clearly be seen to represent mistletoe: *eihwaz* (ᛇ), 'yew tree', and *isa-* (ᛁ), 'ice'. What can this rune 'ice' be if not a picture of an icicle? and icicles hang down from something else (eaves of a roof, for instance). So I take *isa-* to be our 'ixias', mistletoe-loranthus, or bardic Ii. Now, notice the shape of *eihwaz*: ᛇ. If the shape of *isa-* derives from iota, the obvious source of ᛇ is Z (zeta), altered (as is runes' wont) to avoid horizontal strokes that might cut into the grain across which runes were carved when inscribed on their normal medium, wood.

But I settled on zeta or zayin as bardic I or yew (idho) for a better reason than *just* its rune. It turns out that as the initial of *Zeus* (genitive *Dios*) it actually stands for the softening of D *by* I (or *y*) in the Indo-European root *dieus* (Sanskrit *dyaus*), just as English *j* originated as initial *i* and now represents a hard sound (as if from *di-* or *dy-*). Hence I have concluded—and I have seen nothing to challenge this hypothesis except one Greek city that substituted xi (samekh) for zeta in the name Zeus—that bardic I became like our *j* and acquired the hardened sound of Z (originally *dz*) in the Mediterranean region. As we shall see, arraying vowels in phonetic order from "oo" to "ee", with A and I preceding their doubled equivalents Aa and Ii, I (yew)—our Z— actually ends up at the same *sign*, albeit on the Egg, as the original station of D on the Cauldron, the consonantal sound whose corruption corrupted it (so to speak).

The problem, then, stands thus: of the twelve simple letters—heh-vav-zayin-cheyt-teyt-yod-lamedh-nun-samekh-ayin-tzaddi-qof—eleven are completely accounted for by bardic E-U-I-H-?-Ii-L-N-Ng-O-Ss-Kk(Q). This last letter, by the way, shows how ubiquitous the underlying bardic corpus was in the era of the formation of our alphabet: it is quert the apple, whose sound, *qu* in Latin or its Old English equivalent *hw* or modern English equivalent *wh* (sounds linked to interrogative *qu*), is the sound of *biting into* one, and you can easily see that our modern letter (from the Latin) still pictures fruit-with-stem.

So by simple process of elimination we are left with the equation teyt (theta) = Aa. There is no way to make a vowel of teyt, yet this correspondence is unassailable based on shape and on a passage in the book *Bahir* (as well as teyt's shape in Arabic), all of which I will get to shortly. In fact Aa is a dental consonant in *every* alphabet we will be considering *except* the bardic 'root' alphabet we are dealing with here, where it must be treated as the vowel Aa for the indispensible purpose of placement on the zodiac of the seated torso. As for its corresponding to the dental consonant teyt, it is interesting that in Hebrew the word for palm is found in the name *Tamar*, spelled with initial tav, not teyt, yet there are several cases of substitution of one for the other in Semitic roots, so there it is (for what it is worth). Making a dental consonant of Aa has a solid metaphysical basis, as we shall see; but let us turn first to its placement.

EIGHT
Speaking Up vs. Speaking Out

Okay: five of the twelve simples can be firmly placed at their proper signs without any further ado. These are lamedh, nun, tzaddi, cheyt, and qof. Bardic L and N occupy the two months following B the birch (where the year is born), hence lamedh and nun occupy aquarius and pisces respectively. Bardic Ss is the double of S, whose place in the calendar was at taurus in the calendar prior to our labeling it one of the three mothers and giving it aries the head; so tzaddi is at taurus. Bardic Q is K's double, whose station is virgo, so qof is at virgo. Bardic H, hawthorn or may, is at gemini (late spring), which we cede to cheyt. We are left with samekh, plus six of the seven equivalents of bardic vowels—all the vowels except mother letter alef (A).

It occurred to me finally (I am somewhat slow) that if we array the seven bardic vowels in phonetic sequence across the bottom of the Egg (figure 4, bottom) and allow replacement of mother letter alef by simple letter qof at virgo, we obtain a coherent solution to the problem of the ordering of the twelve simples. This presupposes that samekh (Greek xi), the counterpart of ogham 'Ng', is not at Ng's ogham station sagittary, replacing the P of the *bethluisnion*, but rather at head aries, where it replaces the softer version of peh, fearn the alder (F). Since samekh is the only Hebrew letter *shaped* like a head (ס), this is not farfetched. Thus six of seven bardic vowels are stretched across the bottom of the Egg, starting with U and ending with Ii, interrupted only by qof at virgo. This puts summer's vowel ura the heather (U) at summer solstice (cancer); and yuletide's mistletoe (Ii) at winter solstice (capricorn); and vowel of fall eadhe the aspen (E) at mid-autumn's scorpio; winter's vowel idho the yew (I) immediately after it at sagittary—first sign past Samhain (Halloween), where winter was held to begin—leaving one of the seasonal vowels, onn the furze or vowel of spring, out of place at leo or mid-summer. Yet O's being 'out of place' turns out to be a vital key to the underlying Hermetic secret, though the explanation for this must await its proper context.

The beauty of this arrangement is this (figure 4, bottom). Picture the Egg as the inside of the mouth, facing outward towards nature, and each vowel as the column whose base is its month (month starting at its sign). The columns mimic the articulation of said vowels *in* the mouth: Ii and I ('ee') share the shortest column on the far right (within or back), as they contract the throat area at the *back* of the mouth; U ('oo') is the shortest column on the far left (without or ahead), it being the front of the mouth (lips) that contracts; A and Aa ('ah') mark the two middle columns, the tallest ones, the mouth fully open.

Letter Q, the apple, symbolizes fruitfulness. And qof (ק) at virgo pictures a cross-section of the womb, with its two relevant openings, navel and birth canal. So it is clear the interruption of vowels at virgo is from necessity of rebirth. This substitution of Q for A must precipitate the solidification of Aa into dental consonant teyt, from the stamp of the D-T level of air or thought on the solid: this shows the operation of the Law of Thought, wherein physical acts, objects, and events are exteriorizations of thoughts, awaiting their issuers' balancing and dissolving them (as veils obscuring truth). These months lead *to* and *on from* libra, the body, as stops representing birth and death in a sense, twin interruptions of the flow of the vowels.

Only the top five signs of the Egg (plus qof) play the part of Egg-as-tongue in Cauldron-as-mouth *as if facing upward*; the Egg's lower half, the tongue-*root*, is oriented in the rationale of the vowels, *as if facing forward*. Percival, who briefly discussed Kabbalah, said consonants represent the forms through which the vowels as *breaths* act.[31] (How did he know there were vowels in Kabbalah?) Just so, here the consonants of the tree-calendar or 'root' alphabet are phonetically arranged as if the speaker were passively horizontal, *facing the sky*, its vowels as if the speaker were actively vertical, *facing out* (towards nature). Speaking *up* (consonants), versus speaking *out* (vowels).

To further see that vowel sounds shift in the right direction (from "oo" to "ee"), consider vav at cancer. That sign stands for the breasts, what points straight out: to suckle is to pucker as if pronouncing the U, while if you consult table 3 (letter-shapes of ancient Hebrew or Canaanite), you will see that vav bore the shape of a breast pouring fourth milk. In fact, it is the root of the female half of the Great Name (יהוה), as we shall see.

The upshot is that the order of simples on the Egg was originally: samekh-tzaddi-cheyt-vav-ayin-qof-teyt-heh-zayin-yod-lamedh-nun.

Notice that now the shapes of virtually all the simple letters actually *do* fit their stations on the zodiac. The head samekh (ס) is shaped like a head. Shoulders-and-arms gemini or cheyt (ח) is shaped like the shoulders and arms. Backtracking one, taurus the throat as tzaddi has two forms: intermediate tzaddi (צ), which shows the throat while breathing, and tzaddi sofit (ץ), which shows the throat when swallowing. (The shape of ayin will have to wait.) Virgin or womb virgo (pay no attention to astrology on this one), qof (ק), is the womb's side view cross-section. Loins libra or teyt (ט) could perhaps be construed to show a coiled serpent rearing its head—which I relate to the Norse *World-Serpent* or equator, its rune being called 'day'—but see below. Heh's shape (ה) may seem puzzling: I interpret it as the erect male organ reaching across to the female opening. That it occupies this sign is beyond doubt for two reasons. First, it is the letter added to Abram to make Abraham, this to signify the covenant, circumcision: performed on the eighth day of life because it is the eighth sign. Second, its old Hebrew form is a comb, an E facing left with handle, leaning left: Clement of Alexandria said[32] in the Eleusinian Mysteries a woman's comb symbolized the female organ. The terminal filament of the spine at sagittary is pictured in zayin (ז), extending down from the yod that follows, standing for the mid-spine: note to interpret it (standing) as a thigh extending down from knee yod (י) turns things upside down, showing that the primary meaning is the one on the closed, circular zodiac. The spine opposite the shoulders is vividly pictured by the shape of lamedh (ל), the primary meaning of the letter (and word *lemedh*, from the same root as the letter-name) being to teach or learn: a child seen from above moving its arms in learning to walk. Both spine opposite the cervical vertebrae *and* pisces' other meaning, the feet, are portrayed by nun (נ): link between chin and shoulders, or feet seen from above (facing left).

To affix the above picture to a secure foundation (literally), I shall now prove beyond any doubt that teyt is correctly placed at libra (ayin's shape can wait till we have a bit more to go on). When I was studying and classifying meanings of all Semitic roots used in the Old Testament, I used Davidson's (Anglican oriented) *Lexicon* (see bibliography). At one point I noticed that as printed there, mem (מ) and teyt (ט) were hard to tell apart. Then suddenly it dawned on me why: both picture the legs crossed beneath one when seated on the ground! Analyzing them carefully, I realized that ט pictures legs properly crossed in meditation (half or full lotus, in other words), while מ pictures them crossed as one might when just squatting for a moment to visit, with one leg turned out and both knees bending left. This is because teyt is permanently affixed to libra, whereas mem is just 'holding down the fort' for R, whose station it was originally (and will be again), before R got delusions of grandeur and decided to desert that humble station (as guttural R) for a seat at court, so to speak (as the R rolled on the tongue).

Amazingly (as I had read a good portion of it years before), a few years ago I discovered the following passage in the book *Bahir*[33] ('Bright Clarity', published in Provence between 1150 and 1200[34]), p. 31 (§84): "But R. Rahumai said that the belly is like the letter Tet. ¶ He said that it is like a Tet on the inside, while I say that it is like a Mem on the outside." When I read this, my jaw dropped: it was *direct confirmation* that my juggling of the simples was a restoring and not a dislodging, that what I deem to be the original order of simples about the round *was* known in antiquity (or at least the Middle Ages). For by 'belly' it obviously meant 'what you see when you look down' (when seated in meditation). And indeed the wheel that *teyt* is the libra of (Egg) is *within* the wheel at whose libra *mem* is stationed (in the tree calendar), that of the Cauldron. The passage also means, of course, that *mem's* being located there is generally known (from *SY*), whereas *teyt's* being located there is (was) a close secret.

Furthermore, though I find the modern Arabic alphabet much too decayed and simplified in shape to be of help in most cases—often requiring diacritical marks just to tell apart shapes that have grown identical though differing considerably in sound)—*teyt* is a striking exception: it is shaped (ط) like the legs crossed in meditation, seen from the side (facing right).

The reason bardic vowel Aa was a vowel originally will soon become clear. The reason it became a dental consonant in all other versions of the alphabet is because whatever occurs in our physical location (libra, manifested earth) is the exteriorization of some thought that requires balancing (dissolving): thoughts determine physical reality. This is the essence of the Buddha's Wondrous Law: that we are not helpless but can alter destiny from its current path of suffering.

So it is the airy level, that of thought—leo-sagittary of the Cauldron, doubles T and D (before D and P trade places)—that put its stamp on Aa. D is still *thought* even once it travels over to the nature side to show that human thinking, in the spell of the senses, has forsaken the sign sagittary's *approach to self-knowledge* and oriented instead around *other*, around *objects of nature*—attachment to objects outside oneself, which stick to us like so many barnacles, as the Buddha eloquently taught. It would seem incumbent upon us therefore to discover exactly what this self is, as distinct from its 'accretions'.

NINE
The Threefold Self

There is a passage in Plato's *Republic* (book V)[35] of inestimable value in ascertaining precisely what the conscious self is. It tells us there is *that which abides* (translations say 'is' or 'exists'), meaning what is eternal, what time cannot touch (such as relations between numbers); there is *that which abides and abides not*, in other words what has finite duration (thoughts? life forms?); and there is *that which abides not*, what has no duration (the fleeting present instant). He further states that what abides can be known, what abides and abides not can be thought of, but what abides not remains hidden. The reason (which he omits as obvious) is that by the time one turns one's attention to the present instant, it is gone. Poof! Epistemology in a nutshell.

The relatively obvious inference from this is that a conscious self consists of three parts: a *knower*, the part of self cognizant of the eternal; *thinker*, the part of self dealing with what has finite duration; and *doer*, the part of self that must *act in the present instant*. Yet the doer cannot know or even think about the present: it is dark. Only what has duration passing through it can be known or thought of. Hence to act responsibly in the present, the doer must be guided by its thinker and knower. But in the case of human beings, this ideal is not fully realized. For we are estranged from thinker and knower, not by their choice but by ours. The knower still imparts to its doer its sense of identity, the thinker an ability to think (use of three of its minds, see below); but the fallen doer, misled by the senses, thinks sensation can reveal the present instant.

That the fleshly body is distinct from the doer inhabiting it I can attest first hand. For I was fortunate to have the memory surface of when I first entered my body (between one-and-a-half and two), thinking what a new-fangled thing it was I had now to get used to using, compared to my own dimly sensed hoary antiquity. Surfacing of this memory was a delayed side-effect of having taken synthetic mescaline, what Aldous Huxley describes the effects of in *The Doors of Perception*. Although raised as an atheist materialist like my father, since said memory surfaced I have had not the slightest doubt about re-existence.

Add argument to attestation: the conscious identity cannot be *disassembled*. For let us suppose a 'piece' be removed from it: if the piece is not conscious as me, it is mere accretion, not me; if it *is* still conscious as me, how can it be said to have been *removed*? As for where self 'goes' after death, where does the principle embodied in the Pythagorean theorem 'go'?

We only come back as humans, by the way. The explanation for the spark of Light in animals is a bit more involved. A shaman will tell you that each of us has an animal guardian spirit when we are children, else we would never grow up. And evidently certain segments of the psyche get so obsessively attached to the physical that when death occurs they refuse to let go to travel with the rest of the psyche through the after-death states.[36] This is what accounts for the spark in animals; for such 'segments' come in a limited variety of types each fit to animate a particular species of animal (human thinking tends to run in ruts). Insects would appear to be a separate matter: according to Percival they are effluvia that arise from sexual thoughts of the living in some way.[37] I pass this on simply as the best explanation I can give, albeit second hand. I imagine Eastern ideas about being reincarnated as animals are either a distortion over time or else originated as fables created to frighten children into behaving.

The three mothers evoke the three parts of the self: mem the knower, shin the thinker, alef the doer. For the source of the mothers is the Logos: yes, it is a word, *the* Word, whose spelling we shall get into shortly. The thinker, shin being the Cauldron wheel's hub, has seven minds—the Cauldron's seven signs—for the thinking of the three parts. For knower-thinker-and-doer are one, the origin of the Trinity (Father, Holy Spirit, Son). B and P, up on Cauldron's rim, identify the minds of the active and passive aspects of the knower: *selfness*, impressing the self's existence on the eternal; *I-ness*, registering what else exists that is eternal. Below them, D and T identify minds of the thinker's active and passive aspects: *reason*, overseeing the cycling of thoughts a doer creates, even from one life to the next; and *rightness* or conscience, registering when its doer does wrong. Near the bottom, G and K are minds of the doer's active and passive aspects: *desire*, which seeks to control the immediate future; *feeling*, which seeks to interpret the immediate past. R then, straight down (at libra), is the *body-mind*, what links us to the senses, a task R has 'leveraged' into being called 'head' or 'beginning' (*reysh*).

Thinking done through the doer's three minds (G, K, and R) is now ruled by the senses through body-mind R, rather than guided by conscience, T, the thinker's reactive aspect. This explains R's desertion of its original station at libra for the center of the Egg: the body-mind has usurped rulership over the doer's other two minds, those of desire and feeling (G and K). Indeed we see them, in the form of male and female hominids leashed to R's anvil in R's trump, XV The Devil, who has two aspects: the devil itself, of course, but also that 'little devil', meaning a child or offspring—which the Tarot of Marseilles image most resembles—keeping the leashed new parents awake half the night and otherwise dominating their lives. Also, the offspring's first *appearance* is its 'beginning' or 'head' emerging from the birth canal. (Learning that I was *not* the head or beginning in all matters gave me an ulcer when I was eight.)

Based on how the letters' original stations on the Cauldron line up with the zodiac of the torso, it is apparent B and P are on a level with the head, D and T with the thorax, G and K with the abdomen, R with the loins. Based on Percival, self-ness and I-ness (B-P) contact us through pineal and pituitary (rear half); reason and rightness (D-T) through lungs and heart; G or gimel, seat of desire, is the adrenals; K or kaf, seat of feeling, is the kidneys; and R, reysh, seat of the body-mind, is the gonads (for generating new bodies). The Hebrew reysh (ר) shows the male erection and the duct linking it to the gonads. For R's bardic number (15) is the atomic number of phosphorus, and DNA is a series of nucleotides, a nucleotide being "the phosphate derivative of a nucleoside."[38] So phosphorus is the chemical mainstay of chromosomes.

The doubles also double as sense organs, to which they are assigned (in varying ways, from version to version) in *SY*.[39] The main value of this view is to see in one more way how the form of man is governed by the round and its laws: of the sense organs, the one not paired is the tongue, organ of taste; just so, the only elemental triad with *one* sign in the manifested instead of *two* is water. Thus the manifested signs of fire's triad evidently correspond to right and left eye, those of air's to right and left ear, those of earth's to right and left nostril, and libra, the sign Egg and Cauldron (tongue-root and mouth) have in common, to the mouth.

One last note on that passage in Plato: it is the precise logical equivalent of Heisenberg's uncertainty principle, which, stated in terms of energy versus time, says the more you limit the duration over which measurement of an energy state is taken, the less accurate it will be. All Plato lacked was the value of Planck's constant! And it demonstrates the logical *origin* of the uncertainty principle, which is epistemological. Yet this does not have the implication a modern materialist might like, for it proves the epistemological—intelligent matter—has manifestations that are real and substantial (i.e. causative) in nature matter: this is *ontology* in a nutshell.

One can see now the origin of that doctrine—the Trinity, or three-in-one—that caused the Christian religion such trouble over the centuries. In fact the explanation is so utterly simple it is embarrassing that it was ever even controversial, understandable only because of the early loss of Christianity's inner teachings, which were those of the Gnostics, that is, of gnosis.

It is three-in-one because every self, despite the doer's estrangement, is a single self of three distinct parts: ability to grasp the eternal; ability to think about what has finite duration; and ability—nay duty—to act in the present instant, where what it does is judged by conscience (the thinker). Each of us has a conscience, whether we heed it or not. The Son or doer may be estranged from its thinker and knower—"My God, my God, why hast thou forsaken me!"—yet from the perspective of the Father or knower and the Holy Spirit or thinker 'they' are still One.

Terms Kabbalah uses for self's three levels surely originally stood for knower, thinker, and doer: the highest, *neshamah*, must be the knower; the middle, *ruach*, the thinker; the lowest, *nefesh*, the doer. Tradition links the first to the Sefirot Chokhmah-Binah-Da'at, the second with Chesed-Din-Tiferet, the third with Netzach-Hod-Yesod; this would seem to identify *neshamah* as the knower, since Da'at means 'knowledge'. Wikipedia quotes Luria's disciple Chayim Vital as saying: "The *neshamah* shines in the brain in the head of man, the *ruach* is in the heart and the *nephesh* is in the liver, flesh and blood." 'Brain' should be *pineal and pituitary*, 'heart' *heart and lungs*, 'liver' *kidneys and adrenals*, and 'flesh' the *nerves*.

It will be objected by modern Jungians (of which I am one, to an extent) that we have not accounted for the so-called *unconscious*, which many define as an aspect of mind. To the extent that this includes the *supraconscious*,[40] it is accounted for by the doer's (the conscious mind's) estrangement from its thinker and knower. Then there is the '*subconscious*', which, though it interacts with mind, is not mind else it would be consciously registered by one of the three minds of the doer. The 'subconscious' itself—that vast 'shadow' existing in seeming dichotomy with the conscious mind—I think of as the soul or *breath-form* (Percival's term), which is still part of nature. It is roughly what Aristotle and Thomas Aquinas defined as the *substantial form* (of an individual). It is the most evolved being *in* nature (as we shall see) but not part of the conscious self. It will eventually evolve *into* a self but is yet short of that goal. This subject we will return to early in part two, in the context of the Sefirotic Tree, which maps said evolutionary progress and can shed more direct light on it than the letters themselves.

TEN

The Logos

The well known mantra of the East is OM, whose full spelling is AUM. There are traces of this spread across the world. The oldest trace I found (unless Brahmanism is older, which it probably is) is in ancient Egypt. There were only three *single*-sound hieroglyphs, hieroglyphic *letters* if you will, that were birds, though bird signs were otherwise common in Egyptian: they were ' (alef), eagle-like ***Egyptian vulture*** (tool-using bird); ***w***, ***quail chick***; ***m***, ***owl*** (see table 1).

In Greek the Logos would be spelled AΩM (alpha-omega-mu). One is reminded of the expression 'I am the alpha and the omega', which leads to 'mm', sweetness. The A is the doer, the third wheel, operator of the human form; Ω is the thinker or second wheel, our surroundings within and without (what occupies thought); and M is the knower, the first wheel or Monad, a consonant of indefinite duration voiced with mouth closed, symbolizing the all-encompassing.

One trace of the Logos is to be found in the Masonic drama, in the names of the three ruffians Jube*la*, Jube*lo*, and Jube*lum*.[41] A more elucidating indication is the Hindu Trimurti. Percival points out[42] that Brahm*a*-Vishn*u*-Brah*m* correspond to the letters of the Logos, the initial BR standing for the Intelligence (from an original BRAOM). Brahm*a* the Creator (instant of creation), Vishn*u* the preserver (of finite durations that need preserving), and Brah*m*, which becomes (in the Trimurti) Shiva the Destroyer. Well, it *is* the eternal that is still *around* when anything of finite duration gets destroyed. But in delving into Indian alchemy, I stumbled on something that solidifies this correspondence: what distinguishes the followers of Vishnu from the followers of Shiva in Indian practice is that those of Vishnu seek *longevity*, whereas those of Shiva seek *immortality*[43]—it could hardly be clearer than that.

In Polynesia, there are traces of a Libyan presence: inscriptions have been found in New Zealand and elsewhere in the Pacific in an alphabet—Numidian or Maurian (Moorish), whence *Maori?*[44]—used by the Libyan descendents of Sea Peoples who attacked Egypt around 1200 BCE and who settled in Libya after they were defeated, to later become sailors in the Egyptian navy and eventually produce a late dynasty in that country's history.[45] We know from inscriptions this same hardy seafaring people reached the New World via both the Atlantic *and* Pacific in the first millennium BCE,[46] even establishing a culture on the southwestern plateau of North America that lasted into the common era:[47] the Zuñi language is in part descended from Libyo-Egyptian.[48]

Max Freedom Long, in his book *The Huna Code in Religions*, said a living *kahuna* was found among the Berbers of the Atlas Mountains: she was a chieftess.[49] Therein, he describes the Huna teachings of Hawaii, which tell of three selves: a Low Self, answering roughly to what we call the subconscious; a Middle Self, 'the Self that talks'; and a High Self, a personal deity so to speak.[50] The term for this last is Aumakua: Au-makua translates to something like 'utterly trustworthy parental pair';[51] but Aum-akua—an analytical shift intrinsic to the structure of the Hawaiian language[52]—would translate simply as 'AUM-being' or AUM-god'. I interpret the teachings he describes to mean the soul ('subconscious')—the *substantial form* of a material body, according to Thomas Aquinas—the doer (the 'Self that talks'), and the thinker-knower ('utterly trustworthy parental pair'), from which the human doer is estranged. Ostensibly Huna offers a method of remedying that estrangement to some degree, by sacrificing *mana* to the High Self, sending it thither along the *aka* cord,[53] an infinitely stretchable 'cord' connecting us to all that we have touched. This is said to produce truly magical results (of which I have no first-hand knowledge), as in healing, or setting bones.

The grouping of thinker and knower into a pair directly mirrors the doer's reaction to its estrangement: lacking (by its own doing) the clear guidance of its thinker and knower, the doer attempts to substitute its own feeling and desire *for* them. Feeling plays the role of thinker, and desire plays the role of knower. In other words, humans, for the most part, feel rather than think, and desire rather than know. This actually determines the physiological significance of the three mothers, a subject we will get into at the end of chapter 13, by which time we will have a more complete picture of the mothers and just how widespread their influence is.

Another, if slightly oblique, trace of the Logos is the Chinese term *miaou*, which is akin to the Japanese term *myo* (as in *nam myo-ho renge kyo*) and means something like 'mystical': it is simply the Logos with the *m* brought round to the beginning. (The Asians perhaps learned this term from cats.) For the proper pronunciation of the Logos for *us* is not actually 'OM' but rather "ee-ah-oh-um" in a smooth sequence with a slightly nasal tone, the complete spelling for humans being IAΩM, the I standing for the upright body.[54] I am convinced the omission of the initial I when chanting it contributed to Tibetans' loss of their 'ground' or body, Tibet!

The way I describe its pronunciation is this. Smile. Intone this: it sounds as a somewhat nasal 'ee'. Then gradually shift through the entire vowel spectrum, closing with 'mm'. When you do this in a nasal tone, you will notice a 'phase shift' from high to low, which I think is part of its power: from higher frequency to lower, that is, from cycles of shorter duration to those of longer duration. But mere intoning of it without an accompanying mental visualization, say of transmuting from short lived (rhymes with *short knived*) to long lived (or perhaps getting one's country back?), may prove a hollow exercise.

Consider the quite prevalent divine name IAΩ, present in both Orphism and Gnosticism. This is simply the properly pronounced Logos minus the M, perhaps because the M was implied anyway in the nasal tone of its pronunciation (and the closed mouth that naturally caps off the 'oo' sound). The nasal overtone goes from Ng-like through N-like to M-like as one progresses from "ee" through "ah" and "oo" to the final closing of the lips. The name IAΩ conceals a deep-rooted connection between the bardic corpus and alchemy: I, the old moon or vowel of winter, is associated with the color black; A, the new moon or vowel of Yule, is associated with the color white; U, the full moon or vowel of summer, is associated with the color red.[55] IAU translates into black-white-red, signifying the three main stages of alchemy: the Nigredo or blackening, the Albedo or whitening, and the Rubedo or reddening. And sometimes there is a yellow stage in between the white and the red,[56] which would be the yellow-flowered onn or gorse, O.

The scholars of the *nineteenth* century sought to trace the ancient Hebrew-Canaanite alef-beyt *not* from some obscure glyphs called 'proto-Sinaitic', carved in the Sinai by Semitic miners, as is common today (though with little basis),[57] but from early Egyptian *hieratic* (meaning 'of the priesthood'), the more cursive form of Egyptian used on papyrus, specifically from hieratic forms of single-sound signs and, in several cases, of the two-sound signs used in so-called group writing *for* single sounds when transcribing foreign names.[58] In a few cases their reasoning was flawed, but by and large it was a much more fruitful and scholarly approach than today's. I have spent considerable thought and energy attempting to complete their work and feel I have done so (see table 1), the trick being that at least one sound has shifted noticeably (samekh, who else!). But overall, what one ends up with are figures of distinctly similar shape (in most cases, though some are less rounded) *and* almost identical sound.

It is interesting that the hieratic for *'* and *m* (alef and mem) were absorbed into Hebrew, but that for *w* was not; instead, a hieratic form for *š* (*sh*)—the two-sound sign (*š'*) used in group writing, derived from a hieroglyph depicting a *lotus pool*—was adopted and became shin. To offset this subtraction of one of the three single-sound bird signs, two other two-sound signs from group writing were adopted that were bird signs, those for B and T (table 1). And since B and T mark the limits of the thinker's minds *unaffected by the Fall*, this is quite logical.

Interestingly enough, the sign for B was the sign for *b'* (*ba*), the *bird soul* (personality), which is appropriate for the letter standing at the sign of self-knowledge on the Cauldron. The sign for T was from the bird sign showing a *duckling* splashing along in the water, suggestive of a mother overseeing her duckling's learning process, and that is what conscience, the thinker's passive side, does; indeed Sophia the thinker is the ultimate mother figure. There is also lesser Sophia, called *Prunikos* or 'whore',[59] emblematic perhaps of her ability to mold herself to the doer's perverted goals: this may in part explain a substitution of shin for the U of the Logos.

The two doubles for which bird signs were substituted are the two that hold firm while D and P switch places. Switching to the later square-Hebrew letter-shapes for a moment, notice that P's new position as Cauldron's sagittary is right behind yod; so the yod-like tongue inside peh-as-mouth (פ) projects itself onto the Egg at yod or capricorn, thus confirming Egg as tongue. The rest of the peh, the mouth *around* the yod, recalls its sweep from cancer through sagittary— that is, through all the months of the waning year—thus confirming mouth as Cauldron. Could distribution of vowels across the tongue-root be tied to P's swing? The primordial arrangement would surely be the Logos itself: I-A-Ω-M as the four wheels, in ascending order.

The Latin spelling of the Logos, AVM, reveals an affinity between the A of the Logos and the fire triad, and between the U of the Logos and the water triad. Why should this be so? Very simple (figure 6, upper half): the Cauldron's radii pointing to the thinker's two minds, D (at sagittary) and T, intersect the Egg at signs denoting (with libra) the water triad; those pointing to the doer's two minds, G and K, actually form the sides of the Egg's fire triad. The nature side progresses the direction V points, the intelligent side the direction A points: the thinker controls manifestation of thoughts in matter, while the doer controls what is learned from them.

ELEVEN
The Seven Breaths

Now we can tackle what the vowels and their placement represent. Percival called the consonants *forms* and vowels the *breaths* operating through them. What is meant by breaths?

In labeling the meaning of each sign, Percival lists them as follows (starting with aries):[60] consciousness (the ultimate reality); motion; substance (i.e. space); breath; life; form; sex; desire; thought; self-knowledge; conscious sameness; and pure intelligence or abstract will (straight up from desire, but on the unmanifested intelligent side). Ultimately these mark the stations through which every individual must progress, which is where the Sefirot originate; but right now, I just wish to draw the reader's attention to the fourth sign, breath. The sign labeled *breath* is cancer, which points straight ahead, *opposite* the direction of self (self-knowledge): it represents taking-in from without; activity; interaction with *other*—as if taking a breather from oneself.

Now there are fixed wheels, and movable wheels.[61] The fixed wheels are the courses— we know of four so far, those of Ezekiel's vision—and the movable wheels are the clock hands, so to speak, marking the progress of units *around* those courses. Where each unit is focused or working is wherever its aries (consciousness) is currently pointed. The four manifested signs on the nature side are the four manifested elements; so we can surmise that a fire unit would have its aries pointed towards *cancer* of the fixed wheel or world it is in, an air unit towards *leo*, a water unit towards *virgo*, an earth unit towards *libra*. So the *cancer* or *breath* of a fire unit points to libra, that of an air unit to scorpio, that of a water unit to sagittary, and that of an earth unit to capricorn.

This accounts for four of the seven vowels or breaths: Aa the fire breath (palm denotes the phoenix, born in flame); E the air breath (quivering aspen's leaves are stirred by the faintest breeze); I the water breath (yew denotes death and winter, its number that of water); Ii the earth breath (mistletoe being the 'tree' that takes a breather from earth, which it does not touch). The spark-like tiny shape of yod (') expresses well the activity or breath of the one element whose active side is no longer in evidence (remains but a spark). Note that the movable zodiac of each elementary breath expresses the admixture of active-and-passive in its element by how far down manifested nature (the passive side) its aries has progressed, versus how much of the active side of the manifested half is still within *its* manifested half, marked by how far down its cancer or breath is on that side. These breaths represent nature (the senses) usurping the spinal column, which was originally for the use of the Triune Self.

This leaves mother letter A, plus simples O and U. Note these three are the part of the vowel spectrum encompassed by the Logos proper, while the four elementary breaths extend across the other half of the vowel spectrum to initial I. The self for whom the Logos stands is on the intelligent side (being a *conscious* self), the four elements on the nature side. The I of IAΩM is an add-on because I, the body, is of nature, whereas the Logos evokes the self proper. Yet the vowel spectrum from A to U *is* still vowels, meaning breaths. As Percival points out, in addition to the four elementary breaths, there are the three *inner* breaths: the psychic breath (of the doer), the mental breath (of the thinker), and the noetic breath (of the knower).

The doer has undergone the Fall. Its thinker and knower, on the other hand, have not. That is why they can guide the doer eventually to sanity (and why Huna terms them the 'utterly trustworthy parental pair'). Our A is the A of the Logos: each of us intoning it is a doer. But the doer does not in the same way make direct use of the mental and noetic breaths. Yet there *are* two more vowels to account for.

The solution (and this is why I prefer to use omega in spelling the Logos) is that O and U—ayin and vav—are that part of the mental and noetic breaths that are at present *in* the psychic atmosphere or Egg (doer's region of activity). The wheel the Cauldron is the lower half of—the Throne world—maps the thinker's atmosphere; the Monad, wheel whose hub is mem sofit (atop Adam Qadmon's head), maps the knower's atmosphere. These wheels can represent these three atmospheres (in relation to the physical atmosphere or fourth wheel); or they can represent the four worlds of nature acted on *by* those atmospheres; or they can represent an amalgam of *both*, where *within* are self's three parts or atmospheres and *without* are the four worlds.

It is clear that O (ayin) must signify that part of the mental breath that is in the psychic atmosphere, and U (vav) that part of the noetic breath so situated. What little actual knowledge we possess comes from the knower *through* the thinker anyway—which is the O or U (Ω) of the Logos and functions as go-between *between* knower and doer. So it is fitting that the part of the noetic breath to which we have direct access is U or vav, that point in the vowel spectrum where it is just closing off into M, the knower.

O (ayin) is well placed: on the passive side of the mental level, at leo or manifested air, where the thinker as conscience (tav) can be registered. And U (vav) is well placed: the passive side of the noetic level, cancer, light's level, where the doer receives from its knower its sense of identity, of being an individual self (if not yet a fully balanced one, a Triune Self).

Now we can address the subject of ayin's shape (ע). Two considerations recommend it. It resembles the part of a face we watch to determine what a person is thinking: eyes and bridge of nose. And it fits what Percival says[62] about the mental breath in the human: that it has one center in the heart (the stroke at the lower left, echoing that at the lower left of tav, the heart as conscience), plus two centers in the mental atmosphere (part of thinker's atmosphere that is in the doer's atmosphere), which are the two yods hovering above it connected to it by thin lines.

The deeper appropriateness of the above stems from another stipulation of Percival's: that the thinker contacts the body during childhood, as we are in the process of learning; and the knower at puberty.[63] Just so, onn the furze is the vowel of spring and youth, when one is still in school, and ura the heather the vowel of summer and of love's consummation. Now you know the *origin* of the meaning of the verb *to know* 'in the biblical sense'.

TWELVE
The Macrocosmic Hexad

The Ω of the Logos was replaced by mother letter shin in the alef-beyt to indicate that the mental and noetic breaths for the fallen doer are not the same as the sound by which the thinker is evoked in the Logos of a complete, balanced Triune Self, such as we will eventually become. It is saying, "*Shush*, mortal, know your limitations: you are *fallen* Adam, not Adam Qadmon, whom you only *aspire* to be." Adam Qadmon *as an ideal* plays the role of Aristotle's 'Unmoved Mover': every individual mote in the universe is drawn towards that state, *seeks* it ultimately.

This is the only reasonable explanation I can pose for there being any occurrences at all (despite protestations of materialists such as I was when but a lad). The divine Form does not change in the least; it remains the Ideal sought. As a thing of the Monad (object of the knower, of *knowledge*), it is untouchable by time and yet the Mover of all that moves. I have been unable to think up any alternate rational world-view; but you are certainly free to devise your own.

I should point out, as touching on the antiquity or lateness of Greek omega, that the early Egyptian *hieratic* form of **w** (**quail chick**) was virtually identical to Greek *miniscule* omega (ω). (Indeed ancient Hebrew shin is somewhat similar, but with angles instead of curves.) It is quite possible that knowledge of this **w** was preserved in some school amongst the Greeks (the Orphic Mysteries?); its miniscule form entered Greek in the century following Egypt's incorporation into the Greek world by Alexander. It was the *age* of gnosis, that of Pythagoras and Plato that culminated in the brilliance of Archimedes, who even anticipated the methods of the calculus.[64]

As for the singling out of the middle letter of the Logos for special treatment, there *is* something vital which distinguishes it from the other two. First, let me clarify what you surely have already noted: that there is a correspondence between the three parts of the self and the three inner stations of the Cauldron, stations representing minds of the active sides of the three parts. There is a natural division into the four signs on the nature side, representing the four elements delineated by their respective senses—what is seen on the horizon, what approaches within earshot, what is placed within reach (to be tasted), and what is in surface contact with us (the here and now)—versus the three signs leading on from there, culminating in capricorn or self-knowledge (figure 3). (*Gimel* means 'camel', and the great Sufi poet-scholar Ibn 'Arabi said by "full-grown camels" he meant "actions inward and outward.")[65] The reverse of this, then, is expressed on the Egg, the four elemental breaths being stationed at the four signs *starting* with libra: nature's preempting of the spinal column from its original use by the Triune Self.

There are two different *hexads*, or groups of six signs, on the round: one includes the vertical axis, aries-libra, and one includes the horizontal axis, cancer-capricorn. They are labeled male and female respectively in astrology, but this is in error. Male and female more correctly characterize two of the three *tetrads*, or groups of four signs,[66] for a very simple reason: there is also what is *neither* male nor female to account for, Adam Qadmon for instance, represented by the four cardinal signs, the equinoxes and solstices (aries-cancer-libra-capricorn). The tetrad that leans forward from this characterizes the male, that leaning back from it the female—the adult reader should have no trouble seeing why this is the case. Astrologically they are squares, but poetically crosses, symbolizing bodies; and there are three of them. Indeed this is how a Gnostic such as myself interprets the crucifixion story: the Son or doer imprisoned in (nailed to) a body, yes, but the middle one, the one Christ is on, ultimately represents the Adam Qadmon type; for 'He' did not historically 'die on the cross' but had become an embodiment of Uprightness Itself.

The two hexads, on the other hand, refer to what are, clearly, a pair: macrocosm, versus microcosm.[67] The macrocosmic or universal hexad is based on the vertical axis, which extends indefinitely in both directions (going down, it delves into the depths of the earth). The horizontal axis, on the other hand, basis of the microcosmic human hexad, does not actually extend in *either* direction, since the curvature of the earth rapidly renders it no longer horizontal.

There is a sense in which the body is the microcosm relative to the universe as a whole. This stems from the essentially holistic quality of the cosmos, the perspective that the cosmos as a whole is a projection of all the little cosmoses or sets of four wheels that inhabit it. So planets must correspond to individual organs in the body of the universe: the moon is the kidneys, the sun the heart, the stars the nerve endings, this much according to Percival.[68] The ramifications of this can best be treated in the context of the Sefirot of the fourth world or wheel (Asiah). It is a fascinating aspect of Kabbalah, one I am eager to broach; but first things first.

There is also, of course, a sense in which the parts of the self are microcosmic, and the elements of nature macrocosmic.[69] This signals division of the round into macrocosm as *nature* side and microcosm as *intelligent* side. And indeed you can see that the macrocosmic hexad has *four* levels, the microcosmic hexad *three*. But the main point I am leading up to is that one of the three signs representing parts of the self, on the microcosmic or inner side of the round, happens to be on the macrocosmic *hexad*; and this has far reaching ramifications.

Since what manifests as destiny for each doer (if the universe is just) must logically be determined by the thoughts that doer has created, as maintained or preserved (from one lifetime to another) by the thinker, it follows that the thinker's reasoning must be able to take in the 'big picture' if it is going to be able to actually arrange destiny (or karma) so as to both exteriorize its doer's thinking *and* fit that destiny snugly into the general scheme of the destinies of *other* doers living at the same time. That it is able to do this should give you some idea just how poised the thinker actually is, and how great its reach. After all, it did not undergo the Fall, that catastrophe that resulted in, or rather from, the doer trusting the senses alone in navigating the elusive present instant, rather than its thinker and knower.

Those who devised the Elder Futhark (the earliest runes) were quite aware of the different or macrocosmic character of the thinker, as contrasted with the self's other two parts; for they encoded it into the order of the runic sequence, in a way that is unmistakable. And it is to that interesting configuration of letters, based as it is directly on the tree alphabet, that we now turn.

THIRTEEN
Elder Futhark Revisited

I am about to show you something that will come as a complete surprise if you have always thought of the Germanic tribes in Roman times as ignorant barbarians simply because they 'gave as good as they got' in terms of warlike ferocity. The Romans were utterly ruthless themselves, remember, perhaps even more so, for they would often exterminate whole tribes or cities, civilians and all: witness their decimation of the inhabitants of the city of Syracuse, where even though they had orders to spare Archimedes, when soldiers found him he was reputedly so involved in contemplating a problem that he was killed anyway.

The Elder Futhark is usually said to date from somewhere between 200 BCE and 200 CE. There was a much more ancient alphabet used by Low German speakers in Scandinavia in the early Bronze Age, which later became the Tifinag alphabet of the Berbers and Tuaregs of North Africa. These same early Scandinavians also used *ogam consaine*, the consonants-only form of ogham—for example in elaborate inscriptions near Peterborough, Canada, dating *probably* from about 1700 BCE, containing calendar instructions for colonists left there to trade for the copper mined in vast quantities on the north shore of Lake Superior.[70] Poor Wikipedia will never know of such things, because academia polices it to purge it of any of the rich results of the work of the American Epigraphic Society or its founder Barry Fell, and only because his Ph.D. happened to be in another field (Marine Biology, which he taught at Harvard). Furthermore, the prestigious Smithsonian Institute is determined no-one find out Europeans (and others) were here in the New World long before Columbus or even Leif Eriksson: it has even intellectually gesticulated to the extent of branding as forgeries inscriptions in alphabets not yet deciphered at the time they were discovered![71] which is a highly illogical and not very scholarly sort of argument.

Whoever devised the Elder Futhark, sometime near the beginning of our era, was privy to the tradition of letters we are uncovering here, which was evidently still extant then. For they in fact knew the correct original placement of the twelve simples *and* the identity and meaning of the three mothers, as I shall now prove. But first: why are there twenty-four runes, instead of the twenty-two of our bardic 'root' alphabet and its Hebrew permutation? It is actually simple— and may even indicate a post-Christian (albeit Gnostic) origin. One of the extra letters is a result of the incorporation of *both* branches of tree-alphabet, the *bethluisnion*, which includes P, and ogham, which replaces it with Ng: both letters are present in the earliest runes. The other is the division of G, ivy—desire—in two: **jēra* (*j* as in German, pronounced *y*), 'year' or 'harvest', and **gebō*, 'gift' ("actions inward and outward"). They are the desire that acquires, and the desire that bestows. And the latter of the two is shaped like Greek chi, initial of Christ.

First let me arrange them in sequence for you. The last two runes are often reversed, but the oldest inscription has them in this order and I am convinced later *futharks* were merely trying to evade being charged with revealing the whole pie. This order makes more sense, ending as it does in *dagaz*, 'day'—the here and now. But it makes no difference to the argument below.

<u>ᚠ</u> ᚢ ᚦ **ᚨ** <u>ᚱ</u> ᚲ ᚷ ᚹ

<u>ᚺ</u> ᚾ ᛁ ᛃ <u>ᛇ</u> ᛈ ᛉ **ᛋ**

<u>ᛏ</u> ᛒ ᛖ **ᛗ** <u>ᛚ</u> ᛜ ᛟ ᛞ

I underlined every fourth rune (starting with the first), since they indicate the six signs of the macrocosmic hexad: ᚠ and ᚱ are F aries and R libra, R's original station before its delusions of grandeur, marking the vertical axis; ᚺ and ᛇ, H gemini and I sagittary, mark the second axis of the macrocosmic hexad; and ᛏ and ᛚ, T leo and L aquarius, mark its third axis. That the early Christian Chi Rho symbol consisted of these three axes plus a loop identifying the vertical as rho (done here by R's rune standing for libra) is a strong hint that runes originated with Gnostics.

The three mothers I have enlarged in bold: ᚨ and ᛗ are A (alef) and M (mem), standing for doer and knower, whose signs scorpio and capricorn are on the *micro*cosmic hexad, so they are placed just *four* places out from the start of their respective *ætt*s or groups of eight; and ᛋ is S (shin), standing for the thinker, whose sign sagittary is on the *macro*cosmic hexad, so it is placed *eight* out from the start of its *ætt* (at the very end). And the last axis-marking rune before ᛋ is ᛇ or sagittary itself. It is true the runes determining the axes jump back and forth between Egg and Cauldron, but the pattern is unmistakable. And notice the mothers are in the order of the Logos.

Interwoven with (hence reinforcing) the above pattern are two carefully placed sequences of letters where each letter's Greek or Hebrew number foretells the next letter's bardic number. One consists of four runes, the other of two: each of the sequences occupies the exact middle of one of the spaces marked off by the two mother letters representing parts of the self that did not undergo the Fall. (Rune *ansuz*, 'divine being', marks off the first half of the first *ætt* for doer alef, and in that space no such sequence occurs, though the two middle runes of that space, ᚢᚦ, do represent the same sign on Egg and Cauldron.)

Rune ᛋ, mother letter shin, marks off the whole length of the second *ætt*, in the middle of which is the sequence ᛁᛃᛇᛈ. Listing bardic number first, followed by Hebrew (Greek) number, they are: 19-10, 10-3, 3-7, 7-80 (80 being the last number on which Hebrew and Greek agree). And the rune ᛗ, mother letter mem, marks off the first half of the third *ætt*, right in the middle of which appears the sequence ᛒᛖ. These are: 5-2 and 2-5.

The first of these two groups, ᛁᛃᛇᛈ, elaborates on ᛇ's signal that it is the domain of mother letter shin's (the thinker's) sagittary: yod-gimel-zayin-peh, or Egg's capricorn, straight down to Cauldron's scorpio, then straight up its *radius* to Egg's sagittary, then out to Cauldron's sagittary. Note these are the three signs of the self, with sagittary occurring twice. The second group, ᛒᛖ, also marks off the self's three-sign span, Cauldron's capricorn and Egg's scorpio, this time skipping sagittary.

Now that I have your attention, I shall comment on their shapes. Notice the Corn Spirit's fearn the alder is shaped like a stalk of grain (ᛒ): its name *fehu*, 'cattle', signifies wealth or plenty. The vowel of summer, which also stands for the summer of life—coming of age—is named *ūruz*, 'aurochs', and pictures its horn upended (ᛝ), that is, used as drinking horn, since coming of age for a German warrior in antiquity meant trapping and killing an aurochs for its horn. The third rune was later called 'thorn' because of its shape, but early on it looked more like our D and pictured a giant's girth: it is D the oak, rune of Thor (Thunder, Donar), slayer of giants, its original name *þurisaz (þ = th)*, 'giant'. Ailm (alef) the silver fir obviously pictures one (ᚠ): *ansuz*, 'god'. In Ireland, ruis the elder was the wood of magic horses (in witchcraft); and the rune's name is *raiðō*, 'ride' or 'journey'; so there is little doubt in my mind that the rune (ᚱ)—notice it is *not* completely pinched or strangled like our R—pictures the animal mask of the shaman: R at its libra station is evidently seen as taking a journey to the interior of the earth (the Otherworld) to find and bring back knowledge or power. The rune of coll the hazel (ᚲ), *kenaz*, 'torch', is the opened mouth of the poet receiving inspiration from the salmon of knowledge and thus a torch to his or her tribe. The Apollonian or Christ-like aspect of ivy (desire), *gebō* or 'gift' (ᚷ), if it gets its shape from Greek chi, *may* picture the obliquity of equator and ecliptic— characterized in Plato's *Timaeus* as the 'same' and the 'different'[72]— or perhaps the tripod on which a sacrifice is placed. The eighth rune (ᚹ), *wunjō*, 'joy', is an angular form of the shape P, which is also found, a knife cutting the apple in half, w in German being the interrogative letter (*hw* in Old English), making it the equivalent of quert the apple. Indeed of roots starting with qof used in the Bible, *many* have the meaning 'cut'; a couple even mean 'fruit harvest'.

Fence-like *hagalaz* (ᚻ), 'hail' (as in hailstones), evidently represents what blocks the way: H the hawthorn is the hedge that separates things (as does space). The next rune, *nauðiz*, 'need', can be seen in two ways: it pictures (ᚾ) the kindling of the *needfire* (by friction of dry wood, the crosspiece being what spins the vertical stick), but also an oar of ash sticking through the side of a ship. Next, *īsa-* or 'ice', obviously pictures an icicle. The second G (ivy), *jēra* (ᛃ), is often curved and pictures the linked arms of the harvest dance: this shows the Dionysian aspect of ivy. The next rune (ᛇ), *eihwaz* or 'yew tree', I struggled long over till I finally saw the light: it pictures, as does its Greek version (Z), cold air moving down or under the warmer air moving up or over, in a *cold front*, this being the vowel of winter. Scholars do not speculate *what* the name of P the whitten's rune means: it is *perþ-*, a combining form. Its *bethluisnion* name peith suggests the archaic Welsh term *peithynen*, which means divination by a wheel on whose spokes maxims were carved.[73] So combining that with Hebrew peh's picturing a mouth prophesying leads me to interpret this rune's shape (ᛈ) as a rune-cup on its side, having just cast its dice for divination. The next rune (ᛉ) is named *algiz*, elk, and pictures one seen from above (bird's eye view). The next (ᛋ), *sōwilō*, 'Sol' (sun), is a lightning bolt: it often has more than three zigzagging strokes. Its trump (XVI La Maison Dieu) is sometimes called the Lightning-Struck Tower. In the earlier Bronze Age alphabet used in Scandinavia (early Tifinag, table 5), this letter was the alchemical sun-symbol, a circle with a dot in the center. The rune is might not be derived from knowing the sun is electric but merely from lightning's resemblance to it.

The final *ætt* starts with an arrow pointing up; the earlier Scandinavian Tifinag character was an arrow pointing down (named *tagg*, 'barbed arrow'): both remind us that one aims for the heart (tav's station). It (↑) is named *tīwaz* and signifies something like 'divine honor' (duty or conscience), rune of 'war' god Tiw (as in Tuesday), god of the Thing, cognate with *Zeus* and the Celtic *tuatha*, 'people': the Thing was the public gathering at which disputes were judged, issues affecting society decided (tav the heart as crossroads). Then comes the female column (pregnant torso in profile), often angular (ᛒ): *bairkana*, 'birch twig'. The next one (ᛗ), *ehwaz* (Latin *equus*), 'horse', is easy: the underside of a horse (being E, aspen, which is scorpio, the privates). Opposites ᛏ above (taurus) and ᛗ below (scorpio) show bird's eye view versus underside. The similar *mannaz*, 'man, human being' (ᛗ), shows two *wunjōs* (ᚹ) kissing, its trump being VI The Lover. L, rowan, is named *laguz*, 'water, lake' (aquarius, water pourer), and pictures the eaves of a roof (ᛚ), as in south Semitic (see table 3), signifying the sheltering of others (from rain) and suggests that property of rowan wherein it tends to shelter other species that often in the end displace it.[74] Rune Ng (◇), *inguz*, the hero 'Ing', is just a knot, signifying both the flexibility of reed and the strength of the knot; its later runic shape extended sides above and below—like the two shins back-to-back in south Semitic (table 3)—making a latticework or interweaving, as befits ngetal the reed. The vowel of spring, *ōþila*, 'heritage' or 'inheritance', pictures (ᛟ) the hood of one's teacher, or of a schoolchild. To signify the present instant teyt (doer's libra), rune *dagaz*, 'day', pictures (ᛞ) an hourglass on its side. I cannot *prove* they had them, but this one is in the process of being turned over, indicating the instant in which one acts.

Now that the reader has some idea of the power and scope of the three mothers, let us finish defining them. Their origin is the Logos, yet omega, **quail chick**, was suppressed, shin, **lotus pool**, substituted for it, to represent what Gnostics called the lower Sophia or Prunikos ('whore'). But this tells us something else: the three mothers may spring ultimately from the Logos, a complete self, but they function in humans on a level with the doer's *impersonation* of self, desire in place of knowledge, feeling in place of thinking. This is what has drawn both the thinker's minds, T and D, to the nature side, feeling's focus; both the knower's minds, B and P, to the intelligent side, desire's focus. It is what stands behind the Gnostics' feminization *Sophia*. Desire lives in the blood (as in the male erection), feeling in the cerebrospinal nerves.[75] I gather the body-mind resides mainly in the autonomic nervous system (sympathetic nerves). Thus mem stands for the blood, shin for the cerebrospinal nerves, alef for the sympathetic nerves. That is why Semitic shin pictured a tooth (molar), mem a mother clasping us to her bosom (to warm us with her blood), and alef an ox; why in runic *sōwilō* pictures a lightning bolt, *mannaz* a kiss.

Think about the placement of the mothers. Intermediate mem, at libra's loins, suggests blood drawn to sexual organs in copulation; mem sofit atop the head of the standing form means blood circulating to the top of the head when standing. Shin's perch atop one seated meditating reminds us to meditate on isolating feeling from the sensations that seek to distract us from it. And alef, at the heart of the Egg, links sympathetic nerves to the beating of the heart, represented by the cross-shaped tav on a level with it.

FOURTEEN
The Hidden Numbers

The numbers by which bards referred to tree-letters were only revealed up through 16, the number of mother letter shin: saille the willow. Its trump is XVI La Maison Dieu ('The God House'), which depicts a tower's crown being displaced by cannonball (16 is the atomic number of sulfur, important in gunpowder); the two tumbling headfirst from it are perhaps the very twins who were presented by their mother to V Le Pape to be blessed. It is the third in a number series at the onset of spring that means increase, 4-8-16: O (vowel of spring), F (Corn Spirit), and S. It was quite late in the process of figuring all this out that I finally realized what the willow and its trump symbolized: the overflowing fount of spring. This is confirmed by many biblical roots starting with shin that mean 'overflow', 'flow forth', and so on.

After saille, all is dark. Well not quite, though the next number in calendar sequence *is* zero (no number): H, hawthorn, the hedge, meaning empty space, what divides or separates. Its sign, gemini, points just above the horizon, which is where space is. If we but knew how far up the numbers *went*, we could make educated 'guesses' then see how fitting their trumps end up being. But of course we *do* know how far up the numbers go: there are five letters not assigned numbers, so 21 will end the sequence. There is a good reason for this in the periodic table: 21 marks the first of the 'rare earth' metals, a group that several layers down suddenly presents a sequence of fifteen such metals through which valence ceases to progress—a sort of 'vacation' from it, as it were. And there is another important reason (which may be intertwined with this one) stemming from the interplay of number and valence. But first things first.

The numbers that *were* public knowledge are (in numerical order starting with space or no-number): H-A-E-I-O-B-M-P-F-K-G-T-D-N-L-R-S. This is a much more ordered sequence phonetically than that of either the Greek or Hebrew alphabets, though the rationale of the alef-beyt is quite coherent from the point of view of signaling to future generations that the original calendar sequence of letters was known, albeit hidden behind the reordering of the simples (and thus preserved only in the Celtic branch of the tradition). But that must wait a bit.

You can see right off the bat that where one would expect the remaining vowel, U, it switches to B instead; and indeed V (Latin U) was Roman numeral 5. Hence my first 'guess' (which turned out to be right) was to put U fifth-from-the-end, at 17. As vowel of summer—of coming-of-age, of love's consummation—displacement of U by the consonant of birth, B (the silhouette of a pregnant torso in Latin and runic), at 5 suggests impregnation, while the trump XVII L'Etoile (The Star) shows ura the heather to be the (outdoor) bed of trysts, for it shows a naked woman—the only one among trumps with a natural looking pair of breasts (being vav)—pouring fluids from two amphorae into a pond. Now what could that mean, I wonder (besides perhaps someone pouring chlorine, atomic number 17, into her pool)? Confirmation of this first placement can be found in the fact that 17 signified coming of age in ancient Ireland;[76] in the context of Irish mythology, the "seventeenth birthday was the *aimsir togu*, the age of consent, when boys became men."[77]

Since A is 1 (just as in Hebrew) and I is 3, we note the two doubled vowels, Aa and Ii, fall easily into place at first-from-the-end and third-from-the-end: XXI Le Monde (World) and XVIIII Le Soleil (Sun). The former suggests the symbolism of the palm is something like 'far off places', which is what it would have meant to most people in Europe. Hence the interest I take in that 1500s version of Le Monde showing a small hamlet through the porthole of a small jet. And Ii's trump recalls mistletoe's role as Virgil's (and Frazer's) 'golden bough': Ii stands for dark of the moon, when all there *is* is the sun.

One of the two remaining unnumbered leftovers is Kk or Q. Since K is 9 (as in *canine*), it seems logical to put Q at twice 9: XVIII La Lune. For it is *months* of gestation the number 9 counts, and when pregnant there are nine for the child as well, making 18, qof being virgo the womb. Interestingly enough, it is not trump K-9 but the two *even* numerical 'zeros', 0 The Fool and 18 The Moon, that have dogs in their trumps (the Celtic root for 'dog' starts with a C).

This leaves Ss, straif the blackthorn, as 20: XX Le Jugement (Judgment), which depicts Judgment Day, the archangel blowing a trumpet held up to its *throat* (being tzaddi, or taurus the throat), not mouth, surrounded by a bristling phalanx of sharp rays, as befits 'strife' (to which *straif* is surely cognate, blackthorn being the traditional wood of the shillelagh). The number 20 represents two ten-fingereds, the root of strife.

Now that we have filled in the gaps, let us take a look at the number sequence we have ended up with on the Egg; you will recall in the case of the doubles, it proved very interesting. Starting at aries the head, they are: 8—20—0—17—4—18—21—2—3—19—14—13 . . . uh, what? This certainly did not *look* promising to me when I first encountered it. Had I missed a turn somewhere? No, my methods had been utterly rigorous—so much so that it had taken me roughly a dozen years of constantly returning to the problem to get *this* far!

Well, I need not have worried. The *seemingly* haphazard nature of this sequence should however serve to reassure the reader that this whole thing is no scheme contrived by me, since surely I would have chosen some number sequence I could fathom without having to twist my mind around a further mystery for *another* dozen years, that being pretty much what I had done to myself. But once its magnesium signal lamp began cutting through my thick haze to clarify the *chemical* structure adhering to the simples and to how they relate to the doubles out on the Cauldron, I began to see just how haphazard it is *not!*

Before we move on, let us consider the twelve functions *SY* allocates to the simples,[78] though without agreement on their order between the various versions. The seven breaths go part way towards solving the correct distribution. I allot them in this order: speech, laughter, motion, coition, thought, sleep, seeing, hearing, tasting, smelling, working, anger.

Let us start with the four senses: I assign them according to the four elemental breaths. *Seeing* being teyt (bardic Aa) at libra—the palm—calls to mind sight-seeing; and its trump XXI Le Monde frames a dancer. *Hearing* as heh makes sense: aspen, like the ear, is stirred by air; II La Papesse appears to be reading aloud to us; and its atom-type helium raises the voice's pitch.

There is also (I dare mention it) a visual overtone in this card of 'her' either musing on, or being oblivious to, sexual shenanigans taking place in another room (overheard perhaps?), because of the motif formed by what clasps the robe over 'her' breast, its shape an erect phallus issuing from the left and reaching across between the two hangings about her head that resemble the robe of the male and the white-skirted dress of the female. It is definitely there, and fittingly so! since heh represents scorpio, the 'privates', and circumcision (Abram into Abraham): this is why I noticed it in the first place. *Tasting* as zayin the yew calls to mind it is poisonous (requiring a 'food taster'); its tarot trump III The Empress predates modern feminism and thus says the lady of the house is Empress in her own kitchen (where what is to be tasted originates); her shield-eagle extends its feathers out beyond the shield to embrace her about the middle. *Smelling* as yod the mistletoe is obscure to me (I do not recall its odor); but certainly its trump, XVIIII The Sun, shows drops of sweat flying off the wrestling twins.

A, alef, is the fire triad in the Logos, and it is intimately associated with the tongue: in *SY* 3:1,[79] alef is the "tongue of decree deciding between" *pan of merit* mem and *pan of liability* shin. And of course in our model, alef the Egg acts as tongue to Cauldron's mouth. And *SY* 1:3, in the very first translation of it I had the privilege to read, says (right after the five-opposite-five part): "and in the center is set the Covenant of Unity like the Organ of the Tongue, and like the Organ of Nakedness,"[80] speaking of alef, numbered 1 in both the Hebrew and Celtic traditions. Taking alef's fire triad as the tongue, I associate with its three signs the functions related to the tongue: *taste*; and *speech*; plus the function behind speech, *thought*. *Speech* fits samekh's head: speech issued from the head of Orpheus alias Bran after its removal; and its trump VIII Justice is what it proclaims. And *thought* certainly fits ayin, the mental breath at leo; ditto *taste*, the water breath.

Note the phonetic symmetry of this triad (figure 6, bottom). We take its signs, it being an active element, as projecting onto the sides issuing from them: its voiced, active side is zayin (*z*), its unvoiced, passive side samekh (*s*), and its base ayin or O ("oh"). Thus zayin, as *taste*, is a moister sibilant than the dry samekh of *speech*, which needs a glass of water nearby.

Noetic breath vav stands for the function *coition*: no surprise there (ura, heather, vowel of summer and bed of lovers' trysts). Shoulders cheyt (gemini) and the spine opposite them, lamedh (aquarius), are *walking* or *motion*, and *working*, motion's purpose. The former, The Fool, shows a vagabond walking; the latter, XIIII Temperance, signifies learning or working, lamedh being the departure from self-knowledge, a reaching-out from self, a moving-on from current knowledge.

The remaining three help place each other. Nun's trump XIII, nicknamed 'Death' and showing the Grim Reaper, is most fitting to portray *anger*: we can take its station pisces as a backing-off from the start or aries, as befits sound N's role of negation in English, the language fated to be spoken by the most people ever (being the *lingua franca*). Its complement, *laughter*, fits the sign just forward of aries, tzaddi, a sort of whistling laugh, jokes at the expense of others being a form of strife (blackthorn)—the laughter of the resurrection, of XX Judgment. Indeed the back of the neck is the axis of shaking one's head from side to side in negation, the throat what contracts and expands when nodding the head in affirmation. This leaves qof the womb to be *sleeping*, which is what a child in the womb spends most of its time doing. And indeed qof's trump, XVIII La Lune, is the darkest, most nocturnal trump. Quert the apple, in bardic tradition, is glossed 'shelter of a hind'.[81] The 'dogs' in the card look like laughing hyenas: they represent the laughter straight above it, at taurus, from which it is the refuge of sleep.

I should mention the other symmetry in the Seal of Solomon (figure 6). The water triad, as a passive element, has its signs projected *onto* by its sides, with reysh superseding teyt in this context (at libra), making its two sides reysh and lamedh, and its top cheyt. R and L are the only non-nasal liquids (R can be a rolled stop at either end of the tongue *or* the liquid between them), and they are the initials of *left* and *right* in the current lingua franca.

This would seem to solve the problem of which doubles-as-sense-organs are right and which left. That reysh and lamedh line the outer and inner sides of the water triad—fifth in each *ætt* being runes ᚱ, ᛋ, and ᛚ, R and L on either side of water breath I—suggests that the doubles on the *outer* Cauldron are *right* nostril, eye, and ear, those on the *inner* Cauldron *left* nostril, eye, and ear, with P and D at their original stations and reysh at libra in this context. Singling out the left and right sense organs in this way is reminiscent of the manner of casting spells in ancient Ireland—the way Lugh himself did it—which was to stand on one foot, extend one hand, and close one eye.[82]

Notice the sense organs make a pattern like the horns of aries the ram on the human head, branching out from the mouth to first the nostrils, then the eyes, finally the ears. It is apparent each sense organ's proximity to mouth libra is determined by the signs *following* libra, on the inner or active side of the Egg: scorpio, on earth's triad, determines that the nostrils be next on the ram's horn pattern; sagittary, on fire's triad, causes the eyes to be next; and capricorn, on air's triad, means the ears are last, the farthest out on the 'horn'. Since they are on the active side, they are determinative in their respective triads (pairs of manifested signs) in terms of stamping the 'ram's horn' pattern on the human form.

Now that we have a clear idea of the distribution of numbers, and therefore trumps, on our model, I should point out one of the most striking facts about said distribution. The pattern of trumps on the central column is as follows. Beneath The World is The Devil; above it is The Magician (Mountebank); over him looms Justice—the *old* dispensation, Law—which coincides with (and perhaps guards against the destruction inherent in) La Maison Dieu (The God-House or Lightning-Struck Tower); over all of which is The Lover—Love, the *new* dispensation—at its perch, the hub of the Monad. This pattern fully confirms the Christian Gnostic roots of the Tarot of Marseilles.

FIFTEEN

Chemistry in the Ice Age?

Had I not been prompted early on to take note of Kabbalah's implications for chemistry, based on atomic numbers—*nature's* 'numerology'—I might have missed the point. But I had, as I recall, *already* noted most of the trumps of the Tarot of Marseilles illustrated faithfully their atomic numbers, though I admit I was late noticing the most *striking* example of this, namely II La Papesse (The Female Pope), which no-one till now has seemed able to explain: it is obvious (unless you are someone slow like me) that this Pope merely has his voice's pitch raised because he has sucked up some helium.

IIII L'Empereur has a beryl on his breast (4 is beryllium): in fact, it is as close to green as the Grimaud Tarot of Marseilles gets, though it may just be my subconscious adding the shade of an emerald to it (without which, it could still be aquamarine). V The Pope evokes cleansing or blessing, symbolizing boron's best-known ore: borax cleanser. VI L'Amoureux (The Lover) expresses carbon's love of its kind, enabling it to join together in long chains forming the basis of organic matter. VII Le Chariot is the only trump in which someone (its driver) has wind in the face: nitrogen is four-fifths of the air. The scales in VIII La Justice express balance, which is only possible if there is oxygen to breathe. VIIII L'Hermite warns us to keep fluorine away from us, especially when combined with hydrogen in fluoric acid. X The Wheel of Fortune (neon) presages places like the Las Vegas strip. XI La Force (sodium) recalls binding oaths (lion's roar) with salt. XII Le Pendu (The Hanged Man) shows the inverted image on the back of the eye— dancing a jig—to signify sight; for magnesium burns with highly actinic light, used in signal lamps to cut through fog. XIII (nicknamed Death) shows a skeleton (grim reaper) holding his scythe like an oar as he reaps heads and limbs, which refers to that quality aluminum *shares* with bone, and with the wood of ash: lightness combined with strength. XIIII Temperance (silicon) reminds us there is such a thing as tempered glass. XV Le Diable is phosphorus, Phosphorus being another name for Lucifer: both mean 'light bearer', or Venus as morning star. XVI La Maison Dieu (Lightning-Struck Tower) as sulfur is quite obvious. XVII L'Etoile shows a naked woman pouring some chlorine in her pool. XVIII La Lune reminds us that argon is used in light bulbs to exclude oxygen and thus keep the filament from burning up; and I can attest to having done double takes *thousands* of times thinking I had seen the moon only to find it was in fact a street lamp. XX Le Jugement refers to calcium in bone in the only way left after using bone itself to point to aluminum: on Judgment Day, all that will be *left* of us (figuratively speaking) will be bone. XXI Le Monde points to the fact that rare earth metals (scandium being the first of them) are so rare as to often be named for *where they are found*, as is the case with scandium.

I have saved back three that require more than one sentence each in this context: I Le Bateleur, III L'Imperatrice, and XVIIII Le Soleil. (Le Mat, The Fool, is simply ambling along traversing space, *his* 'atom-type'.) It turns out hydrogen is the most common atom-type in the cosmos (though not in earth's crust). This alone might make it worthy to be personified as the magician or sleight-of-hand artist: its ability to be plus-one or minus-one valence (one extra, or lack of one, valence electron) at the drop of a hat allows it to shift in and out of chemical bonds swiftly and mercurially, which serves to quicken the entire universe of matter (and enable such minor details as life, and occurrence). But the specific reference in this card is, I believe, to its use in dirigibles such as the Hindenburg to *levitate*. Of course this could also be the case with helium (minus the Hindenburg), were there not a more striking way to picture that august stuff.

III L'Imperatrice is an especially interesting case, as the aspect linking it to lithium does not seem even to have been noticed or mentioned in all the discussions of this trump at the tarot forum I used to frequent, except by me, whereupon everyone seemed to remain as blind to it as to the mother's arm in V Le Pape. Yet without either of these extremely important details, one simply does not have something worthy to be called tarot. The card V Le Pape has the mother's arm entering from the right so that the viewer might *place his or her self in the role* of a mother presenting her twins to the pope. The eagle on the shield at the feet of III L'Imperatrice extends its left tail feathers subtly *off* the shield to *embrace her about the middle*. The reason these two details exist is because in these two cases and these two cases only (apparently) we identify with the off-card (in the case of Le Pape) or two dimensional (in the case of L'Imperatrice) character of *opposite sex* to the main image and read trump III as the *male* pillar Jachin and trump V as the *female* pillar Boaz. The first and last letters of ogham are B, bardic 5, and I, bardic 3, and they are the only two tree-letters that retain their tree names in runic. These two trumps in fact even picture their respective ancient Semitic letters: Le Pape wears the priest's mitre pictured by beyt, and L'Imperatrice has a zayin-shaped harness on her chest. Needless to say I puzzled mightily for years on the seeming sex-reversal of these trumps. But patience won out, and I was rewarded at last with the truth.

The link between III L'Imperatrice and lithium is that the eagle's extension embraces the Empress to comfort or reassure her, just as lithium is prescribed to comfort or reassure someone bipolar suffering from depression. (I had a friend of many years who, though diagnosed bi-polar, did not want to take lithium, fearing it might dull his creativity.)

The relation of XVIIII Le Soleil to its atom-type potassium appears to be multifaceted. One link seems to be something rather subtle, discovered around 1969 and summarized in the following heading from the National Library of Medicine (online): "Specific Requirement of Potassium for Light-Activated Opening of Stomata in Epidermal Strips" (stomata are the pores found in the epidermis of leaves, stems, and other organs that facilitate gas exchange). A more obvious connection to the sun is that potassium gets its name from potash (ashes of plant life), of which it is the most important ingredient (useful in many ways): it is the tangible end-product of the chief effect *of* the sun on earth, vegetation. Moreover, of most relevance to us, potassium plays sun or center—attractor of the solar system—to every cell in the body: it is *potassium* chloride that holds fluids *within* cells (read solar systems), and *sodium* chloride that marshals fluids in the intercellular fluid (read interstellar spaces). The sun's symbol is gold, 19 times as heavy as water; and there is also the 19-year Metonic cycle synchronizing solar and lunar time.

Note how the three atom-types this involves are placed on Egg and Cauldron (figure 5). The atom common to both salts, chlorine, is at the outer extreme of the Egg; potassium is straight back from it at the inner extreme, linked to it via the Egg's horizontal diameter. Sodium is the extension of that diameter out to the Cauldron, representing the intercellular fluid, the Egg being the individual cell. This discovery was one of those 'gotcha' moments for me, where I realized something profound was afoot. Alef, hydrogen, is the midpoint of this diameter, where it can hijack the chlorine, so to speak (prevent it linking up with potassium, opposite it), to produce hydrogen chloride, which combines with H_2O, (top half of Egg's vertical diameter) to make hydrochloric acid, essential for digestion of proteins and an important barrier to intrusion of microorganisms. Hydrochloric acid is thus configured by the samekh and vav radii of the Egg, limits of the unmanifested half of the outer or nature side of the Egg.

The number structure of letters that correlates them with their atom-types is much more ancient than tarot: at least as ancient as Apollo, and more likely dating from before the end of the last ice age. To continue our chemico-physiological wanderings, note that calcium is perched at taurus: this is because calcium levels in the blood are regulated by the parathyroids, found in throat taurus. They are those four little bodies—Galilean moons, if you will—clustered about the thyroid (which also interfaces with calcium). The horizontal at taurus ties bone's calcium to aluminum, an *abs*traction of bone's quality of lightness-combined-with-strength (once *ex*tracted from its ore) there at back-of-the-neck pisces where the quality is most needed to properly hold up one's head. Next layer down, empty space (The Fool) at gemini, where arms and hands reach out *into* space, has as *its* inner abstraction (by horizontal) the silicon at aquarius, principle (mixed with oxygen) of glass or quartz: a setting-apart or abstraction *of* space. Moreover here at Egg's upper inner quarter-circle—last two signs plus the return to aries, the last three *middot* or divine attributes (see part 2)—oriented as if a hill ahead to be climbed, are silicon-aluminum-oxygen, the three most common atom-types in earth's crust (in the order 2nd, 3rd, 1st).

Below the horizontal diameter we find similar coherence. At leo is beryllium, and beryl (such as emerald) is an outward sign of well-being; straight inward from it is lithium at sagittary, relating to inward well-being (as treatment for the bi-polar). They are the two lightest metals and form the base of the triad pointing up. At the lowest horizontal, approach to and departure from the border *between* outer and inner, it is perhaps a simple matter of the argon in light bulbs (our sleep function) being *outside* us, the helium raising voice's pitch (our hearing function) *inside* us; both are inert gases. And straight down is scandium, named for: location, location, location.

And notice the coherent pattern here of non-metals versus metals. Taking the inner end of the horizontal diameter to belong to the unmanifested—towards which the round is headed there—the four levels of the upper half, starting at aries, alternate non-metal, metal, non-metal, metal. Taking the outer end of that same diameter to belong to the manifested half—towards which the round is headed *there*—the lower half's four levels, starting at cancer, also alternate non-metal, metal, non-metal, metal.

SIXTEEN
The Four Elementary Particles

Now is a good time to come back to the four types of elementary particle and explain exactly how this model puts forth the scheme of placing them at the four cardinal points (figure 10). The presence of oxygen at aries, and of the magnesium in signal lamps on the Cauldron's rim *straight out* from aries, obviously suggests a ray of light linking us to the horizon before: a *line of sight*. Since oxygen is the key to oxidation or combustion, and that is how photons are generated, aries is where the photon of light naturally lodges. It is in the middle, photons being electrically neutral; and one round high, being *spin one*.

The *fermions*, the material particles of which matter is composed, are *spin one-half* when it comes to their (quantized) angular momentum, compared to the photon (at aries) at *spin one*. So we would expect to find fermions halfway up the Egg. Potassium and chlorine—at the two ends of Egg's horizontal diameter, where they marshal the fluids within cells—are halfway up the Egg. Potassium, the inner pole, has one valence electron, meaning one electron *over* what is needed to complete a stable argon 'shell', one that can be loaned out in forming a compound. It forms the salt potassium chloride that holds fluids within cells because chlorine has one *under* what it needs to complete its argon 'shell' and so is ready and willing to *take* said loan. So here we have the obvious implication of an *electron* at the inner pole and its opposite, a *proton*—also one electron short—at the outer pole. The electron stands for leptons generally (which include the innocuous neutrino). The proton stands for baryons generally, which include the neutral neutron; yet neutrons are only stable while inside the nuclei of atoms.

Note that the electron and proton these signs symbolize are *actually present* at the *center* of the Egg (horizontal diameter's midpoint) in the form of alef, hydrogen, which consists of one of each. Lepton and baryon are the two types of fermion. Opposite electric *charge* is measured on the horizontal scale. Our model calls active-inner the 'plus-one' pole (i.e. plus one valence electron), passive-outer the 'minus-one' pole (i.e. minus one valence electron). Unfortunately, we moderns got it backwards: identifying electrons as 'negative' means the direction of current is opposite the direction the electrons are actually traveling.

The atom-type at libra, scandium—atomic number 21—has the largest nucleus of all the atom-types utilized for this model and expressed as trumps of the Tarot of Marseilles. This is quite logical, as the heaviest tends towards the bottom. Anyway, *being* the largest nucleus, it of course calls to mind that which binds nuclei together: the quantum of the strong nuclear force. The pi-meson's discovery (i.e. its mass) was *predicted* (albeit underestimated) based on its being the carrier 'particle' of the strong nuclear force, given the *range* of that force and the Heisenberg uncertainty principle[83] (underestimated perhaps because 'range' was taken as size of nucleus, the *actual* range being a bit less). It is *spin zero*, hence at zero height, and comes in three varieties of charge, electrically neutral, 'positive', and 'negative', which average out to neutral, placing it in the middle.

The exchange of virtual pions (I will not here get into the technical meaning of *virtual*) is *still* credited with what physicists now call the 'residual' strong force *between nucleons*. They call it *residual* only because they are hypnotized by their obsession with quarks as 'particles', instead of as inseparable point-constituents *of* particles. Therefore they think of their imaginary *gluons* as the exchange particles of the (to them) more important force binding quarks together into nucleons, which 'force', that of 'quark confinement', cannot be overcome by a greater force and therefore (to a *sane* physicist) is not a force. The so-called quarks are integral *parts* of a nucleon and were originally called *partons*; they are not particles *compounded into* a nucleon. The problem stems from modern physicists' unhappy choice for the meaning of *elementary*: the logical choice for its meaning is 'indivisible'; but they have settled on 'point-like'.

It is quite true that *motions* must be point-like. If a motion were 'smeared out' over a volume—the idea behind the 'classic radius of the electron' and so on—or even along a 'two-dimensional' *string* (as in string theory), it would mean motion was actually occurring 'at an infinite number of locations', which is quite impossible for the simple reason that *infinite* means 'numberless' and *numberless number* is self-contradictory. What physicists fail to grasp is that a *single particle* might have *more than one* point within its compass at which motion is occurring, a sort of 'local interconnectedness' (akin to global interconnectedness?). This is far preferable to the pseudo-notion of a force that cannot be overcome by a greater force. Myriad physicist-hours are being wasted exploring imaginary edifices such as string theory, based on a current standard model that is physically as well as metaphysically unsound.

Here is a summary of the model implied by the distribution of letter-numbers about the cardinal points of the round in our bardo-Kabbalistic, paleo-Hermetic model.

- The **photon** is on top (aries), at the height of *one* Egg or round, being *spin one*, and midway between right and left, being electrically *neutral*.
- The **meson** is at the bottom (libra), at *zero* height, being *spin zero*, and midway between right and left, since it comes in positive, negative, and neutral and thus is *neutral* overall.
- These first two are on the active or *vertical* axis, making them **bosons** (quanta of force).
- The **lepton** is on the right (capricorn), at the height of *half* an Egg or round, being *spin one-half*, and on the right, being (what moderns, who got it backwards, call) electrically *negative* overall, since neutrinos are neutral and electrons—of which there are many in the world—are 'negative' in charge (*plus-one* in terms of valence).
- The **baryon** is on the left (cancer), at the height of *half* an Egg, being *spin one-half*, and on the left, being (what moderns, who got it backwards, call) electrically *positive* overall, since neutrons (unstable except when in the nuclei of atoms) are neutral and protons—of which there are many in the world—are 'positive' in charge (*minus-one* in valence).
- These last are on the passive, *horizontal* axis, making them **fermions** (particles of matter).

I wish to emphasize I did not figure all this out myself: it was clearly suggested by the structure of the symbol system itself. As for moderns getting 'positive' and 'negative' backwards, should not the direction of electrical current more logically be the direction the electrons are actually moving? Sadly, that is not currently the case. I overcome the problem of how to speak of this model (without constant confusion) by noting that the presence of an extra electron beyond a fixed 'electron shell' means one electron is available to form a valence bond with another atom: I call this *plus-one* valence, which is how nature sees it. When an atom is one electron short of a fixed 'shell', it is *minus-one* in valence, a state mimicked by a proton without an electron (though 'positive' in charge). This terminology will suffice in dealing with the very important number structure at the heart of our model.

The antics physicists have gone through to *cast* their smokescreen hiding confirmation of the four elements are rather comical. Their most ludicrous contortion is the term *hadron*, as in 'hadron collider'. What they mean is 'baryon and meson collider', and I would dare say that at this point their reasons for wanting to build more and more powerful 'hadron' colliders borders on the absurd. But my main point is that the term *hadron* itself is absurd. They group together under this term both baryons and mesons. Again, baryons are *fermions*—particles of matter— whose behavior is to always separate out into distinct energy states in any system of which they are part: this is called the Pauli exclusion principle. Mesons, on the other hand, are *bosons*— quanta of force (exchange or carrier 'particles')—which like to gather in the same energy state, the obvious example being the laser, a gathering together of light rays of the same wavelength.

In our model, note that *bosons* are gathered together in the center, on the vertical axis; *fermions* are pushed off to either side, to their own 'corners'.

Just think how much further along particle physics might be today if its professors and theorists would have just *admitted* the existence of the four elements and moved on. Perhaps a few of them will read this book and realize that the conclusions of the *last* civilization—which surely (judging from this model) had progressed a good deal farther along in its understanding of matter and life than we have—can be used as a sound foundation for progressing deeper in our own understanding of matter, perhaps even to a grasp of the physical-metaphysical mechanics of the interplay *between* thought and matter, and how things came to be as they are.

If you are thinking we have neared the end of what can be said about the sophisticated science contained in our model, you are in for a surprise. There is a coherence here that runs way deeper than we have yet penetrated, so deep in fact that I am of the opinion it actually maps how and why matter attained its current physical and chemical structure—that is, patterns in the doer's thinking that precipitated it. I realize quantum mechanics purports to explain things based on its mathematical analysis of the behavior of matter on the atomic scale (what they can as yet decipher of it), and much of it (except the quark aspect, which is a misstep) may be more or less correct. Still, I would categorize much of that as *symptom*, rather than cause. And I will show you why—beyond the simple fact that much of it seems to resemble circular reasoning of the sort where you measure the parameters of matter's behavior and then turn around and say it behaves thus *because* of the theory constructed out of those parameters.

SEVENTEEN
First Principles

To illustrate the difference between cause and symptom, consider the periodic table of chemical 'elements'. Quantum physics presents rather tedious (and in their way correct) reasons for the periodic table taking the form it takes. But I will give you a simpler model that is just as particular about structure yet simpler to understand, at least for the first twenty-one atom-types we are dealing with here—but also, in a sketched-in way, for the rest. It is a model by which an astute thinker from before the time of modern chemistry could have accurately deduced valence structure up through atom-type 21. If the model were a finished one that accounted as easily for all the big unwieldy atoms as it does for the simpler ones, by Occam's razor it would *have* to be considered the correct theory. (I am hoping one of you will extend it to encompass the whole.)

Taking Adam Qadmon, what appears to us as Upright Sentience Itself, as the sexless type from which this, our mortal type, descended—first by division into male and female (since *one* must precede *two*), then by further degeneration, clearly mapped in Kabbalah (as we shall see)— a plausible view of why matter takes its present form can be pieced together from first principles.

At some point *in the thinking of the doer*, duality, which originated as an aspect of Unity (of number itself), rebelled and separated itself off (in the doer's thinking) *from* Unity. At this juncture, duality as second now pulls against Unity's first, rather than with it. What effect might this have on matter? at least on the type of matter we doers at present are fit to interact with?

To answer this, consider number in *base ten*, humans' natural numbering system (since we have ten fingers). It is pivotal in other ways as well: *ten* is the sum of *one* through *four* and contains an equal number of primes and not-primes, sharing this quality only with *twelve* and *fourteen* but *unique* in that in *ten* they form a symmetrical pattern: 1-2-3-5-7 versus 10-9-8-6-4. Number, remember, adheres to an infinitely recurring pattern of +1, +2, +3, +4, -4, -3, -2, -1, ±0, based on digital summation. One might speculate that this pattern maps the structure of the kind of matter Adam Qadmon interacts with. But what happens when 2 rebels against 1? Since 2 now pulls *against* rather than *with* 1, the first two cancel out, making 2 equivalent on some level to 0. This is precisely what we find in the periodic table: atomic number 2 is helium, an *inert* gas. By inert, we mean its valence—how many more or less electrons it has than needed to form the nearest stable 'shell'—is ±0, a stable shell.

The next few atomic numbers also have their valence stuck two paces behind number, 3 being +1 in valence, 4 being +2, and so on. This discrepancy places intense pressure on matter to bring valence back into sync with number. Number cannot change, being unaffected by time (or anything else). So this tension can only affect matter itself, meaning valence.

This tension precipitates a compression of +4 and -4 *valence* into one *number*, 6, whereas in *number* +4 and -4 occupy two places (4 and 5). This rectifies only *half* the pressure, bringing valence to only *one* step behind number: 7 (-2) is nitrogen, -3 in valence; 8 (-1) is oxygen, -2 in valence; and so on. Since tension, albeit reduced, is still present, +4 and -4 are *again* compressed into a single number, 14, which causes the following sequence of atomic numbers, 15-21, to at last be in sync with number. This sequence of seven numbers just happens to be the third and final sequence of seven (atomic) numbers included in the trumps of the Tarot of Marseilles. The 'crunching together' of +4 and -4 into 6 gives carbon its ability to join with itself—+4 with -4—in those carbon chains our bodies depend on for the organic matter of which they are made. Is silicon's similar ability what enables silica to be 'smooth as glass'?

Taking the problem out beyond our current limited needs, it is interesting to speculate about the origin of the iron-cobalt-nickel sequence that carves out the eighth and last column (beyond inert) in the periodic table as it was displayed back before we moderns decided to base its array on *series*, instead of *periods*: displayed the old way, the numerical patterns are much more clearly discernible (figure 9, bottom). Altering the display of the periodic table may well have been another defensive reflex, like quark theory, in this case covering up the 'surprising' coherence of chemistry's number pattern lest some not properly indoctrinated thinker like myself notice it and doubt it had a mindless origin.

Since +4 and -4 have learned to share, they do so again, which increases tension this time by pushing valence out *ahead* of number in the sequence starting at 22 (number of letters in the alef-beyt) leading up to the iron-cobalt-nickel sequence. So matter must contrive to fall behind again if it is to avoid getting ahead of number by *two*. This it accomplishes via the iron-cobalt-nickel (26-27-28) sequence—running in place, so to speak (same valence)—after which matter repeats the tension-relieving process that brought it into sync with number in the first place (thus oscillating between one ahead and one behind). This 'running in place' starts at iron, 26, key to the oxygen-toting ability of hemoglobin: iron's strength comes from being the lightest atom-type with 8 valence electrons (albeit not all utilized at one time in chemical reactions).

Tentative justification for the above might be gleaned from Rupert Sheldrake's theory of formative causation: that patterns of development in the past have more likelihood of recurring (when circumstances allow) than of being replaced by some new development also possible but not already imprinted on the all-pervading morphic or morphogenetic field, with whose earlier 'stamp' only repeated occurrences resonate.[84] Instead of embarking on *new* territory—valence jumping from one pace ahead to two paces ahead (and beyond)—matter or nature, by simply relaxing a few paces, can again traverse the familiar ground of the previous two periods, where, being behind by *one*, it relieved that tension (at 14) to get itself in sync with number.

Rupert Sheldrake's theory, by the way, provides a simple, elegant explanation of the correlation in particle physics between increased frequency and increased inertial mass:[85] at higher frequency, each cycle finds things closer (than at low frequency) to where it was *last* cycle, increasing its resonance with the field and thus its inertial mass (resistance to any change in momentum).

It is clear that the pattern of *squares*—25, 36, 49, 64, and 81, the squares of numbers 5 through 9, a set that has particular significance amongst Sefirot of the physical world (being the cycles of inner planets Mars-year-Venus-Mercury-moon, the 'watery' or form layer)—has a coherence that can surely help explain the pattern of the periodic table. But that can wait.

The pattern amongst the letters of our model that most strongly suggests first principles rather than mere symptoms is that of G and K, desire and feeling, and their relationship to the potassium chloride that binds fluids within cells. For G, 10, is numerically +1 but 0 in valence, while K, 9, is numerically 0 but -1 in valence. Straight up from these two on the vertical lines extending upwards from them are the two atom-types in potassium chloride, yod and vav, inner and outer extremities of the Egg's horizontal diameter and roots of the two halves of the Great Name (יהוה): *these* two are +1 and -1 respectively in *both* valence and number.

The obvious inference is a fundamental polarity between *numerical* +1 and -1 *valence*, which cannot interact as they are but must project themselves onto surrogates that are +1 and -1 in *both* number and valence. The interaction that then results is what keeps fluids within cells and makes life possible. I find this compelling stuff!

Moreover, the arcs connecting G's and K's stations to the signs *preceding* them—that is, extending towards the nature side—mark their *valence* heights, as measured by hydrogen's ±1 as well as potassium's +1 and chlorine's -1. Arcs linking them to the signs *following*—extending towards the intelligent side—mark their *numerical* heights, by that same measure. This shows a dynamic the ramifications of which we will see further developed in part two: valence expressed as height-off-the-ground. While the scale of spin puts *spin one* (the photon) atop the Egg at the center of the second wheel (the Cauldron's), the scale of *valence* places ±1 at the center of the Egg: these two heights obviously represent two kinds of 'unit', related to each other in the ratio 2-to-1. Carbon then, at ±4 valence up at the center of the Monad, is a further type of unit, a unit of light let us say (as in coal *or* diamond)—earth-light, according to Percival—related to a unit of spin in the ratio 2-to-1.

This polarity between G and K gives rise to the sexes. For when G, desire—what seeks to determine the immediate future—has the upper hand in the doer's psyche, the body is male; but when K, feeling—what seeks to grasp the immediate past—has the upper hand, the body is female. Both are present in each, but the one that is stronger determines the sex. Thus they are the ultimate source of pillars Jachin and Boaz, to which we now turn our full attention.

EIGHTEEN
The Twin Doorposts

In the Masonic drama, Boaz is represented by a *broken* pillar next to which a woman weeps.[86] What this symbolizes is that Boaz is the front column of the body, which has been *broken off* at the sternum to allow for the womb's enlargement in bearing offspring. Jachin, the intact column, obviously symbolizes the other column, the spine.

Considering this obviously two-columned structure of the human form, is it not fairly obvious that the original from which we are descended—that of Adam Qadmon—must be-or-have-been a two-columned form that in *us* was modified by the Fall to have its front column broken off at the sternum? How else would it have been two-columned in the first place? And it is further apparent that this original type was in need of no replacement bodies, else the front column would not have originally been intact (as it seems to me it must have been). Having now glimpsed this apparent truth, I could not personally ever go back to believing in a neo-Darwinian 'ascent' from some lower creature. The 'odds' of that are infinitesimal, making it certain such a complex being as man must have degenerated or devolved from a superior being—by the second law of thermodynamics, if nothing else! yes, I mean that in jest, since I suspect that that law is itself overturned by the behavior of plasma (a gas of charged particles), as in the stellar reaches.

What academia would like to forget is that Darwinian theory predicted *gradual* change over time, whereas what geological evidence actually reveals is long periods of stasis punctuated by *sudden, sweeping* change. It was a serious theory, I grant you, not an absurdity on its face like the 'big bang'; the fossil evidence simply did not bear it out. The model of human origins evidence supports is the Kabbalistic one, based on the Fall (or Hindu, also based on a universe that is eternal), the view explored in greater detail here and in part two (and its ramifications in part three).

Traces of fully 'evolved' humans extend back in time with no real limits, with evidence of technology (perfectly machined metal spheres) going as far back as the *pre-Jurassic*![87] If the Creator (the doer, the A of the Logos) is eternal, it follows that creation too is ongoing, not just a lone event in the past. So thought Johannes Scotus Eriugena, "considered the most considerable philosopher of the Western world between Augustine of Hippo and Thomas Aquinas."[88] And in the words of Bertrand Russell, "His view of creation as timeless is, of course, also heretical and compels him to say that the account in Genesis is allegorical,"[89] meaning—surprise, surprise— the Bible was written by poets, not professors (though perhaps the professors of their day). With no arbitrary limit to man's antiquity, the paucity of early fossil evidence simply means countless civilizations have already culled through it.

We now must confront another anomaly contradicting what professors preach: a subtle, intricate number pattern showing utter mastery of the periodic table centuries, perhaps millennia prior to the modern age. We have encountered such sophistication in portrayal of atom-types by the Tarot of Marseilles, and in placement of potassium, sodium, chlorine, and calcium on Egg and Cauldron. What follows has a sophistication and subtlety dwarfing even that.

If we trace the month or arc leading *on from* the sign each simple occupies then look at the six columns marked off by vertical lines connecting pairs of signs, we find more columns than chance would dictate show agreement in valence between 'ceiling' and 'floor' (arc on top and arc on bottom): three out of six. And they are *every other one*. The innermost (rightmost) and outermost (leftmost) columns on the *intelligent* or *active* side of the Egg have, respectively, potassium-lithium and aluminum-scandium as ceiling and floor, the first pair both +1 in valence, the second pair both +3. And the *middle* column on the *nature* or *passive* side of the Egg has calcium-beryllium as ceiling and floor, both +2 in valence. By themselves, these facts are remarkable. But it all becomes *really* interesting once fitted into the greater pattern, which involves the rest of the simples plus the doubles and the mother letter mem.

Arcs play a crucial role in all that follows. We must pay close attention to them with regard to all the letters, not just the simples, including the ramifications of where the radii of the doubles and mem, emanating from the Cauldron's center (shin), sweep the Egg in approaching or leaving each sign. Only by means of arcs and radii is this symbol system able to convey as much information as it does (much yet to be explained), including: valence by height off the ground; columns of planetary metals in the alchemical vessel, which determine the planetary rulership of signs in astrology; the dynamics of the solar system itself; a mapping of elements onto the four types of elementary particle (chapter 16 above); key aspects of Sefirot in the lower three wheels or worlds; important correlations between this number pattern and salient points of chemistry and physiology; all oriented around the human form and a complete inventory of its parts.

I defer the matter of the seven planetary metals to the context of the fourth sefirotic Tree, that of the physical world, where said planets and metals *are*. But before we move on to part two (the Sefirot), I need to explain just how pillars Boaz and Jachin are indicated in this scheme. I will then conclude this first part with a chapter on exactly how the alef-beyt got arranged in its present order, which I am sure has been puzzling many.

We have seen that only two of the original runes retain their tree names: B and I, birch and yew. Since the runes' order reveals familiarity with the original order of letters about the round (something missing even amongst Kabbalists today), it should not surprise us in the least that these two stand for the doorposts of Solomon's Temple, Boaz and Jachin. These, as I have pointed out, represent the two columns of the human form: broken front column, and spine.

The male and female roots of the Great Name, yod and vav, do stand for these two pillars in one sense: they stand for the versions of them that are more or less intact: a man, who has a spine, and a woman, who also has a spine. It takes two, a man *and* a woman, to invoke the Great Name—the divine creative power—because in us it has devolved into *pro*creative power; that is, humans do not create from scratch. That is why the Name is ineffable. For the creative power originally resided in the two-columned form, whereas we have but one intact column apiece. The passage in scripture about Adam's 'rib' or 'side' must mean the front column, suggesting the backbone of the female form inherited its uprightness from what *had* been the front column in sexless Adam Qadmon. This must have occurred not upon Adam's initial division in two but upon the choice of these two to couple for the purpose of procreation, which is what necessitated the breaking-off of the front column. More on this in parts two and three.

In the individual mortal, the Boaz column is broken. Hence our model represents it *in potentia*, waiting to be rebuilt (the Great Work, the goal of alchemy). For I, idho the yew, is one of the twelve simples and occupies the terminal filament of the spine, sagittary, with its double, Ii, at spine's mid-point, capricorn; whereas letter B, beth the birch, resides on the Cauldron, but on its inner horizon—correlating with pineal gland and left ear—as if a mere notion 'in the back of the mind'. However, there is clear purpose in its being so placed: the Cauldron's radius as it approaches B's station sweeps the 'ceiling', nun, of the nun-teyt or aluminum-scandium column, which shares B's valence (+3) and is the part of the intelligent side right up *against* the nature side (see figure 8).

Thus in fallen Adam, the Jachin column, originally for the use of the Triune Self (being towards the intelligent side), is denoted by the Egg's innermost planetary column, the terminal filament and mid-spine (water and earth breaths); whereas the Boaz column, originally for the use of nature (being towards the nature side), is denoted by that second column on the intelligent side marked by ceiling and floor of matching valence, bordering on, but not of, the nature side.

It is imperative that I point out that the choice of intelligent or active side as the 'male' side and the nature or passive side as the 'female' side has absolutely nothing in it of chauvinism or misogyny. What differentiates male and female is whether desire or feeling currently has the upper hand in the doer, as this determines the sex of the body born for it to inhabit or operate. Both are obviously equally necessary for the doer to function, since the Ideal in Adam Qadmon is for the two to be in balance. The real cause of the alignment of desire with the intelligent side and feeling with the nature side is quite simple: desire is that side of the doer that is trying to determine or influence the immediate future, which is still *on* the intelligent side (not having occurred yet); whereas feeling is the side trying to grasp the immediate past—sense it, perceive it, project the doer's thoughts onto it—which, having already occurred, is on the nature side. A man tends to be slightly more concerned with what *will* happen, a woman slightly more with what *has* happened: both are present in both, but somewhat out of balance.

Since doer's A is linked to the intelligent side and thinker's Ω or U (V) to the nature side, the letter standing for Jachin is on the Egg, and that standing for Boaz is on the Cauldron, yet linked by valence and radius-sweep to one particular column of the Egg. So since the Egg is the zodiac of the seated torso and the Cauldron its surroundings, note that B, initial of the column that is broken, is not on the Egg or current human form, whereas I, initial of the intact column, *is*.

NINETEEN
Alef-Beyt Letter Order

Okay, I have held you in suspense long enough: I will now address how the alef-beyt got put in its current order. It begins with how the simples were rearranged, a somewhat involved yet intriguing story. Once we get past the simples, the rest really *is* rather simple. The simples were reordered to hide a secret (their proper sequence) but in such a way as to convey additional vital information to the contemplator. To grasp the method of it, we must first clarify our view of the four triads.

Since most of the human beings we know anything about live in the northern hemisphere, *up* or aries means north (to humanity as a whole) and *down*, libra, means south, just as on most maps (my apologies to those living 'down under'). The tricky part is identifying east and west. Symbolically there is an affinity between *outer* and west, *inner* and east: I doubt many would disagree with this. And cancer is where the cycle of seasons descends, as do stars in the west, capricorn where it rises, as do stars in the east. And this—cancer west and capricorn east—is the proper orientation of the Masonic Lodge, according to Percival.[90]

There is one *slight* problem: when seated in meditation *facing* west or cancer, the zodiac of the torso is oriented *opposite* that of the heavens. Now I think I have an idea why this makes perfect sense, but it involves a stipulation by Percival which many might think farfetched and which I cannot confirm (though it seems certain). I will simply offer this twofold hint. One, the side of the zodiac on which signs continue down the legs to the feet in the broken-and-extended zodiac (down into earth, if seated on it) *is* oriented the same as the zodiac of the heavens when facing west. Two, that is the side of the intact pillar, Jachin. That is all I will say for the nonce.

So with cancer to the west, we have: fire-north; air-east; water-south; and earth-west. This is, in fact, how the *Zohar* assigns elements to directions,[91] reasoning in the case of fire and water that fire is needed in the cold north and water in the more arid south. To this we can add that east is where heavenly bodies rise into the air, west where they fall again to earth.

There are actually *three* distinct traditional ways of assigning triads to elements. There is their natural order, the primordial arrangement known to the knower and confirmed in the *Zohar*. There is astrology's way, which keeps fire in place, element of the knower (unaffected by time), while the other three drift ahead to the next available triad: this way of identifying triads we will identify with the thinker, weaver of the threads of destiny spun by its doer. Third is the poetic method, that of ceremonial or seasonal magic, elements assigned quarters by affinity with annual and diurnal seasons: fire-summer-south-day; earth-winter-north-night; air-spring-east-morning; water-autumn-west-evening. This we will associate with the doer.

For what brought about this third arrangement was the Fall: divine creative power, or alchemical fire, 'fell' from head to loins to become the procreative power. For here fire's triad points to loins libra (south), displacing water's triad to the next sign, scorpio (west), thereby displacing earth's triad to the next sign, sagittary (north), thus filling the gap left there by fire.

Officers of the Masonic Lodge, according to Percival,[92] represent the seven minds: the Master in the east and his assistant are the knower's two minds, our B and P, in the east (at capricorn); the Senior Warden in the west and his assistant are the thinker's two minds, our T and D, in the west (at cancer); and the Junior Warden and his two assistants in the south are the doer's three minds, R and the G and K it dominates, in the south (at libra).

So, in juggling simples, the Egg was divided into an *upper-inner* quadrant, capricorn-through-aries; an *upper-outer* quadrant, aries-through-cancer; and a *lower* 'quadrant', meaning the underside of the Egg, leo-through-sagittary. Upper-inner was assigned to the knower and the primordial arrangement; upper-outer to the thinker and the astrological arrangement; and the lower five to the doer and the poetical arrangement.

These three stations—inner, outer, and below—perfectly express what Georges Dumézil and his school of comparative mythology identified as *tripartite* division of proto-Indo-European mythology and class-structure:[93] priests or spiritual power, our *within;* warriors or secular power, our *without;* and commoners (artisans, farmers, laborers), our *below*, this last being essentially economic, correlating with the chthonic, with fertility and prosperity. All this is confirmed by the trumps associated with the doubles: B a Pope, P a Chariot (Plato's? Bhagavad Gita's?); D the Hanged Man, T Force; and K the Old Man or Hermit, G the Wheel of Fortune, R the Devil. The three mothers confirm it as well: mem sofit, the tefillin atop the head of standing Adam, for the knower or *upper inner*; shin, a crown (secular power), for the thinker or *upper outer*; and alef the ox, who raises water up out of the ground for irrigation, for the doer or *lower* (chthonic).

The reassignment of elements in astrology I interpret as a mapping of the doer's flawed thinking: earth and its senses flipped to control the triad of air or thought (east); air's thoughts pushed down by this into the triad of water and the emotions (south); water's emotions dragged out towards earth and the senses (west). This places air-water-earth at the manifested cardinal signs such that slow revolution of the heavens (Great Year) around the zodiac (see chapter 9 of part 2) exerts relentless pressure to rotate them by one cardinal sign back to their proper stations. Meanwhile, the upper-outer quadrant borders the lower half at the triad it has in common with the doer, water or west; the upper-inner quadrant borders the lower half at the triad *it* has in common with the doer, air or east; and upper-inner borders upper-outer at their common triad, fire or north.

Funnily enough this suggests a mysterious fourth or 'working' arrangement: fire north, air east, water west, earth south—a *poetic* east-west, but with fire raised back to the head!

We are now in a position to track how the simples were shuffled about (chart 1). Letters originally occupying signs capricorn-through-aries (upper-inner) were moved back one sign on their respective triads, for the knower (Master and Senior Deacon). Those originally occupying signs aries-through-cancer (upper-outer) were moved where their respective elements end up in astrology, for the thinker (Senior Warden and Junior Deacon). And those originally occupying signs leo-through-sagittary—the underside—were moved where their respective elements end up in the *poetical* scheme, for the fallen doer (Junior Warden and his two assistants); but the first three, leo-virgo-libra, manifested air-water-earth, transport these, not their respective triads.

You may have already noticed that string of four letters from the *upper-inner* quadrant that were moved back (on their respective triads) as a block: yod-lamedh-nun-samekh. With regard to those of the *upper-outer* quadrant, the astrological, fire's aries, sign it has in common with upper-inner, is already accounted for; water's cheyt, gemini, 'drips' down one sign to cancer (west), displacing earth's vav or cancer up to its new perch taurus, which displaces air's tzaddi or taurus over to aquarius (south), thereby generating the elementary triads of astrology.

With regard to the lower 'quadrant', note that here there are five remaining letters or signs, not four, to express the popular misconception that there are five senses: earth is moved *twice*, once for smell and once for touch. From leo, ayin carries *manifested air* (hearing) east, to capricorn. From virgo, qof carries *manifested water* (taste) west, to pisces (directly opposite): Raphael Patai quotes the *Zohar* as saying sun and moon *faded* when Adam emerged "because the apple of [his] heel . . . darkened their light"[94] (qof is apple, pisces the feet). From libra, where we contact the ground, teyt carries *manifested earth* (as touch) north, to leo—note both thinker's *and* doer's earths get displaced back two signs. Then from scorpio, on earth's *triad*—which points forward, like the nose—heh carries earth north again (as smell), to aries (olfactory nerves being in the head). And from sagittary, on fire's triad, zayin carries fire (sight) south, to gemini (here water and fire are both moved directly opposite). All this is plotted in chart 1.

The rest is straightforward. We start with alef, the doer, the creative beginning of the Word: Brahm*a*, the Creator (of thoughts). Next come the three doubles that reproduce, on the Cauldron, the signs the three letters of the Name, yod-heh-vav, originally occupied on the Egg: beyt-gimel-dalet. (The deeper import of this we will tackle in the context of the Name, in part three.) Then, starting at the first sign aries, the height measured by Cauldron's outer rim dalet, come the simples of the nature side of the Egg (in their new order): heh-vav-zayin-cheyt-teyt-yod. Having ended at virgo, we repeat virgo on the Cauldron: kaf. Then follows libra: lamedh. We repeat *that* on the Cauldron: intermediate mem. Then come scorpio-sagittary-capricorn, the three signs of the conscious self: nun-samekh-ayin. Having reached capricorn on the Egg, we follow it with the nearest sign on the Cauldron *to* Egg's capricorn (*Cauldron's* capricorn, beyt, having already been used), namely its sagittary: peh, which faces Egg's capricorn and points its yod-like tongue at ayin (to remind us it has replaced yod). Then come aquarius-pisces, finishing off the Egg: tzaddi-qof. Note here the two doubled consonants are juxtaposed, just as the two doubled vowels, teyt-yod, were earlier, these two pairs being last on their respective sides of the Egg. Next, upstart reysh ('head' or 'first' in Hebrew) asserts its usurped position here at the head of things. Mother letter shin, as Prunikos, crowns him. Whereupon tav, conscience (sense of duty), speaking through the heart, condemns whatever reysh orders that is wrong. Remember this final jump over to the Cauldron's leo, as it will become relevant later (part 2, chapter 8).

PART

TWO

:

THE

SEFIROT

Truth's Champion

Eyes, stand with the poets of an elder age
Against the sprawling currents of the lesser fields
That rampage over times present and counted on
Where deeper shadows lie. And champion the man
Against the herd, eternity in place of time,
The unseen rather than its vague appearances.

Surprises not that others stick their forks at us
And prod us with their voices like a steaming iron
Come to take the wrinkled edges off my mind.
Their own wrinkles are labeled folds and then paraded
Before us as examples of the smooth. I balk
At such deceptions. Why not call things what they are

And leave the rest to others.

ONE
Preliminaries

Barddas is a rather uneven collection of bardic transcriptions (some say forgeries) first published in 1862 and eloquently defended against its detractors by Lewis Spence in his book *The Mysteries of Britain*.[95] In it there happens to be a strong indication that the numbers applied to the letters in medieval Ireland (according to Graves) was a tradition also in Wales: one Welsh poet therein lists them (1 through 16) in the same numerical order.[96] Considering the profound ramifications of that numbering (not all of which have yet been elucidated), this goes a long way towards rehabilitating poor Iolo Morganwg (*Barddas*'s author) from the charge of being a forger. Other poets therein offer them in differing order; one,[97] listing them correctly except for 9-13 (the middle five of 1-21), relates that *after* A E I O B M P F (D T N G K) L R S were added U and H, the two which *enclose* 1-16 at 17 and 0 and which spell out the first name of a Celtic 'Hercules', Hu Gadarn. Another 'Hercules', Ogma Sun-face, reputedly invented ogham.[98]

A recurring theme in *Barddas* is ten 'principal cuttings'[99] "secret from the age of ages among the Bards,"[100] which preceded and are distinct from the regular alphabet. The book also discusses what Spence describes as the "three circles of spiritual evolution,"[101] and these appear to be the precise equivalent of our three mothers (first three *Ofanim*).

The most important source to be published around the time and place of the Kabbalah's initial flourishing was the book *Bahir*. Its description of the ten Sefirot is largely ignored by modern Kabbalists—as is, more surprisingly, the description of them in the even earlier *SY*. Yet both are essential to penetrating the mystery of the Sefirot—essential to both Kabbalah *and*, I dare say, the earlier Work of the Chariot, or *Ma'aseh Merkavah*, Kabbalah's roots. The book that gets all the glory is the *Zohar*, a long-winded work that is nonetheless quite useful in spots. It is very clear the *Bahir* is a knowledgeable source. There is, for example, that passage I quoted earlier about teyt and mem, clearly part of a much deeper corpus that has since largely been lost.

Kabbalists today, on those rare occasions when they do speak of the description of Sefirot in either of these earlier works (for example when translating them with commentary), act almost as if they need to *apologize* for their content, even dismissing them as listing Sefirot in a *different order*[102] in an attempt to explain discrepancies in the naming of them in these works as compared to the (later) tradition of the *Zohar* and Lurianic Kabbalah, shown in the commonly seen diagram of three triads plus a tenth (figure 7).

Now excuse me for being an upstart, but that is just plain nonsense. The Sefirot are first and foremost ordinal, not cardinal; the *Bahir* labels them *first*, *second*, *third*, and so on. The idea that they would be listed out of order in such hallowed tomes does not make sense. It is true that *SY* contains a jumbling of letter correlations to hide secrets, and it takes deeper understanding on our part to build up a completely accurate picture of the alef-beyt. But the Sefirot? The authors of *SY* and the *Bahir* certainly would not jumble their order.

The explanation for the discrepancies is that each text describes the Sefirot of a different wheel or world: the *Bahir*, those of the Monad; *SY*, those of the second wheel, the Throne world or Cauldron circle; and the *Zohar*, those of the Egg, the form world of the fallen doer. We can add to these that corpus which, though it attracted charlatans like Aleister Crowley, did preserve certain valid traditions, namely the Hermetic Kabbalah: its attribution (from Christian Kabbalah) of planets to Sefirot leads to an accurate view of the fourth world as well. (Judaic tradition offers several competing sets of these correlations.[103]) The occultists also preserved a pattern of 'paths on the Tree' that appears to have merit (figure 7), again out of several set forth in Judaic lore (see chapter 8, below). Such sparks of Light demonstrating survival of hidden knowledge reinforce each other, another being that passage in the *Bahir* concerning teyt and mem, and of course there are the square Hebrew letter-shapes themselves.

The *Bahir* describes Sefirot as they first appear, on the wheel centered atop the standing Adam Qadmon. Here each Sefirah is a power unto itself, based on its position on the round, not tied to any scheme of pairing, tripling, or quadrupling. Those are for later worlds. Only the last two are paired, and while there is an important internal reason for this, it also prepares us for the pairing that will prevail in the following world, where they are all paired.

Concerning the Sefirot, *SY*, verse 1:5, Short Version, says: "Their end is imbedded in their beginning, and their beginning in their end, like a flame bound to a burning coal."[104] This clearly means they are circular, like the worm Ouroboros. Yet I do not think anyone has quite described their origin accurately. A description has survived of them as spokes on a wheel—rays arrayed in a circle—yet the key, that they are the first ten of *twelve* such spokes, has not, I think, been passed down to us. The diagram I have seen of them merely shows a ten spoked wheel.[105]

The twelve signs are just as present on the first wheel—the Monad—as they are on the other three. That no letters delineate them signals that in this first world they form an undivided whole, rather than a set of pairs, or three triads, or articulations of four elementary layers. The Monad is the world corresponding to the first of the elements, fire, a Oneness: the light world. From the human perspective—as opposed to that of the Intelligence by whose Light a conscious self thinks—it constitutes the Whole, the all-encompassing. *In* that Whole, the starting point is 'on high', the direction Up, towards the divine—Uprightness or Consciousness itself, the upward impulse on the vertical axis of the one Form (in the Platonic sense), that of Upright Sentience, Adam Qadmon. Everything that is arises *from* Consciousness (in a sense) and will eventually return to aries *as* Consciousness, according to Percival.[106]

The thirteen *middot* (divine attributes) early Kabbalah speaks of can only be the twelve spokes of the primordial Monad plus a return to the first. We conscious selves have progressed only as far as the *tenth* spoke and have yet to traverse the last three. We have yet even to make good our attainment of the tenth in a sense, being *fallen* doers, not yet balanced Triune Selves. But we have arrived there, after all, and the knower, which did not undergo the Fall, still resides at that spoke, identifying our ultimate identity as conscious self even if we doers are estranged from its direct realization, being divided (male and female), mortal, and very troubled.

TWO

The Soul

The ten Sefirot represent steps through which each conscious self traces its long journey from first distinguishing itself from (in) Consciousness—aries, the ultimate reality—by virtue of motion (taurus) acting on substance or 'no-thing' (space, gemini) to manifest as a (fire) unit of nature at cancer,[107] from there progressing on eventually to libra in its development as a nature unit, and, after long ages as a nature unit, crossing over to the intelligent side at libra, eventually to become a conscious self at the (Monad's) tenth sign, capricorn. We will see how Kabbalistic tradition explicitly backs this up.

But I want to take a moment to describe, and rigorously define (a rare thing in esoteric literature), the soul, introducing as well a term coined by Harold W. Percival, the *aia*.[108] I think the rigor of the compound definition will go far towards convincing the discerning reader that we are here privy to a profound mystery relevant to every human being, not just to a special class of initiate or member of a particular religion.

As a unit progresses in nature, it becomes more and more sophisticated in function as it approaches libra, the point of contact with the intelligent side. On each wheel, once it *reaches* libra, being still a nature unit, it has nowhere to go but up: up the vertical diameter dividing nature side from intelligent side till it reaches the aries of the next smaller wheel (having begun on the largest) and disgorges onto it to progress along the nature side of that wheel. On reaching the libra of this new wheel, it does the same thing again, progresses onto the next smaller (more refined) wheel, and so on.

We know of four such wheels. Percival stipulates twelve altogether,[109] which can be derived (my reasoning, not his) from the saying of the revered *Emerald Tablet* (attributed to Hermes Trismegistus): "That which is below is like that which is above and that which is above is like that which is below to do the miracle of one only thing" (Isaac Newton's translation, given in Wikipedia). This is often paraphrased as: 'as above, so below' and 'as below, so above'. So we postulate another set of four wheels above our four, and a third set of four below. Percival identifies the four above as the spheres of the primordial elements, domain of the Intelligence; the next four as the four worlds (light, life, form, and physical); and the remaining four (those below) as the light, life, form, and physical planes of the physical world.[110]

Once a unit progresses to the libra of the twelfth wheel—the last four stages of which are the senses, sight, hearing, taste, and smell[111] (controlling the generative, respiratory, circulatory, and digestive systems, respectively[112])—the unit once again climbs the center-post, the vertical diameter, but this time it finds no lesser wheel onto which it can issue forth in its progression *in nature*. It thus gets stuck (my terminology) *on* the center-post, an upward impulse or pressure thereon, still part of nature but now its most subtle and powerful kind of unit: a soul or *breath-form*. It *is* the uprightness of the body it animates and determines its form or type (upright man or Anthropos) based on its myriads of ages of experience as a nature unit fulfilling every natural function there is to fulfill. This experience is not yet in the form of knowledge but rather what one would call *automatic* behavior, its seat the front half of the pituitary, according to Percival.

As the current Triune Self progresses on to become an Intelligence, the next unit behind the current *soul* on its ladder of progression—the sense of smell or touch—progresses onto the center-post to become the new soul, dislodging (my terminology) the one previously there over to the intelligent side *while still on* the center-post. It is that center-post still, but in relation to the intelligent side, rather than to the nature side: it is what Percival terms the *aia*.[113] The origin of his term seems quite transparent (though Percival does not explain it): being the same center-post as the soul but in relation now to the intelligent side, it acts as the means by which the doer, A, communicates its desires to the body or breath-form, I, whose feedback, then, makes its way back to the doer, A.

It is only once the next shift occurs and a new soul dislodges the old one to the intelligent side (to become the aia) that the erstwhile aia gets dislodged from the center-post altogether and progresses clear up to capricorn or self-hood, already familiar with the three levels leading there (which become doer, thinker, and knower): it has become a conscious self. Percival calls all this the Eternal Order of Progression.[114] What precipitates each shift is the current self progressing on to become an Intelligence.

The self's capricorn is that of our first wheel, the light world. Until a unit has become an Intelligence, the spheres (of the primordial elements) are beyond its ken. For they consist of the 'purely determinative', the 'predominantly determinative', the 'predominantly determined', and the 'purely determined', and it takes all four in combination to constitute an actual occurrence. While we can reason about them and postulate their existence, we cannot operate in them as Intelligences do. And before we progress to that point, we must first pass a test of balance, our failure at which produced the Fall.[115] We shall consider this test of balance and all that stems from it in the context of the triadic Tree (Tree of forms).

The Sefirot we are about to explore correspond to the pips of the Tarot of Marseilles: the numbers 1 through 10 in each of four suits. Atzilut is clubs or staves (originally polo mallets). Beri'ah is swords, curved scimitars except on court cards, ace, and one each in odd-numbered pips, these being straight broadswords. Yetzirah is cups. And Asiyah is money, its round coins signifying the planetary cycles governing the physical world. The fourth wheel symbolizes the (dark) present instant in which the doer acts, or on which it stamps its will. This is expressed symbolically by the fourth wheel being centered on the womb, making it a copy of the parent or third wheel. Corresponding suits in modern playing cards: clubs, spades, hearts, and diamonds, respectively. In each suit, there are ten pips standing for the Sefirot of that world, and (in tarot) four court cards standing for the letters of the Great Name (יהוה) resonating in that world.

THREE
The Sefirot of the *Bahir*

In Lurianic Kabbalah, that of sixteenth-century followers of Isaac Luria (known as the Ari, 'Lion'), a vestige of the teaching we are about to consider starts with the idea of *tzimtzum*: retraction of the *Ein-Sof*—Deity without limiting qualities, what we might roughly equate with the ultimate reality, consciousness—from a hollow or round within Its omnipresence, leaving a residue of Light therein yet allowing existence 'also' of something 'other' than *Ein-Sof* in that space.[116] Perhaps it is a way of describing an individual unit of nature distinguishing itself from or in consciousness. For nature matter is only conscious *as* what it is (in whatever consciousness of it there happens to be), as contrasted with intelligent matter, which is conscious *of* existence.

Into this hollow of relative 'non-Deity' a ray of Light enters, to organize things. Two aspects of it take shape: one, a *round*ness (the movable wheel of the unit itself?) conforming to the hollow left by the *tzimtzum*—which is the more harmonious of the two—and two, a "straight ray of light [that] goes back and forth to seek its ultimate structure in the form of man," the latter of higher degree, as it "comes directly from *Ein-Sof*."[117] It is with the Form thus brought about, Adam Qadmon, that the Sefirot originate, their character determined by the round.

We begin with the standing figure of sexless Adam Qadmon, which logically precedes-or-is-coeval-with the worlds.[118] What is the *point* of Adam Qadmon? It is the point *to* which Upright Sentience *tends*: the summit of the head, uprightness's *extent*. Relative to this point, the direction *down* points towards the body whose uprightness the point expresses. This point is the fount from which all Light of understanding, in the form of 'rays',[119] flows. This touches on Celtic lore, for I strongly suspect that the name once greatly revered amongst bards in Britain, *Taliesin*, since it meant 'radiant brow' and was as much a divine name as that of an individual[120] (for whom it may have been a title), referred originally to this same Adam Qadmon.

The impulse initially *at* that point is *up*, the first logically discernible direction relative to it being the upward impulse in Adam Qadmon of which it is the expression. Yet the very body whose Uprightness it is lies in the *opposite* direction, to which the innate impulse *at* that point must logically connect itself. A body, straight down, is inherent in the definition of the point—*where it is*—but has yet to be incorporated into the impulse at the point—*what it does*. Hence the *impulse itself* must pivot or rotate: this rotation, which *unifies* that initial dichotomy between straight and curved, is necessary for it to become *whole*, that is, to progress. The initial hollow embodies the thirteen *middot* or divine attributes—the fixed course—and pivoting about it are the Sefirot, the steps taken so far *on* that course.

The *first* of the 'Ten Sayings', the *Bahir* tells us (starting at verse §141),[121] is the Highest Crown (figure 1): have we not said this? The *second* is Wisdom; the reason for this is in part the fact that, being departure about the *round*, it constitutes the wisdom to *return*; and certainly said departure is the ultimate cause of motion itself, which is what Wisdom must regulate. The *third* is called Wisdom's *treasury*, the quarry of the Torah; for it corresponds to gemini, space, the 'field' of Wisdom's departure from straight up, the 'treasury' where motions are 'stored'.

The triangle in the Seal of Solomon that points *down* is traditionally associated with water;[122] water is likened to Torah because, like Torah, it flows from the higher to the lower.[123] This makes crystal clear why the third station, the point of that triangle's inception, is called the '*quarry* of the Torah': it is the point *out of which* the triangle pointing down *issues*. This implies Torah's (Law's) omnipresence. It reaches *beyond* matter to its very substance or substratum: space—no-thing, to human eyes. Is this not what the Buddhist concept 'void' originally meant, that *space itself* is the domain throughout which the Wondrous Law holds true, that law of cause and effect (called karma) by whose grace we are *not* mere pawns of whimsical fate but ourselves the ultimate cause of what occurs in life? What is needed to profit from this Law is to cheerfully take responsibility *for* our thoughts and our life, not shift blame to others. Believe me I am not blind to how difficult it is to accept *either* law—Torah *or* Buddha's—after a catastrophe of the scale and horror of the Holocaust. I mean only to express my view; you are free to reject it.

The *fourth* is called Kindness, *Chesed*. For it is straight ahead, which signifies *towards other*. It is not called Kindness simply because as a divine attribute it could never be *un*kind: the *middot*, being self-contained, are both positive *and* negative—"thirteen pairs of opposites" they are called.[124] No, it is Kindness because *as yet*—that is, in this, the first world or Monad—the Sefirot are entirely radiative, not held back or limited in any way. Any reaction back *from* the direction each points—centripetal limitation—is an aspect that can only arise from other worlds or wheels in addition to the first. For such centripetal limitation to occur, this original world must first grant 'other' its origin, that back from which it *can* occur: hence, Kindness.

The next station, *fifth*, represents progressing on past or away from the direction *towards other*. This attaches to *fifth* the quality Severity (Gevurah) or Judgment (Din)—even here in this first world, evidently—as described by verse §145:

> The fifth is the great fire of the Blessed Holy One. Regarding this it is written (*Deuteronomy 18:16*), "Let me see the great fire no more, lest I die." . . . This is the Left Hand of the Blessed Holy One.

Fifth is called the 'great fire' because it is on the triangle pointing up, and it is the first point to complete a side of any elemental triad, namely the one beginning at *first* (Highest Crown). It is the fire triad's first point in the manifested half. (Of the two triangles in the Star of David, the one pointing up is traditionally associated with fire, since it points the direction flame tends.)

Sixth the *Bahir* calls the Throne of Glory, this undoubtedly because it is the approach to straight down and therefore symbolizes descent: it is what makes it possible for there to be a second wheel, that of *seated* Adam. It represents form, what logically and immediately precedes or prefigures the physical. The passage (verse §146, p. 53) goes on to call it 'the house of the World to Come', which gives this expression new meaning. *Seventh*, then, is called Holy Palace (verse §154, p. 56)—"and it supports them all"—being straight down, towards the body itself.

One reason for the departure from *up* to travel about the *middot* in the first place is to link uprightness to the body in which it is. Upon reaching *down* the impulse, in order to complete the job, must return to *up* (cf. the *aia*). Assuredly, seen in terms of thirteen divine attributes, the round does return to the beginning, as the symbol linking Uprightness to the body it uplifts. But the Sefirot, these stations as acquired attributes (steps progressing towards selfhood), do not yet extend all the way around but for *us* only as far as the sign signifying self-knowledge, where we are currently working.

Thus in *eighth* through *tenth*, the last three Sefirot, the *Bahir* has described for us a great truth, one mysterious *without* the key but which opens up to reveal 'the Kingdom' once that key is produced and turned. Here in the *Bahir* it is *eighth* that is called Foundation (Yesod) and the Righteous One (*tzaddik*), not *ninth* as in the more commonly known Tree. Why the 'shift'?

Here, *ninth* and *tenth* are both called Netzach, often translated 'victory' but essentially meaning 'endurance' or 'permanence'. This is the name assigned the *seventh* Sefirah in the commonly known Tree (that of the Egg). Now how does one get *that* simply by shifting the order about? by *seventh* dividing in two as it shifts to *ninth* and *tenth*? It is claimed these two Netzachs differentiate into Netzach and Hod[125] (7th and 8th) in the common scheme, but this overlooks the *reason* there are two of them. The *Bahir* identifies *ninth* and *tenth* with what it calls the *two* wheels of the *Merkavah* or Throne-Chariot: a lighter, more battle-worthy version of the one with four, I take it. Pairing 9 and 10, remember, is nothing new, for among the doubles they are K and G, the minds of feeling and desire, the fundamental polarity (-1 valence versus numerical +1), which stands behind the vav-yod polarity of the Great Name.

The reason for how *eighth* through *tenth* are described in the *Bahir* resides in how the conscious self—eighth through tenth signs—manifests in this, the first wheel. The explanation for the last two Sefirot here being 'permanencies' and *eighth* being the Foundation is quite simple: the knower, *tenth*, and thinker, *ninth*, did not undergo the Fall, being 'permanencies', and it is the doer that is the Foundation on which progress rests (on whose shoulders it is borne). The ultimate goal of alchemy is to turn *eighth*, the doer, into a third 'permanency' or Netzach. As will become clear from the Tree as it is on the third wheel, upon graduating to selfhood the doer must pass a test of balance, this by not losing sight of the inner horizon (the one opposite the outer) even while the senses only inform it of the outer. To give the reader a glimpse over the horizon, in the third wheel (the common Tree) it is the doer's thinking, *sagittary*, that must serve as foundation (and *tzaddik*), by leading towards self-knowledge. As the Buddha made clear, between thought, word, and deed, it is thought whose modification will have the most effect, this against the Jains, who argued deed was most important (were they behaviorists?).

Lest anyone think we are not on firm ground here, Scholem stipulated that to thirteenth-century Kabbalists the Sefirot represented "stages in the manifestation of the personal, individual identity of God."[126] The first Sefirah is equated with nothingness—*Ayin*, alef-yod-nun—and "through the process of emanation 'Nothingness changes into I' (*Ayin le-Ani*)"[127]—'I' being *Ani*, alef-nun-yod, thereby transposing the yod and nun of *Ayin*. Further, "God reaches His complete individuation through His manifestation in *Malkhut* [Kingdom, *tenth* Sefirah of the commonly known Tree], where He is called 'I'."[128] This is the 'I' of the *divine Form*, Adam Qadmon, Upright Sentience, model for all sentient beings and the state from which we fell. *Tenth* is also known as *Keneset Yisrael*, 'community of Israel' (perfectible man), and is associated with the *Shekhinah*, the divine Immanence or Presence (in us). No, we are not *departing* from tradition but *explaining* it.

Foundation is associated with the Righteous One or *tzaddik*,[129] what supports the self. In fact, the *tzaddik* is the pillar that supports the world;[130] for (say the wise) it is only the righteous *in* the world that keep it from being destroyed. *Righteous* means self-governed with regard to sex; for its covenant is *circumcision*, marked by insertion of the simple letter heh (eighth sign, scorpio, the privates) into the name Abram to make Abraham. Foundation *is* associated with the male organ in the common lore, but it is as *eighth* that it acquires this association, the eighth sign being scorpio. In the *Bahir*, it is in the context of *eighth* we are reminded that circumcision is on the *eighth day*.[131]

It is rather curious to read in Scholem that "[i]n the *Sefer ha-Bahir*, and in several early texts of the thirteenth century, the *Sefirah Yesod* [Foundation] was thought of as the seventh."[132] For the *Bahir* (in Kaplan's translation) definitely calls it *eighth*. Yes, much ado is made therein over whether eighth is actually seventh or is really eighth—verse §157 (p. 57) says, it being the "Foundation of all souls", it is written (*Exodus* 31:17), "And on the seventh day [Sabbath] He rested and souled," hence "it is the seventh"—yet the very next verse (verse §158, p.58) says: "Is it then the seventh? It is not." Note that the seventh spoke *is* where each progressing unit 'rested and souled'. Perhaps solving the mix-up is as simple as noting that while scorpio, the foundation of righteousness, is the eighth sign, it is at the end of the seventh arc. This has the deeper meaning of presaging that in a lower world, because of the Fall, each Sefirah that is in the manifested half will drift, via the arc leading on from it, to the sign following; but we are not yet there. What is *seventh* here, the body, will, as body-mind, gain control over *eighth*, the doer, and thereby erode this Foundation, forcing *ninth*, thought's approach to self-knowledge, to serve as Foundation (Yesod) in the common Tree till the doer completes the Great Work and consciously joins its thinker and knower *as* the Triune Self.

The pairing of *ninth* and *tenth* as twin 'Victories' recalls the 'utterly trustworthy parental pair' (Au-makua) of Huna. It is also a lead-in to the next world, that of creation (Beri'ah), where Sefirot are generated as pairs of opposites. Pairing numbers 9 and 10 presages feeling-and-desire (K and G) in the *fallen* doer acting as *substitute*, inadequate though they be, for the parental pair (*ninth* and *tenth*, or thinker-knower), 9 and 10 being the 'fundamental polarity' described earlier.

The ten Sefirot of the first wheel (Atzilut) progress to the point of being a full-fledged (if not yet fully balanced) conscious self: a capricorn unit of the light world. Here in the Bahir, the Monad's ten are described as they manifest to the fallen doer; for any doer who has *avoided* the Fall, who *passed* the test of balance, would hardly need to read about it in a book.

FOUR
The Sefirot of *Sefer Yetzirah*

It is called *Sefer Yetzirah*, yet the *Sefirot* described herein are those of the second world, Beri'ah, not the third, Yetzirah. True, Beri'ah means 'creation' and *SY*'s title is often translated 'Book of Creation'; and as the source of the doctrine of the three mothers and twelve simples, it certainly treats of the third or Yetzirah world. But the Sefirot are here generated in pairs: first-last, good-evil, up-down, east-west, south-north. The third wheel is 'still in its belly' (in logical succession, I do not mean in *time*) and has yet to give rise to triplicity as organizing principle. The dichotomy here is between macrocosm and microcosm, the hexads. The Throne world's macrocosmic hexad marks where the spokes (radii) of the signs of the manifested half of the Monad intersect it (figure 6, upper half). The first of each pair of Sefirot is on the macrocosmic hexad.

That it is the second wheel is confirmed by *SY* delegating, albeit in jumbled manner, the seven doubles to the six directions (last six Sefirot) plus the 'holy palace in the center' where the axes meet. For the doubles just happen to wrap around the bottom half of the *second wheel* (the Cauldron) in a way that aligns smoothly with up-down, east-west, and south-north.

The determining factor in each of the first two pairs is easy to grasp. First comes aries of the second wheel, the hub of the Monad, while the next sign embarks out onto the second wheel itself. 'Depth of the first' thus refers to the eternal, which precedes all beginnings; and 'depth of the last' takes us into the realm of the temporal, where all things come to an end. The 'depth of good' is gemini of the Throne world, realm of the thinker, source of conscience, last sign of its unmanifested half, whereas the next sign marks the start of its manifested half, the beginning of the next smaller wheel within it, the 'depth of evil' being this upper limit of the fallen doer.

An echo of this coincidence of evil with the advent of the level of the third wheel is the description of the three circles *Ceugant*, *Gwynvyd*, and *Abred* in *Barddas*,[133] the same source that speaks of the ten 'original cuttings' that remained secret, mentioned earlier. The first, *Ceugant*, a note in the text calls "the perfect rim that bounds the entire space of existence."[134] Lewis Spence describes *it* as containing only God, the *second* "all animated and immortal beings," and the *third* all things corporeal and evil, which, however, "God does not hate."[135]

The remaining Sefirot are easy to picture. The 'depth above' is the angle approaching leo, up being the direction its triad points, towards the fixed stars or macrocosm; and the 'depth below' is that approaching virgo, the approach to straight down, symbolizing descent towards man the microcosm. The 'depth of the east' is the angle approaching libra from virgo, on the triad pointing east; the 'depth of the west' is the angle departing libra for scorpio, on the triad pointing west. The former is on the macrocosmic or nature side leading *to* libra (the present), the latter on the microcosmic or intelligent side leading *on from* libra: east is where stars rise up into the macrocosmic heavens, west where they fall back into memory, the microcosm. Finally, the 'depth of the south', the angle leading to sagittary the thinker, references the U/V of the Logos, which points south; the 'depth of the north', angle leading to capricorn the knower, references the mem sofit of the Logos, which is as far north as it gets: south is towards, north away from, the ecliptic, the bulk of the population, north thus being where one might more easily commune with self. This would seem to associate the pole with the knower, with what abides, suggesting we regard it as stationary, with the entirety of the heavens wobbling about it like an immense drunk (every 25,772 years or so)—not *physically*, but *actually*.

How came the second Sefirah to mark the 'depth of the last': could it be, as the reverend rabbis claim, actually the tenth Sefirah emanated *out of turn*?[136] Of course not. The 'depth of the first' is the logical beginning of all we know—the eternal—while the 'depth of the last' takes us out into the realm of the temporal, of things (such as thoughts) which actually *come* to an end. Moreover, as the first arc departs aries to approach second sign taurus, the round's innate balance brings about a counterbalancing arc, the one *approaching* aries: this illustrates that quality of the second Sefirah wherein it is the *wisdom to return* (being departure *about the round*). Thus this is not meant to point just to the last *Sefirah* (on whose triad the second sign finds itself) but to the end of the entire round, the (arc leading to the) last of the *middot*.

Let us consider the further terminology *SY* applies to the first four Sefirot. It tells us the first is 'Spirit' (*ruach*), Spirit of Living Elohim, the second 'Spirit from Spirit': does this latter not mean Spirit's (temporal) *continuation*? Both are Holy Spirit (*ruach ha-kodesh*),[137] being what emanates directly from the knower and pervades the thinker to the 'depth of the last'. In other words, it is what unites the Au-makua, the 'utterly trustworthy parental pair'.

Continuing, third is 'Water from Spirit'—in which earth itself solidifies (see below)— and fourth is 'Fire from Water'. This strongly confirms our model; for the third is gemini, start of the water triad that manifests in earth or libra, and the fourth is cancer, the first manifested sign, that of manifested fire.

The fourth element, earth, was not skipped in designating fourth as 'Fire from Water', for the description of the third Sefirah in *SY* 1:11 (in the most revered version, the *Gra*) says:

> And He poured snow over them
>> and it became dust
>> as it is written
> "For to snow He said, 'Become earth' " (Job, 37:6).[138]

So the fourth element, earth, is included merely as eventual *result* of the triad established in the third Sefirah (water's), which manifests in libra, where it will gather to leave an earthy sediment as it evaporates. You will notice elemental breaths are similarly structured, earth breath Ii (yod) being the double of water breath I (zayin) and numbered third-from-the-end (water as reflection).

Following 'Fire from Water', and parsing the manifested half as it were, is the sealing of the six 'directions of space'—one for each remaining Sefirah—by the six possible permutations of the three letters used in the Great Name. The order of the combinations of yod, heh, and vav used in most commentaries (though there are several other variant traditions) is the one in the 'short version': yod-heh-vav *above*; yod-vav-heh *below*; heh-yod-vav *east*; heh-vav-yod *west*; vav-yod-heh *south*; vav-heh-yod *north*.[139] Here the order of initial letters as well as the order of the remaining two letters in each pair follow their order in the Name.

I have concluded this is the exact reverse of the original, correct order, which goes as if starting from the tenth Sefirah and working back up the Tree. This was forced on me by having finally solved the assigning of doubles to the six directions. Schemes of *this* in variants of *SY* fail to even get voiced and unvoiced equivalents on the same axis, to me an obvious requirement. I was late solving this, distracted by bardic numbering, tarot images, and other clues. Then one day it became obvious: the six directions are the last six Sefirot on the second wheel, the arcs leading to which *form* the Cauldron; and the order of the doubles thereon (skipping naughtily absent reysh) is D-T, K-G, P-B. I do not see how it can be otherwise than that dalet-tav are up-down, kaf-gimel east-west, peh-beyt south-north. Traditionally, pillars Jachin and Boaz were south and north—or right and left, viewed out the Temple's eastern entrance—just as south-north here link year's end (south)—P—to year's start (north)—B—at the cardinal sign *of* the east.

Duir the oak forms the canopy above, tinne the holly the bush at our feet. Coll the hazel and gort the ivy mark the directions of their triads, the former a kernel of wisdom, the latter the Dionysian revels. Peith the whitten or ink-maker's tree (Hebrew peh is a mouth speaking) points to the gregarious (more populated) south, beth the birch to the less populous north, being the sign turned away from others towards self. The latter's white bark suggests the lesser pigmentation of northern ancestry, while the ink-maker's tree is reference to that pigmentation (I hope I have not offended anyone, which seems easy to do these days). This should remind us of the absurdity of prejudice based on skin color, since all it signifies is *latitude of ancestry*.

My apology to readers from 'down under' for *SY*'s being northern-hemisphere oriented, but that *is* where most people live. Perhaps that is why twice *SY* lists *north* first,[140] to let folks from the southern hemisphere know it is okay to reverse the two. (I would be loath to exclude Australian aborigines, who seem to have a very sophisticated culture, albeit an endangered one.)

The remaining double letter reysh obviously occupies the meeting place of the three axes. One might speculate that the three distinct ways of pronouncing R—liquid, guttural, or rolled at tongue's tip—arise from the fact that there are three axes passing through it, each pronunciation relating to a particular axis. Rolled at tongue's tip, the sound is close to D and T; guttural R is close in sound to G and K. That leaves *liquid* R, perhaps drawn by the liquid L counterbalancing it on the water triad, striving towards (though never reaching) P and B. Thus while the guttural R 'knows its place' (body-mind as servant to the doer), the R rolled on the tongue's tip denotes the body-mind lording it over feeling, liquid R the body-mind lording it over desire. The liquid R adhering to the nature side of the water triad (opposite L) must be the liquid form's reflection as it reaches out to unite the two rolled forms. Confirmation of the above consists in the fact that liquid R is the one that is voiced, the rolled forms being repeated voiceless 'interruptions'.

FIVE
SY and Tarot of Marseilles

There is an odd phenomenon involving *SY* and tarot trumps: the latter appear to portray some of what *SY* says of the first few Sefirot. The language in *SY* relating to Tarot of Marseilles images is not quite definitive, yet it is suggestive. It involves something we will take a closer look at later on, namely coupling the first trump with the first-from-the-end, second with second-from-the-end, and so on.

Concerning the second Sefirah, called 'Breath from Breath' in verse 1:10,[141] *SY* says, "He engraved and carved / 22 Foundation Letters"—II La Papesse shows her reading a book—"Three Mothers / Seven Doubles / and Twelve Elementals [simple letters]"—XX Judgment shows three foreground figures, a *mother*, her *'double'* in the form of a father, and a *simple* child emerging from a coffin (it is Judgment Day). Note the three mothers include the knower or Father, while the doubles are of the thinker Sophia, so male-female sort of melt into each other symbolically. It says, "And one Breath is from them," there being in trump XX an archangel with a trumpet, and in trump II the impression that La Papesse might be reading aloud to us.

The third is called (in verse 1:11)[142] 'Water from Breath' (meaning from breath*ing*, as in condensation on a mirror?): "With it He engraved and carved / chaos and void / mire and clay," and indeed the odd-looking 'throne' in trump III L'Imperatrice *looks* as if it is carved from mud or clay. It continues, "He engraved them like a sort of garden / He carved them like a sort of wall / He covered them like a sort of ceiling," and trump XVIIII Le Soleil shows a wall topped by what *looks* like an attempt to roof it, the text leading us to believe this wall exists to keep the sweaty ('Water from Breath') exertions of the twins (the year's two halves) from trampling the garden hidden behind it.

The fourth is called (in verse 1:12)[143] 'Fire from Water', and "With it He engraved and carved / the Throne of Glory"—on which IIII L'Empereur shows him seated, albeit in a field (where he is obviously campaigning, being O, vowel of spring)—"Serafim, Ophanim, and holy Chayot"—this last oft translated 'living creatures', there being two dog-like creatures in XVIII La Lune, baying or barking at the moon, as well as a crustacean of some sort in the pool in the foreground—"and Ministering angels"—*obliquely* represented by the eagle on the shield at the emperor's feet (signifying angels waiting to serve God?), the angel in XX Le Jugement being an *arch*angel. It then says, "From these three He founded His dwelling" (the 'three' being Breath, Fire, and Water, according to Kaplan[144]), and indeed XVIII La Lune has a pair of tower-like edifices flanking pool, moon, and dogs—the only edifice in any trump save XVI La Maison Dieu, where the tower is being shaken by a cannonball and two figures tumble out of it. Trump XVIII La Lune's *bardic* theme is refuge from hounds—the "Ogham Tract" from *The Scholar's Primer*[145] calls Q, quert the apple, "shelter of a hind"—hence the face in the moon has its refuge or 'dwelling' *there*, taking refuge from two dogs, who dwell in the twin towers, the crustacean's 'dwelling' being the pool. The dogs' breathing—their moist breath visible issuing from their jaws (as dots) in the cold, damp evening air—is *between* the towers, just as the text (verses 3:4 through 3:6)[146] has breath deciding (balancing the scales) between fire and water.

The following verse[147] (1:13), setting forth the remaining six Sefirot, also seems relevant: simples yod, heh, and vav are chosen "in the mystery of the three Mothers," and much in trumps V and XVII (fifth-from-the-end) *bespeaks* motherhood. V Le Pape has the mother's arm enter the card from the right to *present* her twin sons to the pontiff to be blessed (this being the trump of beth the birch, the *birth* of the year, and of Boaz). And XVII L'Etoile (The Star) shows the conjoining of fluids poured from two amphorae, suggesting conception, this being ura, heather, bed of trysts under the stars (vowel of the full moon, of love's consummation). The nude woman in the trump pours from two 'jugs' or amphorae and is the only figure amongst the trumps with natural looking breasts (fit to suckle)—those in XXI Le Monde look pasted-on, rather than real. (Old Hebrew vav, remember, pictures a breast pouring forth milk.)

Trump V Le Pape somewhat implies the next line, "And He set them in His great Name," after which it says, "and with them, He sealed six extremities," XVII L'Etoile having seven stars forming a cup (or pendulous breast) around a larger one. These stand for the seven manifested signs, which start at vav or cancer: the doubles occupy these seven signs on the Cauldron and are delegated by *SY* (verse 4:4)[148] to the six extremities plus "the Holy Palace precisely in the center / and it supports them all."

Which of the last seven Sefirot is to be singled out as the Holy Palace depends on what world one is in. In Atzilut it is *seventh* the *Bahir* calls Holy Palace: the body, libra. Here in Beri'ah, *SY* would imply it is the fourth Sefirah, out of which the last six as extremities spring. And in the Lurianic Kabbalah it is the first six of the last seven Sefirot (the 'broken vessels') which are said to span the Yetzirah world (when one Tree is spread across all four worlds) and which are identified with the six spatial directions, leaving the last Sefirah (*tenth*, Malkut) as the Asiyah world and thus 'odd man out'. I find it interesting that the knower's world has the Holy Palace in the middle, libra, while the next two worlds, those of thinker and doer respectively, position it on the nature-side rim and intelligent-side rim respectively, just as the thinker's U (Latin V) in the Logos symbolizes the nature or descending side, doer's A the intelligent or ascending side.

All this seeming reference to *SY*'s imagery in the trumps is rather subtle, almost obtuse, as if describing Beri'ah as perceived through the *fog* of Yetzirah. Yet it is quite striking in its way and surely not the work of the god Chance. But here, as in all questionable things, I leave final judgment to you dear reader, though I will say that XVIIII Le Soleil's wall leaves little doubt in *my* mind what is hidden behind it: the Garden (shielded from the young scalawags).

SIX

The Tree of Forms

Even with the Tree in its commonest form, seen in practically every book on Kabbalah (figure 6), the core meaning is never elucidated. (Is it even grasped?) Perhaps it is only obvious from a certain viewpoint, realized in my case by having read Percival. I should point out that this Tree can be seen in two ways. It is commonly viewed as three triads plus a tenth, which is quite useful, as we shall see. But its original signification is as the (triangular) tetraktys of the Pythagoreans: one by itself; followed by a pair; then a triad; then a tetrad. When we do view the first three Sefirot as a triad (which is permissible), overall it prefigures transition from triadic to tetradic (in preparation for the next Tree), for it still ends with a group of four (just as the second Tree prepares us for triplicities by ending with the three axes).

I will cut to the chase: these Sefirot, being those of the doer's third wheel, represent the path of the Fall. Now should you be too much the skeptic to take the Fall seriously, there is an alternative interpretation, perfectly compatible with that of the Fall but quite valid in itself, that will suffice to still derive great psychological value from the model. This also is not, as far as I can tell, specifically to be found in currently available expositions of the Tree. For the benefit of the skeptics among you, I shall commence with that alternative description.

There is, in human thinking and behavior, a hierarchy of modes, shall we say. There is: (1) A completely sexless mode, as when accessing Uprightness itself. (2) A chaste male mode, as that of a small male child. (3) A chaste female mode, as that of a small female child. (4) A procreative male mode, seeking to conjoin for purposes of offspring. (5) A procreative female mode, seeking to conjoin for purposes of offspring. (6) A procreative neutral mode, the linked state or issue of two thus conjoined. (7) A lustful male mode. (8) A lustful female mode. (9) A lustful mutual mode or issue centered around the nine months of gestation. (10) A lustful mutual mode or issue centered around what can be grasped with the ten fingers.

The other, more 'biblical' way of viewing the Tree needs an introduction. If the Prime Mover is the divine Form every individual unit of existence ultimately seeks, each instance of that Form must be a sort of Jacob's Ladder or path of ascent towards that goal for all the units involved, the conscious self inhabiting it having currently achieved the tenth step on our wheel, that of selfhood. According to Percival, on having graduated to selfhood, along with concurrent shift of every unit progressing through the various functions of nature on that ladder (enabled by the previous self's having brought it into balance and moved on), there is the test of separation into a desire body and a feeling body, so that the doer might bring its two sides into balance.[149] This last is accomplished only if the doer manages *not* to be deceived by the senses into thinking itself two separate beings. Once balanced, the two reunite into the single sexless immortal body the doer will use to fulfill its responsibility of overseeing operation of the Law of Thought: that all physical acts, objects, and events are exteriorizations of thoughts, which continue to cycle about till balanced (dissolved) by the one issuing the thought. This is essentially the Buddha's Wondrous Law: that we ultimately forge our own destiny and are not mere pawns of fate. A doer's passing of this test is a first prerequisite to progressing on to become an Intelligence (a capricorn unit of the fire sphere), by whose Light the conscious self can see within itself.

Unfortunately, we mortals failed this test, hypnotized by sight's outer horizon (and its concomitant sounds, tastes, smells, and tangibles) into losing sight of what we actually are, the inner horizon opposite it. Believing the senses' reports from without that seem to show desire and feeling as two, not one, yet sensing they somehow belong together, the desire and feeling bodies then conjoin for purposes of offspring, prompted I imagine by signs of physical decay resulting from 'their' new mode of thinking. This coincides with the introduction of death into their world[150] (birth comes from death), though not of suffering.

The original (immortal) type constitutes the first Sefirah: the first 'earth'. The desire and feeling bodies constitute the second and third Sefirot: the second 'earth'. The male and female bodies altered to conjoin for the purpose of procreation constitute the fourth and fifth Sefirot, their capacity to produce offspring being the sixth: these three constitute the third 'earth'. After the initial pair perishes, the bodies produced presumably would be (as with us) dwelt in by an admixture of desire and feeling, predominance of the one or the other determining sex.

This conjoining is evidently pleasurable, for the doers of that third 'earth' who seek to conjoin *because* of the pleasure it yields[151] (rather than its original purpose) cause the physical type to undergo a further transformation into the types represented by the seventh and eighth Sefirot and their twofold issue: ninth, the prospect of offspring (nine months' gestation), and tenth, what the ten fingers can grasp. The female, presumably, is more focused on a potential nine months' pregnancy, the male on what his ten fingers can grasp.

It was only upon entry into this fourth 'earth' that pain and suffering entered our world. This Tree is relevant also to those who have *passed* the test of balance, being a map of all the various types that these balanced, poised, immortal beings are tasked with governing.

It is easy to see how the first three Sefirot here got their names. First is Keter, 'Crown', being aries the head (atop the seated form, where shin is), that which links us to the original type, Adam Qadmon, at least when seated in meditation. Second, the chaste male type, is Chokhmah, 'Wisdom', for governance of desire. Third, the chaste female type, is Binah, 'Understanding', for governance of feeling. These seem self-explanatory. They are the first signs, respectively, of the cardinal, male, and female tetrads, the one leaning forward being more expressive of desire, the one leaning back more expressive of feeling. But what happens with the next one? For the fourth Sefirah is male, yet the fourth *sign* is on the cardinal tetrad: what gives?

Here we encounter the origin of that elusive quasi-Sefirah Da'at, 'Knowledge', a neutral station between the 2-3 and 4-5 pairs. In the proper course of things, the doer passes its test of balance and types 2 and 3 merge back into 1, now 4, a body of four balanced elements. This calls to mind the oldest axiom of alchemy, attributed to one Maria the Jewess, the earliest known alchemist in the West: "One becomes two, two becomes three, and out of the third comes the one as the fourth." Indeed tradition offers a *version* of the Tree with middle column 1-4-7-10.

But doers who fail the test, on entering the manifested half of the Egg—realm of time and decay—occupy forms determined by the arcs or months extending *on from* their signs. Thus 4's arc, starting at fourth sign cancer, ends at fifth sign leo, on the *male* tetrad; and 5's arc, starting at fifth sign leo, ends at sixth sign virgo, on the *female* tetrad; and so on. Note that sign cancer thus remains unused: being vav's station, the noetic breath in the psychic atmosphere or Egg, it bears the name Da'at or Knowledge.

At the end, 10's arc gets nipped in the bud—as pictured by its letter, yod (ʼ), Hebrew 10—at the limit, capricorn, which it would have to share with 9 but for one of them projecting back across to the sign opposite, cancer, the only sign of the first ten that is yet unoccupied. It must be 9 that projects itself across, if the fundamental polarity between 9 and 10 (K and G) is any indication, a result that parallels, on the Egg, transference of D from sagittary to cancer on the Cauldron. The process this pattern embodies will be revisited in the context of the Name, but suffice it to say it maps thought being lured from its station at sagittary over to cancer by objects of the senses to which it is drawn. The mechanism of its crossing over is the fact that in the third world the impulse in the direction a radius points is weaker than the impulse *back from* it, water being more passive than active: *prior* to 9, the sign opposite is in the unmanifested; but when time's maelstrom pushes 9 to capricorn, it reverses itself to the first manifested sign. As the nine months of gestation, it *redefines* knowledge, so to speak, as knowing 'in the biblical sense'.

Since here in the Yetzirah world this process involves 9 (-1 valence) and 10 (numerical +1), the minds of feeling and desire, we begin to glimpse just how feeling ends up being a stand-in for the thinker or *ninth* and desire a stand-in for the knower or *tenth*. These last two Sefirot are the only two that have remained paired from the beginning: they are the two 'Victories' or Netzachs in Atzilut, the polarity south-north in Beri'ah, and the fundamental polarity in Yetzirah.

The *procreating* male and female types are called Gedulah and Gevurah, 'Glory' and 'Power', or else Chesed and Din, 'Mercy' and 'Severity'. For the male gives freely of his seed, while the female 'imprisons' it in her womb. The result is Tiferet or 'Beauty'.

The *lustful* male and female types are called Netzach, 'Victory' or 'Endurance', and Hod, 'Splendor'. It is apparent surely that desire fully expressed is power and feeling fully expressed is beauty. That is how their representatives in this fourth 'earth' acquire the names Victory and Splendor. Their conjoined states are Yesod, 'Foundation' or offspring, and Malkut, 'Kingdom', what can be grasped by ten fingers. This last has both an outer and an inner meaning, the latter being for the instruction of the doer. Association of the Shekhinah or divine Presence with this last Sefirah signifies the ethical *reining-in* of what the ten fingers seek to grasp.

This Tree's triads are linked to the parts of the self. For in the first and second 'earths', a doer is still in communication with its knower or *neshamah*. In the third, it is still in communion with the thinker or *ruach* (*ruach ha-kodesh*, the Holy Spirit). But here in the fourth 'earth', the doer or *nefesh* is 'on its own', if only from its own flawed point of view. Tradition agrees with this allotment of parts to Sefirot, adding that the body is tenth (what the ten fingers can grasp).

SEVEN
The Broken Vessels

Looking online just now, it amazed me how much hot air is spilled on this teaching: it was not until the eighth site down the list—Architizer Journal, to give credit where it is due—that I found even a mention of the fact that "of the ten vessels of light, which correspond to the ten Sefirot, the upper three, being stronger, did not break." After exploring the origin of this Tree of Forms (vessels) in the last chapter, it should be clear why this is so: the first three are chaste forms, those *preceding* the Fall. We may presume that the front column Boaz was not broken in any of the first three forms, and that the breaking off of Boaz is what is meant.

There is a fascinating artifact of this teaching that arises from the numbers representing letters in bardic tradition, as expressed by their trumps and atom-types. You will recall that the language of *SY* seemed to describe aspects of trumps corresponding to the first few Sefirot when counting from beginning and end: first paired with last; second paired with second-to-last; and so on. Well, a very interesting phenomenon surfaces thereby with respect to the first three.

The three groups 1-11-21, 2-11-20, and 3-11-19 each exhibit a clearly coherent pattern: 1-11-21 are one thing, one thing in relation to *one* ten-fingered, and one thing in relation to *two* ten-fingereds; 2-11-20 are all numerical +2s; and 3-11-19 are all +1 valence! After that, there is no pattern similarly aligned, though 7 and 15 (but not 11) share a valence. This phenomenon is clearly a relic of the *shevirat ha-kelim*, the 'shattering of vessels'.

Indeed by the *last* three Sefirot, there is some hint that what little coherence remains has been displaced or offset by one, judging from northern European tree-lore—as if the reflections had slipped down one and crashed into the original fulcrum, XI Force. They appear to be paired like this: trumps XI and X are the holly and the ivy, traditional rivals at yuletide;[152] trumps XII and VIIII are the oak and the hazel, alone singled out by the east Goths as being immune from felling and at the same time said to dislike one another and be unable to agree;[153] and trumps XIII and VIII are ash and alder, from which male and female human beings were fashioned,[154] according to Norse myth. The name of the woman, Embla, is often translated 'elm', but ash and alder make much better sense, as ash tends to strangle plants growing in its shade,[155] while alder is beneficial to them (nitrogen-fixing), like a mother, and its wood is softer than ash.

So while reysh at 15 does share 7's valence, it shares its digital sum with mem or 6: both 15 (R) and 6 (M) evoke Cauldron's libra. And libra is both the seventh sign *and* where the sixth arc ends up (which is what makes 6 neutral on the triadic Tree).

Consider, for a moment, the 'arrows' suggested by the first two Sefirot seen as pairs of trumps or letters. Listed head first, arrow 1, alef-teyt, points up, to the center of the Egg (fourth wheel's aries) or, as the triad pointing up, to aries itself, with its tail teyt at libra. Where one might expect 2 to point to second sign taurus, heh-tzaddi points instead to its opposite, scorpio, its *tail* at taurus. This is a reference to the reversal of 2 resulting from duality's rebelling against

Unity to pull against it and cancel it out (inert gas helium). And that is what has occurred, if we measure valence by height: heh or helium connects, via its approach arc, to libra, zero height, while its tail, tzaddi or calcium, connects via its approach arc to its valence height, +2, at aries (occupied by oxygen's -2). The remaining numeric +2 in this second of three *un*broken vessels, the 11 of 2-11-20, is at its valence height (+1) as leo on the Cauldron, same level as alef's ±1 at Egg's center, and connects to its *numeric* height, +2, by approach arc on the Cauldron. T or tav, is physiologically the heart (which sodium affects), seat of conscience; hence it projects onto the center of the Egg, midpoint of 2's arrow. Its shape is an arrow in runic (↑), in the Scandinavian Tifinag an arrow pointing down (table 5): arrows target the heart (tav). Ancient Hebrew tav is one's mark or X—one's bond—or alternatively +, a crossroads or center (the heart of things).

Two heights missed so far are the *numeric* +2 of heh's helium, and the valence as well as numeric heights of teyt (+3). Heh can be understood to have briefly *been* at its numeric height of +2 as it departed aries, just before flipping its arrow about. And teyt is the floor of the Boaz-in-potentia column that, along with ceiling nun, share the valence of beyt, the double whose radius sweeps said ceiling in arriving at its station and whose *departing* arc marks the valence height of +3 (as well as teyt's +3 *numeric* height) at its upper end. Nun's +4 and beyt's -4 numeric heights are unmarked; it happens that *numeric* +4s and -4s, all four of them, are consistently *not* directly marked by height, as if the crunching together of +4 and -4 valence toppled them. One of the two *valence* ±4s is carbon: as mem sofit, it occupies its valence height at the hub of the Monad. Carbon's *numeric* height, -3, is marked by intermediate mem's sweep of the floor of the Boaz-in-potentia column as it departs libra, thus linking it to beyt's reach up to ±3 height. The other ±4 valence, lamedh, is a special case, as we shall see in the context of the planetary metals.

Consider the two 'arrows' zayin-yod (3-19) and ayin-qof (4-18). Each of these 'arrows' consists of one of the two manifested signs of alef's fire triad plus the sign following—as if each arrow gets flipped about between one sign and the next. The 3, zayin, points to the sign after 2 (heh), that is, sagittary, the sign opposite the third sign; so its arrow starts already flipped about, then flips back about by the time it reaches the end of its arc at capricorn. The 4, ayin, points not to the fourth sign (opposite 3's 'tail') but the fifth—end of the fourth *arc*—then flips about again at the next sign to plant its *tail* at 18, qof; this 'skipping ahead' we can interpret as the beginning of the breakage, this being the first 'broken vessel'. And if the last three Sefirot set the pattern for the lower seven, the *broken* 4 would now pair rather with 17, *fifth*-from-the-end, which just happens to reside at the *start* of the fourth arc (cancer, the fourth sign).

Now note that the three +1s by *Hebrew* numbering, 1-10-100, are alef-yod-qof: fire triad alef plus those two 'tails' (by bardic numbering) of arrows 3 and 4. Is that not interesting? And the Hebrew +2s (2-20-200) are beyt-kaf-reysh: those same two 'tails', on the Cauldron this time, plus the tail of the first 'arrow' (taking reysh as libra).

EIGHT

'Paths on the Tree'

There are various schemes of applying letters to the 'paths' (figure 7) of this Tree. Some say there is one way of applying them for descent and another for ascent, meaning the *tikkun*, the restoration of what has been shattered. That it is with regard to this Tree that *tikkun* is frequently discussed confirms it is indeed the Tree of the fallen doer.

I cannot tell you with certainty there is any one right way. If I were to invest time and effort to try to solve this puzzle (with no assurance even that I could), I would most likely start from versions (or my own scheme) that put the three mothers on the three horizontals, the seven doubles on the seven verticals, and the twelve simples on the twelve diagonals.

There *is* one scheme that has survived the test of time. In contrast to the many suggested solutions given in Judaic lore, it is the main *commonly accepted* scheme in modern-day Hermetic Kabbalah. This latter some occultists (e.g. Crowley) would like us to believe is their inviolably correct inherited corpus of Truth, sometimes claimed to be of Egyptian origin, and on far weaker grounds than I present herein for what I have traced back to that hoary past. The actual origin of much of their lore resides in Christian Kabbalah, from the Renaissance.

Their scheme of 'paths' (shown in figure 7) starts at the top, using letters' normal alef-beyt order, and basically just fans out in a natural way till it reaches the bottom. The interesting thing about this scheme is the order in which letters feed into the central Sefirah, Tiferet, namely: gimel-heh-zayin-yod-lamedh-nun-samekh-ayin. Starting with the desire mind, on the intelligent side of the Cauldron, it climbs that side of the Egg, using letters' *original* order, all the way to the top, followed by leo, the 'vowel' of the season it has reached (spring). My first discovering this was another of those jaw-dropping moments, as I had long dismissed occultists' version of things as mostly spurious, all except the Tree itself of course, and correct assignment of planets to Sefirot.

You may recall (chapter 19 above) that the alef-beyt's pattern following mem is much the same: simples climb the inner Egg, this time in their jumbled order, from scorpio to aries (with one interruption at capricorn), their arrival at aries accented by the double usurping that station (reysh) and the mother residing there (shin), then jump over to the *Cauldron's* leo. I have yet to explore all the ramifications of this scheme of 'paths', but note that gimel (desire mind) links 6 to 1, or alef the doer, and that heh and zayin link 6 to 2 and 3 respectively, their bardic numbers!

The final jump to leo (ayin) brings up a vital aspect of things I have left till now because it is best tackled in the context of planetary metals and the alchemical Egg: exactly how spring's vowel O (ayin) manages to *manage* spring from way down there in the Egg's lower half where the vowels *are*. It does so manage, and exceptionally well, as we are about to see.

NINE
The Planetary Metals

The key to the Hermetic or 'metallurgical' side of all this is the planetary attributions to Sefirot preserved unambiguously in occult tradition (from the Christian Kabbalah), also listed as one possible solution in Jewish tradition.[156] They are (following Giordano Bruno): the Primum Mobile; the fixed stars (firmament); Saturn; Jupiter; Mars; Sol; Venus; Mercury; Luna; and the sublunary sphere (earth and its atmosphere). These are mostly correct; the only errors are the attribution for Sol and for the 'fixed' stars. The best way to visualize it is as follows.

They bridge the gap between 1, eternity or Unity, and 10, today, the present (what can be held in ten fingers). The Primum Mobile is the source of the stars' (electrical) energy, which is conserved, plasma's electromagnetically determined behavior almost certainly overcoming the effects of the second law of thermodynamics (which decrees that thermodynamic systems 'run down'). All these cycles are in a forward sense, not retrograde; for by Great Year we do not mean drift of equinoxes backwards about the 'fixed' stars (what physically triggers the cycle as we understand it) but rather the end result of that: progress of the entire physical heavens *in a forward sense* about the zodiac, that is, around our projection of the zodiac of the seasons (and seated torso) on the stellar heavens. Each such revolution takes about 25,772 years, by current reckoning. This reveals an important secret that physicists lack: the universe, though not *earth*-centered, is *anthropo*centric, for it is centered where intelligent side and nature side *meet*.

The proper place of the sun in this Tree is 2, for 'precession' is defined as the change in the relationship between 6—the ecliptic or year—and 10—the equator or day. I can even prove this is how it was originally viewed, using the tradition preserved in astrology of which planets are exalted in which signs. Assigning planets to Sefirot as above, then pairing them as on the third Tree, each male-female pair are exalted in signs opposite one another: the sun and Saturn, 2 and 3, in aries libra (gold above, lead below); Jupiter Mars, 4 and 5, in cancer capricorn (or without and within); and Venus Mercury, 7 and 8, in pisces virgo (back of the neck and womb). (Luna, 9, the odd 'man' out, is exalted in taurus, connected to 'parents' Venus and Mercury via horizontal and vertical, respectively.)

Skeptics may object that we have not taken into consideration the three (now two my foot!) outer planets not visible to the naked eye. But I assure you they are here as vividly as if they had been listed by Bruno himself (though he was probably unaware of them). There is a sense in which they are extra-cyclical, for all three go about the sun in a *reverse* sense when plotted onto the *central frame* of the solar system, which itself revolves roughly once every thirty-one years.[157] So they are mainly counterweights to the angular momentum of the visible planets. And note the planetary cycle that marks the limit of non-'retrograde' planets, beyond whose orbit lie the three not normally visible to the naked eye, bears the number 3, count of what lurks beyond (we are not yet finished with these).

If we take asteroids, which occur mostly between Jupiter (4) and Mars (5), as remnants of a planet since destroyed by catastrophe (the reason for which may become apparent shortly), it is tempting to identify this fragmented planet with quasi-Sefirah Da'at, meaning vav, whose month just happens to span the gap between the fourth and fifth signs.

It is quite striking how this Tree matches the structure of the periodic table. Cycles 2-6-10—Great Year, year, and day—form its framework: corresponding atom-types are helium (2), byproduct of radioactive metals' long decay periods—comparable to the Great Year—carbon (6), life itself—whose cycle is the year—and neon (10)—switched on and off daily (nightly).

Let us pause for a moment and consider how appropriate these planetary assignments to Sefirot are. The innocent male mode is the sun: brightness itself (Chokhmah, Wisdom). The innocent female mode is Saturn: ruler of the mythical Golden Age, when life was peaceful and agrarian (Binah, Understanding). The procreative male is Jupiter, god of many offspring, from which comes the term *jovial* (Chesed, Kindness). The procreative female is Mars; for the martial *ideal* is a mother defending her young, since she *will not yield* (Din, Severity). What these two produce is the year or cycle of vegetation (Tiferet, Beauty). The lustful male mode is Venus, or what he lusts after. The lustful female mode is Mercury, what *she* is most drawn to, a mover and a shaker (god of commerce and trickery). What they produce concerning pregnancy is Luna, for obvious reasons; and concerning hands' grasp, the earth or day, again for obvious reasons.

Even the directions given in *SY* are appropriate. North is just earth, the pole; south, the ecliptic, is where the moon provides two-thirds of the tidal pull in that plane that is the physical cause of the precession. West and east are the two planets closest to the sun (thus tied to sunrises and sunsets), Mercury and Venus, the latter called Phosphorus or Lucifer as morning star. The 'depth below' is the year, meaning crops or harvest; the 'depth above' is Mars, one's iron helm. The 'depth of evil' is Jupiter, god who overthrew Saturn's Golden Age (precipitated the Fall); the 'depth of good' is Saturn's Golden Age itself. Finally, the 'depth of last' is the Great Year, which outlives us all; and the 'depth of first' is the eternal, out of which all things spring. This clashes slightly with allotment of doubles to extremities, as dalet, the depth *above*, is Jupiter's oak (though note that *Zeus* is cognate with Norse *Tiw*, usually identified with Mars) and so on. Doubles T and K stand for sun and moon, this much is certain (see below).

Let us return to the columns that share floor and ceiling of like valence. By a scheme of exquisite subtlety, the columns bordered by vertical lines linking signs, plus the vertical diameter or center-post itself, are assigned, in orderly fashion, to Sefirot 3 through 9, reading from within to without. They fix the planetary metals in the Egg-as-alchemical-vessel in a way that explains planetary rulership in astrology (figure 8): a sign is ruled by the column the round just passed through to get there. Means of assigning the columns alternate: the middle columns within and without are determined by valence of *planetary metal*, the rest by column number (Sefirah) and *its* valence. The ramifications of this are enormous!

Planetary metals are gold (2, or 2-6-10), lead (3), tin (4), iron (5), copper (7), mercury (8), silver (9). Columns 3 and 5 are our Jachin-Boaz pair, determined by the numbers 3 and 5 and their valences (+1, +3), the columns of Saturn (lead) and Mars (iron). Jupiter's tin column between them is identified by its ceiling, lamedh or silicon, which, though not a metal, shares tin's valence of ±4; and by its floor being swept by the Cauldron radius at the end of the arc departing intermediate mem or carbon, also tin's ±4. Lamedh itself is on the border between lead and tin, both of which share silicon's ±4 valence.

Column 8, the middle column without, is the calcium-beryllium (tzaddi-ayin) column we encountered earlier, reinforced by the third letter of that valence, D or 12 (magnesium), at the Cauldron's outer rim, the radius departing which sweeps that column's roof as it approaches its terminus (at Cauldron's leo): all three are the +2 valence of the *metal* mercury (column 8). The column to its right is 7, Venus or copper, fixed by P (7), nitrogen, and R (15), phosphorus, which is seventh-from-the-end and shares 7's valence; they accomplish this from their original stations at the Cauldron's cancer and libra, since the radius as it departs the one and approaches the other sweeps this column's ceiling and floor, respectively. The last column is 9 (-1 valence), Luna or silver, fixed by its floor vav, 17 (-1 valence), and by 9 itself, kaf, whose radius as it approaches its Cauldron station sweeps both the ceiling and floor of its column.

The center-post, vertical diameter aries-libra, is marked as 6 at *both* extremities by mem: below by intermediate mem, the mem of the calendar (bardic 6), and above by mem sofit, 600 in Hebrew. Though this column itself only extends up to half the latter's height, mem sofit reminds us this is the one column that *can* be extended upwards without any alteration of its axis. It is the one reliable 'channel' to what is above: Uprightness; the high self; the AUM-akua. Could this be the aka cord by which mana (reclaimed Light) is sent to the parental pair, the Au-makua?

The Tree of the fourth wheel is intertwined with the third, as in coincidence of water and earth breaths I and Ii, and earth's inclusion in water (as *third*) in *SY*: doer's third wheel stamping its character onto the fourth, the dark present instant. In the fourth the outward thrust of a radius is completely overcome. Starting with 2's reversed arrow, the Egg sets the pattern; 3 is Saturn's floor, 19 (third-to-last, 3's tail) is Saturn's roof. Why? When the reversed direction enters the unmanifested, the original direction reasserts itself, leading to 4, ayin, marking the end of the fourth angle, the one making 4 male in the Tree of Forms. (The fourth wheel's total reversal is perhaps seen in light rays coming *back to* us along a line of sight being what produces an image.)

Amazingly, there is only one real leftover in all of this, one letter that might have been used to help determine a column (by the rules here established) but was *not*: tav the heart. It is over on the opposite side of things from the column that shares its +1 valence (the Saturn column within). But tav, the center or pivot of the trumps, has a special role, as we shall see.

Remaining atom-types not needed to determine columns fall into two groups: three inert gases, all within one arc of libra (±0 height), and two that share -2 valence, both at ±2 height (at aries). This raises two questions. First, since all 'leftovers' are at (or express by arc) the proper valence heights, might the rest express their valence heights in unmistakable ways? And second, since they had no role in initially determining columns, what role might oxygen and sulfur, the two -2s, fulfill besides expressing increase as the 8 and 16 issuing forth from 4 (O) at the start of spring? The answer to the second question is one-third of the answer to the first. We shall start with the other two-thirds of the first question, and let the remainder serve as *coup de grace*.

TEN
The Alchemical Egg

We already touched on how 5's column marks its valence height. It and 7's column do so in the same way: B and P (5 and 7), acting for their respective columns *as a whole*, reach up like horns from their original stations on Cauldron's inner and outer rims via their arcs on the Cauldron-circle extending up into the unmanifested to aquarius and gemini respectively, which are at the proper ±3 height. Mem sofit marks the ±4 height of the center-post; and intermediate mem's radius sweep links this also to the *tin* column (though lamedh's oblique marking of its own valence height remains to be seen). And the innermost and outermost columns are *at* their +1 and -1 heights. Well, we made quick work of that!

The remainder of the answer is one of the key 'tricks' of this entire model. It is how onn the furze—O, ayin, vowel of spring—*rules* spring. Though D jumps over to the nature side and by radius sweep anoints the roof of mercury's column, thus linking it to its +2 valence level (the outer horizon), we are about to see how the column itself attains this valence height, which it does not at present quite reach. It demonstrates in no uncertain terms that alchemical symbolism is an integral part of the model, implying that Hermetic symbolism is of great antiquity, since it is here found woven in with knowledge that can only be a survival from many thousands of years ago. Or would you argue that this whole sophisticated model could have been devised by the not-so-ancients, those for whom even light bulbs and steam engines were apparently rare and/or secret things?[158] My own take is that this model is palpable evidence of that *prisca sapientia* Newton and his fellow alchemists searched for:[159] that pristine, *very* ancient wisdom predating the current state of affairs traceable by history and archeology. But draw your own conclusions.

While it is the *metal's* valence that determines the 8 column to be mercury's, the columns to either side of it are determined by sefirotic number, rather than metal. And it just so happens that Mercury's sefirotic number, 8, is the *bardic* number of the next roof inward (to the right of it) and the *Hebrew* number of the next roof outward (to the left of it). Fearn the alder—and since the head is outlined in gold in VIII Justice, samekh evidently as well—affixes bardic number 8 to the ceiling of the copper or 7 column. And huath the hawthorn, cheyt, which is Hebrew 8—and being bardic zero is happy to do *something* to contribute to the work at hand (the Great Work)—affixes 8 to the ceiling of the silver or 9 column. Putting 2 and 2—or rather 8 and 8—together, there appears to be a takeover of the upper halves of these two columns by fumes of the volatile metal mercury, whose column they frame (see figure 8, top).

How does this happen? Any alchemist knows that when you heat mercury, it flies up into the air: this is what necessitates the Egg be a hermetically sealed vessel (since mercury vapor is poisonous). And look where the mercury column's floor is situated: it happens to be the hottest month of the year (leo). It represents where *nature* places the fire under the vessel. So, as the floor of the mercury column gets heated, its vapors fly up from the lower half of its column to take over the entire upper half of the outer vessel—which constitutes spring—thus reaching at last its valence level, already marked by D, the oak of Jupiter (whose messenger Mercury is). So once mercury is heated and leaps into the 'air', its floor, spring's vowel O, onn the furze, finally captures its season, spring, so that it can share the top of the outer Egg—aries, spring equinox—with the other two numbers there that together with it express increase or a gushing forth from the fount of spring: 4-8-16, aries being the valence height of all three *and* of mercury itself.

This leap of mercury's vapor into the 'sky' of the outer vessel also symbolizes filling-in of trees' foliage in spring, which has to be what Newton and his fellow alchemists meant by the 'Greene Lyon', since it is rooted in leo (perhaps on a practical level it is a search for how to tint mercury's vapors green?)—this represents summer's recurring heat reaching back in time (so to speak) to *cause* spring. If we picture the *outer* Egg by itself as spherical, then the shape taken by mercury's column once these vapors are included happens to be that of a mushroom or toadstool with a hollow stem. Graves in *tWG* makes quite a point of postulating a mushroom or toadstool cult in the Dionysian lineage of bardic tradition. I have never imbibed the *amanita muscaria* mushroom, but I have experienced synthetic mescaline, and I can testify to how the psychedelic experience can facilitate *seeing* in the sense of transcending inborn intellectual and psychological limitations. It certainly helped me lift myself above my atheistic, pagan-leaning teens to change into the Gnostic I am today. *Ayahuasca* is used to initiate shamans in parts of South America—a toxic dose, to test whether the initiate has the presence of mind to ask for the antidote (or else fail to return from this raid into death's realm). The book in which I read this (Harner's *The Way of the Shaman*, see bibliography) says that in North America, shamanic initiation through visions was usually induced by fasting, not than drugs, the peyote cult of Kiowa and Comanche being a fairly recent exception (post Civil War). That Mercury's column takes the form of a toadstool explains why in early Greek times Hermes was simply a phallus,[160] the kinship between the two shapes being fairly obvious.

Notice the arrangement of columns, that is, before mercury's takeover of the upper half of the outer vessel, and relate this to which planets rule which signs in astrology: each sign is ruled by the planetary column the year has just traversed to arrive there. But there is a glitch: the column the year traverses just prior to leo is Luna's (she has just conferred her rulership on cancer), yet astrology says Sol rules it.

Tav, at his station on the outer Cauldron far from the column of his fellow +1 valences, zayin-yod (Saturn's column), will now come to our rescue to set things right. For the Cauldron's radius as it departs tav (the arc approaching kaf) sweeps silver's entire column, and 11's valence is +1, that of both the *metals* silver and gold. This is the *hierosgamos*, the sacred marriage of sun and moon, a recurring theme in alchemy: tav—the sun or heart, being a numerical +2 (11) and a sefirotic 2-6-10, at the passive end of air's level of the Cauldron—by its sweep restores Luna to the upper half of her column (after mercury's usurpation of it) and, allowing her to rule there, steps in to rule in the manifested. Each time Luna is displaced from her sky (sound familiar?) by fumes of volatile mercury, Sol will be there, on the Cauldron and thus out of mercury's reach, to restore her rule. She brings her domain to the marriage; what he brings is the strength to rule it.

How might lamedh mark its valence height (besides through mem)? It signifies to *learn*, to *teach*, as the sign progressing *on* from self. Its shape and grammatical significance in Hebrew (and of several roots starting with it) signify a reaching out beyond oneself. Stationed in the gap beyond the tenth sign (last Sefirah), L senses that if it were to extend its side of the water triad (figure 6, bottom) up to the *Monad's* aquarius, its approach arc there *would* link it to its valence height, Monad's capricorn. And the vertical at Monad's aquarius—what in the Egg divides lead and tin (L's valence being that of both)—happens to be the precise length (as measuring rod) to mark its valence height if placed on the ground—perhaps thought of as a plumb line? So here is a plausible double rationale linking lamedh to its valence height (and numeric height, -4).

Confirmation this is what was actually intended to mark L's valence height comes from considering how the metal iron, the first +8 atom-type (first with eight valence electrons, even if not all are used simultaneously), marks *its* valence height: height +8 corresponds to the *aries* of the Monad, so the only way iron could possibly mark this height is if we take its column, the one right up against the center-post within, and project it also onto the Monad. Such trickery is only possible, perhaps, on the inner or intelligent side. This projection of the iron column contrasts with both the copper and silver-gold columns having their metals' valence height (+1) marked by being chopped off halfway by mercury's volatile takeover of the outer Egg's upper half, which would seem to be concurrent with P's swing across to end up at that height, Cauldron's sagittary. This completes valence-by-height to include also the metals.

I guess I should point out that the remaining numeric ±4s could also express their heights if we allowed each to project onto the next larger wheel. Nun's (13's) +4, when projected onto the Throne world, reaches height ±4 via the arc progressing on from it. Beyt's (5's) -4, projected onto the Monad, is *at* said height. And both of these are on the voiced or inner side, on Egg and Cauldron respectively. Ayin's +4 can reach that height by projecting mercury's vapors' takeover of aries onto the next larger wheel—able to do so from being right up against the center-post?

Consider how the Venus or 7 column—first Sefirah of this fourth 'earth', that of lust— compasses the two mothers not (to begin with) solidly on the central vertical axis. Alef was the floor of the column whose inner border is the central axis on which resides the hub of the Egg (where alef as one of the mothers is), replaced at virgo by qof the womb: might this not refer to the advent of procreation, our third 'earth', linked to Egg's summer quarter by the *un*reversed aspect of radii 4 through 6 (since the reverse points to the unmanifest)? And shin marks the 7 column's outer limit taurus in the tree-calendar, which tzaddi displaced across 7's roof to aries to be mother letter shin, a crown (the Irish call S the queen of consonants, the only one having no others equated to it in rhyming). It seems probable shin's move over from the tree-calendar's taurus (as Prunikos) to replace omega at the Cauldron's hub occurs with the advent of our fourth 'earth', represented here by columns 7 through 9. All the columns' limits are projected onto the Egg by reversal of radii (the outward impulse being no longer in evidence in the fourth 'earth'): for 3 through 5, opposite each Sefirah is the sign where its metal's column begins; and 7 through 9 have roofs directly opposite the arcs along which their Sefirot drift to end up male, female, and neutral respectively (see chapter 6 above).

ELEVEN
Cosmology (Planets and Elements)

What was that about Sol (as tav) being on the *passive* side of the airy level? The usual way of talking about the sun is to describe it as active and fiery; the indications of this model are otherwise. Percival briefly describes the distribution of the planets to their respective elementary layers,[161] and from his incomplete sketch I have deduced what I take as the underlying Hermetic or proto-Hermetic model of the heavens (figure 9, top).

Percival said earth's crust is permeated by a fluid layer that extends beyond it on both sides (the inside is hard to visualize and need not concern us here), permeated by an airy layer that extends beyond that (on both sides), permeated by a radiant layer that extends to the stars and to earth's center, gravity being nil there as well.[162] Traditional (not modern) cosmology says that fire-air-water-earth form the layers descending towards us from the heavens. Percival again: stars belong to the radiant or fiery layer (which plasma cosmology confirms); sun to the passive (its 'atmosphere' to the active) side of the airy layer, other planets being also of that layer; moon to the passive (its 'atmosphere' to the active) side of the fluid layer, other planets also being of that layer. These layers extend within earth's crust as well, but beyond insisting geologists are certain of little yet surmise much about earth's interior, I will not argue the point.

In the macrocosmic projection of the human form, stars are nerve endings, sun the heart, moon the kidneys, earth the gonads (Mercury the spleen? Venus the liver? Mars the pancreas? Jupiter the thyroid? Saturn the thymus?). Now what many will resist is the notion that the sun is not a star: I will argue briefly for this distinction's compatibility with the evidence. One of the points I consider to have been confirmed by modern plasma physics is that the stellar heavens are fiery, not earthy, meaning there is no longer any question but that *electromagnetic* forces form the stars and galaxies (if indeed there *are* more than a single galaxy and the reflections of it at various stages), not gravity. This is so well established (i.e. everywhere but in cosmology and science classes themselves) that I will simply suggest the reader research EU (electric universe) theory for his or her self: an open mind will discover that current standard cosmology based on gravitation no longer has a leg to stand on, as it ignores the known behavior of plasma (a 'gas' of charged particles), which even *they* admit constitutes 99.999% of visible matter in the cosmos. For electromagnetic forces are *several dozen* orders of magnitude stronger than gravity, which is thus completely negligible in the stellar reaches. Given such gross error in the standard model, how much stock need we place in mushrooming declarations of planets orbiting stars (as if they were suns)? I remind you there are no close-ups; *most* stars are (at least) binary; and what is sought by astronomers are effects of gravity, not the more appropriate electromagnetic Z-pinch.

My own view is that the stellar heavens form the power plant—size is no object, hence determined by function—and the sun is the transformer. This is the coherent structure suggested by our Hermetic or sefirotic model. Taking the squares of the numbers denoting the first three elements as their layers' limits, 1 indicates the fiery layer, 2-3-4 the airy, 5-6-7-8-9 the fluid, and 10 the earthy; and in order for each elementary layer to retain the character of its element, two of the three airy 'nodes' must be active and at least three of water's five fluid ones must be passive. What, I asked myself, would account for a different number of nodes in the airy and fluid layers? The answer proved quite enlightening.

A point can act (determine position) on any of the other three elements: line, angle, or solid surface (but not on another point, obviously, without being the same point). A line can act on an angle or solid surface, but when intersecting another line it is the point of intersection that acts on it, not the line itself. An angle, though, *can* act on (subdivide) another angle, *or* a solid surface. Thus the breakdown of planets as Sefirot must be as follows. Sol (2) is air *as receptor to fire*: it focuses the starlight (which is what acts). Saturn (3) and Jupiter (4) are air's ability to act on water and earth, based on number. Mars's number (5) is -4 numerically (with water we are dealing with reflections): water's ability to act on earth. Year's number (6) is -3: water's ability to act on water. Venus's 7, -3 in valence, Mercury's 8, -2 in valence, and Luna's 9, -1 in valence, must represent water's capacity to be acted on by water, air, and fire respectively, based on valence. Early Kabbalah, by the way, stipulated 6 and 7 (water acting on water in the above) as groom and bride[163]—analogous to the marriage of Hephaestus and Aphrodite?

We can now get a better understanding of another interesting couple, namely 4 and 5, the couple that procreate (in the Tree of Forms): the male, 4, is air's ability to act on earth, while the female, 5, is water's ability to act on earth. Since the Fall is a loss of balance, the active-passive male form is stamped on the body (earth) by active-passive air, the passive-active female form by passive-active water, the basic form thus determined by this first procreating pair.

The asteroids mainly occur *between* the active-passive airy layer and passive-active fluid layer: may I suggest originally they were some organ having to do with *balance*? Whatever this organ, which may have some connection to Da'at, its remnants are surely the lymph nodes. But what is especially interesting is this. Fire's ability to act on *all three* lower elements is contained in one Sefirah, fire, which is 1 or unity; but it seems logical that the *differentiation* of its abilities to act on air, water, and earth must await the duality of air to find their articulation. And through serendipity or synchronicity, or by the direction of Intelligences working through human beings, which is the same thing, the outer three planets, judging by their names, seem to claim their roles as these three distinct modes of fire, expressed on the unmanifested side of air: Uranus, channel through which fire acts on air; Neptune, channel through which fire acts on water; Pluto, channel through which fire acts on earth. They have no corresponding metals (that I know of).

Notice active planets all have metals on the active side of the Egg, passive planets all on the passive side. Moreover if you look at the periodic table as it *used* to be projected—by period, rather than by series (figure 9, bottom)—a similar pattern emerges: passive metals are all on the left, active ones in the center or to the right'. The three greatest lights are all in tav's (sodium's) +1 column, with Mercury (80) right next to Sol (79), as we would expect. Saturn and Jupiter (lead and tin), air's active side, are both in lamedh's ±4 middle column (82 and 50), Mars (iron) *way* over to the right in the eighth (shared) column (at 26, first atom-type to have eight valence electrons). The active metals all follow immediately on squares: lead (82) on 81 (9^2); tin (50) on 49 (7^2); and iron (26) on 25 (5^2). The square in between lead and tin is 64 (8^2), the exact center of the group of fifteen rare earth metals occupying a single place in the scandium column, thus throwing numbers 'off'; directly above and below it are those squares of 7 and 9 preceding tin and lead! And the square (6^2) between iron and tin is the middle of three inert gases (18-36-54) that are even 9s (numerically ±0). I am not sure what exactly to make of all this, but I suspect there is a key in there somewhere. Each of the three active metals is separated by three places from one of the three great lights, the airy ones three greater, the watery one three less.

How does air, in the guise of Saturn, act on water or form as Mercury? Take Mercury as the sealed vessel, which mercury's toxic vapors make necessary: form as compression, close up against the sun's transforming of stars' energy into turbulence. *Taking* air as turbulence, air's active aspects, Saturn and Jupiter, would be the dissipative or 'outward bound' aspect and the concentrative or inward bound aspect, respectively, of turbulence. So Saturn is the embodiment, in air's active layer, of the solar wind that beats against the inner surface of the vessel or planet Mercury, that which (symbolically) catches and confines it. Jupiter marshals the asteroids (big rocks) into a well-defined belt within its orbit,[164] this influence extending surely to earth itself, being how the airy layer (gas giants) *acts* on solids. Part of the mechanical structure of the fluid layer is glimpsed in the orbital resonance of the year and Venus (Hephaestus and Aphrodite), the former acting on the orbit of the latter. And I imagine much more goes on in terms of magnetic envelopes and electromagnetic dynamics than we moderns yet grasp.

A quick note on creationism—both kinds. I take the universe, and Upright Sentience, as having always existed: there is certainly no evidence to the contrary, despite what is taught at all levels of education. John Scotus Eriugina reasoned that if the Creator is eternal, so must the *act* of creation be an ongoing thing. As for scarcity (though not absence, as is commonly thought)[165] of evidence of advanced humans from the *very* distant past, this is quite easily explained: most of what evidence there was in the fossil record would already have been culled through by the countless civilizations that have risen and fallen *between* then and now. Is this not obvious?

The problem with a 'big bang', all of matter supposedly originally contained in a single point—an absurdity in itself—*or* with creation at a single point in time by a deity (I have always wondered why deities are so eager to take 'credit' for this mess) is that both contradict virtually all the conservation laws of physics, its only solid basis. I can understand religion's tendency to believe in creation *ex nihilo*; but the big bang is pure pseudo-science. It is *assumed* the redshift of light from distant galaxies is Doppler effect (of receding velocity) when it is much more likely that light loses energy interacting with the intervening plasma: the mechanism has perhaps been explained recently by 'Plasma Redshift Cosmology', the brainchild of Icelandic physicist Ari Brynjolfsson.[166] Intrinsic redshift, such as the high redshift of quasars—which are connected by filaments to galaxies of much lesser redshift[167]—strongly reinforces a non-Doppler explanation.

TWELVE
Egg Psychology

It is easy to see the *origin* of the tale of Aphrodite's adultery with Ares (Hephaestus caught them in an iron net): the Egg's two middle columns of any width, Mars and Venus are separated only by Hephaestus (Vulcan) himself (6), so thin a column he would be easily missed.

Distribution of columns in the Egg mostly reinforces the cosmological hierarchy just described. In the unmanifested, Saturn's column—air's ability to act on water—ends at (rules) aquarius, last sign of the water triad; and Jupiter's column—air's ability to act on earth—ends at (rules) pisces, last sign of the earth triad. In the manifested, Mars's column—water's ability to act on earth—ends at (rules) scorpio, the middle sign of the earth triad. In the manifested on the passive side, air as leo acts on Mercury's column as its floor, ayin; and water as virgo acts on Venus's column as its floor, qof. On the unmanifested passive side, the air triad's first sign acts on Mercury's column as its roof, tzaddi.

Sol and Luna are a special case. It would appear both are acted on by manifested fire at cancer, on either side of which they hover. However the watery one, Luna, is *above* or *before* the fire that acts directly on the sun's half of her column (as its floor): she, being the silver of mirrors, merely reflects the sun apparently. I can only point out that when mercury's vapors have risen into the upper half of the outer vessel, they do edge Luna out (dark of the moon), crunching her down into the manifested half of her column (closest approach to the sun), where she *can* be acted on by manifested fire. At the alchemical wedding of sun and moon, it is the queen that brings title to the realm (it is *her* column), only granted to Sol through wedlock, after which she rules the heavens—Urania, Queen of Heaven—and he the earth, which makes him the tanist, king of the waning or manifested half of the year, as befits his tree (tinne the holly). This is reminiscent of the Egyptian goddess Nut, the sky, and her brother and consort Geb, the earth.

It is easy to picture what the seven metals mean symbolically and psychologically. First, we find all the passive metals are malleable, the odd man out, mercury, being *super* malleable (i.e. liquid). The positions of the columns give the psychology. The copper column represents what is close, and thus common. The Sol-Luna (gold-silver) column represents what is far off, and thus rare. The mercury column between them represents power to transmute, on the nature side. The opera*tor* or alchemist is of the intelligent or active side: the lead column holds back, the iron column steps up, and the tin column between them produces, when mixed with common copper, bronze instruments which when sounded summon the operator from one to the other. Iron means the brute instruments for beating the malleable metals of the passive side. And lead is the plumb by which uprightness is measured (or downrightness perhaps, if one is digging a trench): the masons' tool. For further clarity, apply the terms *saturnine*, *jovial*, and *martial* to these three active columns.

It remains to consider the stages of the Great Work as expressed in metals: they are lead, mercury, silver, and gold.[168] One can see a parallel with the color stages: beginning at lead is Nigredo or blackening, what makes transmutation by mercury necessary. Albedo or whitening is the transition to silver. And Rubedo or reddening (coloring) is the final transition to gold.

Let us tie up two loose ends: the seven pairs of opposites *SY* assigns the seven doubles; and the planets *SY* also assigns them. Both correlations appear in varied order in the different versions of *SY* and thus require a bit of sorting out.

Judging in large part from the trumps involved, the seven pairs of opposites should go in this order: life and death (D, XII The Hanged Man); peace and strife (T, XI Force); wisdom and folly (K, VIIII The Hermit or Old Man); fruitfulness and sterility (R, XV The Devil); wealth and poverty (G, X The Wheel of Fortune); dominion and servitude (P, VII The Chariot)—reminding us of the symbolism of the chariot in Plato, where the soul has to drive a team consisting of one horse of noble breed (the blue one?) and one of not so noble breed (the red one?)—and grace and sin (B, V The Pope). This last is sometimes translated 'beauty and ugliness', but 'grace and sin' appears closer to what the inventors of Tarot of Marseilles had in mind. These pairs of opposites are even more revealing when juxtaposed with the six directions plus center they represent: life and death is above us, peace and strife beneath (meaning under our control); if east (morning) is wise, and day is fruitful, then west (evening) will be well-off; south (towards people) represents dominion or servitude (not of people but of one's passions), and north (away from people, that is, dependent entirely on oneself) grace (purity) or sin.

The *planets* assigned the doubles are more problematical, as their proper place is really the fourth Tree. But if there is a correct set of attributions for them, it is perhaps: G-gimel-ivy, Saturn; D-dalet-oak, Jupiter; B-beyt-birch, Mars; P-peh-whitten (and F-alder), Mercury; T-tav-holly, Sol; K-kaf-hazel, Luna—these last two at least are solid—R-reysh-elder, Venus. Some (Graves, and perhaps Norse myth) would associate T with Mars, but dynamics of the planetary columns say otherwise. The above implies that R, as repeated stop (rolled), be thought of as intermittently *un*voiced, as there are four passive planets and only three active (voiced) ones. It also places holly and ivy, paired in the carol, as the first pair, chaste male and female: 2, Sol, and 3, Saturn (exalted in aries and libra).

One final reminder: the above clashes with alignment of planets of the fourth Tree with the Sefirot of the second that generate the six directions. For instance, in the second Tree, D the oak dalet is the 'depth above', yet this is the fifth Sefirah, which aligns it with Mars. As Jupiter's fourth immediately precedes fifth, it must put its stamp on the 'depth above', before delegating to Mars the localization of that in one's iron helm. And Mars, as fifth, must (following Graves) put its stamp on T, holly, the 'depth below', before (in the logical sequence of things) delegating it to the sun, the localization of that: tav the heart (Sol). The sun puts its stamp on the 'depth of the east' as it delegates said depth to Venus, the morning star, which is not kaf but the following double, reysh. The rest loses clarity. This is a tough problem, one I have not yet solved; hence I leave it to the reader to solve, for now.

PART

THREE

:

THE

NAME

A Little Help

Now when the music rises
On hillocks bold and bright,
My joy uplifts itself in triumph
And day engulfs the night.

The little spritely natures
Of things come bursting out.
In celebration of the sun,
The moon tumbles about.

Time, the impulsive hunter,
Harvests and sets his traps,
But I walk on without my feet
And fly above perhaps.

The eagle lands on certainty
But soars with the help of the wind.
And so for one who finds himself
Enamored of a friend.

ONE
'In the Mystery of the Three Mothers'

The Muse of Life returns to me in form.
The cause of life awaits me with her fire.
The fuses of life's candle wax me down
With eyes that single-focused face the night.

You are about to learn secrets concerning the Great Name—key secrets—that no-one who has not pieced together the original order of the twelve simples, or divined something of the nature of self and its relation to the three mothers, would know. It has evidently been centuries since any of this was taught (unless some selfish secret society knows but keeps it hidden). It is a difficult aspect of Kabbalah even for me, yet I can offer insights no longer extant in the Jewish tradition, if the current literature is any indication. Percival, from whom I have lifted a few hints, appears to have understood the Name yet gave virtually no details. What follows is what I have been able to work out to my own satisfaction.

Percival said the Name stands for the divine Form, in which the divine creative power is invested or embodied. It is spelled yod-heh-vav-heh: *SY* (1:13)[169] stipulates that simples yod, heh, and vav were chosen "in the mystery of the three Mothers," this in context of sealing the six directions. Clearly this 'choosing' was for use in the Name as well. There is little elucidation of this passage, commentary merely referencing *SY*'s assignment of elements to mothers (shin-fire, mem-water, alef-air)—which was no mystery, as it was stipulated openly later in the same tome!

We are fortunate to possess two indispensible keys: (1) derivation of the mothers from the Logos; and (2) knowing yod-heh-vav and beyt-gimel-dalet are the same three signs on Egg and Cauldron respectively. To complicate matters, we know *SY*'s assignment of elements to mothers is *not* all there is to it: mem's omnipresence is not just the 'belly' but, as mem sofit, carries blood clear to the top of the head when standing (center of Monad); shin, though fiery (cerebrospinal nerves), replaced the U of the Logos (*w*, *quail chick*), which as Latin V is the water triad (or astrological air, being the thinker). It is the *mothers* that *SY* assigns to 'fathers' yod, heh, and vav, meaning the first three wheels (those with other wheels in their bellies).

First, note that a very interesting valence-by-height pattern emerges from switching to Hebrew numbering for 3 and 4, the two that form the pair *good* and *evil* in *SY*. It was 3 and 4 whose 'arrows' earlier revealed a striking crossover with Hebrew numbering, the fire triad and its 'tails': bardic 3-19 and 4-18, versus Hebrew 1-10-100 (and 2-20-200).

Starting with alef at height ±1 (hydrogen), 2 (duality) as heh or desire rebels against 1, *canceling it out* to fall back down to within one arc of ±0 height (ground libra) as the inert gas helium. Switching to Hebrew in response to this catastrophe, gimel-dalet begin the climb again as 3-4, climbing to their valence heights (+1, +2) by the arcs going *on from* their signs, this with

D at sagittary (its original perch). Reverting back to bardic numbering, B and *mem sofit* and P (at *its* original perch), as 5-6-7, go up and over (+3, ±4, -3), B and P marking valence heights by the arcs extending upwards from their signs. Then F (or samekh), 8, brings us down to -2 height (Egg's aries). Finally K and G, 9 and 10, descend back to earth marking valence heights (-1, ±0) by the arcs approaching them: the fundamental polarity. And it is not difficult to see that this up-and-over pattern might well be related to determination of planetary columns in the Egg.

This journey is quite eye-opening: it uses gimel (scorpio) twice, once as 3 and once as 10. Just so is heh (scorpio) used twice in the Name *and* assigned by tradition to Sefirot 3 and 10 (see below). It tells us beyt-gimel-dalet paralleling yod-heh-vav is no fluke. Hence we should apply D's hearkening from sagittary also to the *vav of the Name*, linked to sagittary via the U of the Logos. This solidifies a connection between yod-heh-vav and the three signs of the self, the one on the macrocosmic hexad being the one moving over to the macrocosmic side.

Tradition applying the Name to the Tree has yod extend from 1 down to 2: beyt happens to be 2 in Hebrew. It has the first heh at 3: gimel happens to be 3 in Hebrew. And it has vav as the six Sefirot beginning with 4: dalet happens to be 4 in Hebrew. This is strong indication that this tradition assigning the letters of the Name to Sefirot is worthy of serious study. And yet if it is correct, we must acknowledge that bardic numbering reverses yod and heh, since heh is 2 and yod is third-from-the-end (19); yet this has a plausible explanation, as we shall see.

There is an ancient clue that appears to confirm my solution to the problem of which mother goes with which father. My solution takes the words of *SY* as definitive and therefore joins each mother or wheel with the 'father' corresponding to the part of the self of which that wheel is the atmosphere: mem with yod, alef with heh, shin with vav. But without knowledge of the real relation between mothers and Logos, there would be a strong temptation to couple mem with heh, so that the two forms of mem might be divided between the two hehs of the Name—as is done in Hermetic Kabbalah, as I recall. Our ancient clue *acknowledges* this other way while directing us to the correct solution.

The clue is the letter-order of the Sabean alphabet, what I take to be the standard version of south Semitic letters, used in the Yemeni region (Sheba) during the last millennium BCE (see charts 3 and 4). As near as I can tell, Sabean had two forms each for letters samekh-cheyt-ayin-teyt-shin-dalet-tav. See a pattern here? The macrocosmic hexad on Egg's macrocosmic *side*, plus the thinker (i.e. the mother letter replacing the Ω of the Logos) and the minds of its active and passive aspects. The first two of these divide Sabean into unequal halves: the first *fourteen* letters are framed by the two cheyts (first and fourteenth); the last *fifteen* are capped off by the two forms of samekh. Note bardic 14 and 15 are L and R (left and right). (The middle letter of this alphabet is one of the two forms of shin, the one that happens to have some affinity also with samekh and thus can be seen either as divider or as the other bookend of the 'samekh half'.)

Yod is fourth-from-the-end, mem fourth-from-the-beginning. Heh is third-from-the-start, alef third in the samekh half. Finally vav is sixth (same as Hebrew) and shin seventh, right next to it. Juxtaposition of these last two suggests misdirection towards mating heh with mem, since these two are *also* juxtaposed, at third and fourth, which would leave alef free to mate with yod, which makes sense if we merge the two samekhs at the end into a single place thus transforming yod into third-from-the-end, to match up with alef's being third in the samekh half. I interpret this as a 'hat tip' to this other 'exoteric' way of pairing them, which is perhaps based on the two Ls (L = 14) in Apollo's name, since it divides letters into two groups of fourteen. But the fact that L and R are 14 and 15 points those privy to bardic lore towards the correct choice.

Percival tells us that the Name is divided into a male half and a female half, the male half containing the female, the female half containing the male.[170] So I take the original sense of the Name as male half yod-heh conjoined to female half vav-heh: that much, at least, is clear.

Complicating the picture is the doctrine of the *Partzufim* or 'faces' (façades?), a tradition which appears to run counter to our firmly established polarity yod-vav. This Lurianic doctrine calls *yod*, flowing from Sefirah 1 to Sefirah 2, *Abba*, 'father'; the first *heh*, at Sefirah 3, *Imma*, 'mother'; *vav*, Sefirot 4-9 (with 9 identified as phallus), the son *Ze'ir Anpin*, or 'Short-Face' (Mr. Impatience); and the second *heh*, Sefirah 10, *Nukvah*, his 'female'. In speaking of each *Partzuf* as containing *all ten* Sefirot—a teaching too complex for me to even *grasp*, let alone *expound*, except in that it joins each letter of the Name to a world—"[R. Chayim] Vital [Luria's trusted disciple] informs us that in the feminine *Partzufim* the *Sefirah Yesod* [9], which is the phallus in the male, is the womb and female genitalia."[171]

Remember, it is *eighth* that originally signified the male member, heh being the eighth sign. Heh *is* the feminine singular ending in Hebrew, consistent with being *Partzufim* mother and bride. Yet the feminine plural ends in -*ot*—vav-tav or common salt—the masculine plural in -*im*—yod-mem, yod wed to mem, with which Judaic tradition concurs.[172]

Though the Partzufim are closely associated with the name Isaac Luria, I discovered that his (the Ari's) 'unifications' of God with his Shekhinah are said to be between the YaH (yod-heh) and the WeH (vav-heh) of the Name.[173] The Name is *ineffable* because the divine creative power in *humans* is *pro*creative and requires a man and a woman to invoke it.[174] The yod-heh (the divine name Yah) seems more suggestive of the male's exertion, the vav-heh ('oo-eh'?) more suggestive of deep feeling. If the High Priest of old did indeed (as reputed) invoke it, he would have needed help to do so, which accounts for the difficulty prophets had in dislodging God's 'consort', Asherah, from the Temple.[175]

Placement of yod-heh-vav on the round is suggestive of columns Boaz and Jachin. Yod-heh mimics intact Jachin by measuring its whole length on the next smaller wheel (the womb or offspring). Vav, without the qof that would extend it down to balance yod-heh, mimics Boaz, broken off at the sternum to make *room* for qof, the womb. That this placement of these four letters was known recently enough in the past to have shaped religious practice is proved by the customary substitution of *qof* for *heh* in the Name outside of Bible-reading and prayers.[176] This shows that it was once known that qof shares heh's level in the Egg, fills the gap in the female half of the Name, and stands for the womb.

TWO
King, Queen, Knight, and Knave

Tarot of Marseilles courts do not consist of the pablum of *some* modern decks, namely King (Crowley's *Knight*), Queen, *Prince*, and *Princess*. Instead it was the forerunner of courts in *most* current decks: King, Queen, Knight, and Knave, this last nowadays called the Page. This is because they originally represented the yod-heh-vav-heh of the Name, of which one is on the female side and three on the male side. This original tarot (the scholars' theories to the contrary notwithstanding) was designed by Christian Gnostic bards in the Provence region, fairly early in the fifteenth century I should think, to encapsulate the entire corpus they had worked with the Jews of that region to *reconstruct* back in the twelfth century, when Kabbalah first flourished. The greater region (Provence-Langedoc) had seen hard times in the interim: the Albigensian Crusade, the Inquisition to rid the world of Cathars (who were more like the early Christians than the Christians themselves, yet were ruthlessly hunted down and tormented), and enough harrying of Jews (I would guess) to drive their esoteric schools over the Pyrenees into Spain.

The trick is to place the three male figures of the court correctly. The two keys to this are (1) the member of each court that is most striking should be the one standing for the letter that is key to that suit, and (2) the Knave of Money is the second heh, for in his picture are two coins: one in hand, and one lying on the ground. The benefit of solving this early is to solidify for us which suit goes with which letter. The King of Clubs and Queen of Swords stand out most in their suits. That King's throne has but one column, the Jachin column, but he is prefiguring the other with his very large scepter (held at a pronounced slant). The Queen of Swords' throne has *both* columns; in other words her presence provides the other one; and she holds her suit symbol upright (at only a slight slant now) on the Boaz side, *and it is red* (recently used). The Knight of Cups is the Grail Knight (the crippled Grail *King* ruled over a crippled land, remember). And the Knave of Money looks the most prince-like of his court, the rest all appearing utterly bourgeois!

Consider gimel standing for the two hehs in that up-and-over trip through valence heights that switched to Hebrew numbering for 3 and 4: do we see in this how the runic G got divided up into Knight's 'gift' and Knave's 'harvest' in the Elder Futhark? Indeed the Knight of Cups (Grail Knight) is clearly offering his large chalice as a gift, while the second coin on the ground in the Knave of Money suggests it is waiting to be harvested. In runes, there is a funny twist, in that the rune 'gift' is X-shaped, like Roman numeral 10: a small joke by the rune-masters? or misdirection? or a reminder that even when posing as 3 (the Knight), G's *bardic* number is still 10? I just do not see how the Grail Knight could be the *second* heh.

Courts exist in all four worlds to express how the Name resonates in each, I presume. Could court figures *other* than the striking one in each court be how the other letters of the Name appear from the perspective of that world? This suggests that the Name Itself consists of the four most striking figures, each from a different suit. The root of the male half, yod, resonates with the knower or Monad, that being what desire is trying to imitate. The root of the female half, vav, resonates with the thinker or Throne world, that being what feeling is attempting to imitate. The two remaining letters of the Name must represent (in us, anyway) aspects of the body-mind as it plays *doer* to feeling-and-desire's imitation of thinker-and-knower, there being two aspects to reflect human bodies being male and female.

Representation of the female within the male half must be the Knight: propensity of the male to act chivalrous towards the female. This certainly resonates with the world of forms or psychological states (the Egg). The male within the female must be the Knave: his emotional, physical, and potentially pregnancy-inducing presence in her. This resonates with the world of action (fourth wheel, that of making babies). (Note that both the female within the male half and the male within the female half characterize the shifting role of the male.)

Jewish tradition mates the initial *yod-heh* with mem's *water* and shin's *fire*, and the vav with alef's *air*.[177] Yod is here matched with the correct mother, yet with mem tied to its role as 'water' from intermediate mem's holding down truant R's station at libra. Yet we are trying to return reysh to its proper role by directing the gonads (reysh) to their actual purpose, procreation. Mem is the blood, seen as the medium of desire hence as stand-in for the knower or Monad, its station *as mother* (wheel with another wheel in its 'belly').

Percival says, "Jehovah is properly worshipped when a Jewish man and woman breathe alternately each his and her own part of the name, to propagate. They desecrate the name of their God when they are in union not to propagate; then they use his name in vain."[178]

Hermetic Kabbalah, surprisingly, seems to have gotten something else right. For the convention therein is that the elements adhere to the four letters of the Name in the order fire-water-air-earth. This follows our attribution of worlds to letters of the Name, as confirmed above by the court cards. It is different from the natural order of elements and worlds, and just what this might mean we shall explore shortly. First, however, we must air the remaining major teachings extant surrounding the Name, thus filling out the picture.

THREE
The Partzufim

To add some credibility to the doctrine of the *Partzufim*—where yod the 'father' is 1-2, the first heh or 'mother' is 3, vav the son or 'short face' is 4-9, and the second heh, his 'female', is 10—let me point out that letter vav links itself to all the numbers to which it is attached by that doctrine: it is the fourth sign, its number fifth-from-the-end (17), the difference in whose digits is 6, whose ones' digit is 7, its digital sum 8, and it shares 9's valence (-1). And if it were not for the irreducibly feminine nature of vav and the obvious distribution of the court cards of the Tarot of Marseilles, the doctrine of the *Partzufim* might lead us to believe vav was the male presence in the female half of the Name. What would this look like?

Vav, Hebrew 6, has been associated with the six directions of space,[179] so it might mean the space *in* the female *for* the male (*one* of whose aspects is his member). I would be willing to admit vav in part does symbolize her receptivity to him. Could it have been to make way for him that Hebrew vav was banished as an *initial* from almost every root but 'and' (vav itself)? Still, the overwhelming impression I get is that the masculinization of vav was to cover and conceal the truth—like the lapwing's deception Robert Graves muses over in *tWG*, who goes limping off in the direction opposite that of her nest, hoping the intruder will follow—and that it most likely happened in the era when the prophets were trying to remove every vestige of Ashera, the roots in vav being purged like Ashera from the Temple!

The few roots starting with vav that I have been able to turn up (most from their survival in Arabic, labeled 'A.' below) form a rather coherent group. Three obviously arise from vav being the sign where the round is descending straight down: וקר (A.) 'be heavy', ועף (A.) 'run swiftly', and וזר 'laden with guilt' (A. 'be loaded, commit crime'). Two stem from its being on the passive side of the Egg: וקה (A.) 'obey', and וקע (A.) 'wound, mark, brand'. Two reinforce ו as 'and', vav being the root of the half of the Name that *conjoins* with Yah: וו 'hook, pin (for suspending the curtain in the tabernacle)', and וזה (A.) 'assemble'. Another suggests the result, once conjoined: ופת (A.) 'be entire, perfect', and perhaps (in a name) והב 'gift' (A. 'give')—note this last has heh in it. Four are suggestive of Urania, Queen of Heaven (vowel U in the 'Orphic' hymn of table 4): וחש 'be empty', ורם (A.) 'be high', and in names, collated with Persian, ויזתא 'pure', and ושתי 'beauty'. And the clincher: ולד (= ילד 'bear, bring forth') 'child, offspring'. I believe it clear from these few surviving roots that the thrust of meanings starting with vav was distinctly feminine, strongly indicating they were suppressed not so much to 'make space for the male' as to hide the fact that vav is the root of the female half of the Name.

It is at least clear that 9 as phallus would not *switch* roles in the female, as Vital asserts: it is already in the root of the female half (taking vav as 4 through 9), as is 8, the original position of the phallus (eighth sign, eighth day). Could 9 in some sense represent the male member in the female, being, in the Tree of Forms, the result connected with gestation? If the characterization of the Partzufim evolved to conceal vav's being the female root (God's consort), then the cover-up was sly, still giving her the two hehs. Could the 'impatient one' and his Nukvah have ever been thought of as the male's presence in her (vav) and her exultation therein (the second heh)?

It seems much more likely that from the beginning it was an effort to mislead. Taking 10 and 9 as the fundamental polarity (numerical +1 versus -1 valence), 10 is desire and 9 is feeling. And fluorine's -1 is a hollow or lack, a *space* for 1—whose ache to be filled is the strongest such electro-chemical 'ache' there is—while neon signifies what is desired: completion of the neon 'shell'. So *10* must be the male presence in the female (echoing yod, *Hebrew* 10), not 4-9.

Vav is the *root* of the female half, her essence in this context *being* that she has space (in heart as well as body) for the male. I am forced to interpret the male presence in the female half as the heh. This means the feminine Shekhinah ('Immanence') traditionally associated with the tenth Sefirah, gets its femininity from being in the female half of the Name, the masculine nature of this heh implying that in a deeper sense the divine presence is in the conjoining itself.

If here, as in Abraham's name, heh means *covenant*, it adds another, sort of contrapuntal meaning to Knight and Knave: her presence in him, heh being Hebrew 5, means his hand given her in wedlock, whereby he is sworn to be her Knight; and his presence in her means her hand given him in wedlock, whereby he is transformed into her Knave. (Do I detect a bit of humor here?) The *yod* of the Name—as *Atzilut* and as Hebrew 10—surely represents the ideal, in him, of their two hands being joined; and the second heh's link to Sefirah 10 must be the realization of that ideal in her. In fact, interpreting *Sefirah* 10 as their hands being joined reveals another side of 10 (besides that of grasping fingers), as perhaps better befits its housing the Shekhinah.

Yod being placed by the doctrine of the Partzufim at 1-2, heh at 3, vav at 4-9, and the second heh at 10 accompanies a tradition that the Name portrays the human form: yod the head and neck (first two signs), the first heh the shoulders (third sign), vav the torso (fourth through sixth signs?), and the second heh the loins and legs (seventh, or seventh through twelfth signs?). One can see that this doctrine goes at least part way towards confirming placement of Sefirot on the zodiac of the human form. Yet yod's placement there *alphabetically*, on a level with the aries of the fourth wheel, suggests the head of one's offspring. The first heh, like the first gimel in that up-and-over scenario, reaches *up* by its arc to sagittary, whose spoke intersects the fourth wheel at aquarius, spine opposite the shoulders. Vav's month extends down into the hollow left by the breaking off of Boaz, filling it with the torso of the infant. The second heh, then, like the second gimel in that up-and-over scenario, reaches *down* by its arc to libra, the loins.

There is a theme in all this that I have not yet mentioned, and that is the motif of a tiny male entity (י) wooing a large female entity (ו): tiny sperm seeking immense ovum; tiny electron seeking immense proton; and now, tiny 1-2 and 3 wooing 4-5-6-7-8-9 and 10. Note that these latter, all the Sefirot included in the female half, are the forms after the Fall, all those that ended up as 'broken' vessels (Boaz being broken off). That must be how vav and its heh swept them up to be included in the female half of the Name (vav being the sternum).

If so, then vav as the six directions of space (being 6 in Hebrew) must refer to the space created for procreation *by* the breaking off of Boaz. The second heh, then, would be the point inside that space where the three axes meet (the Knave *within* the Queen). It cannot possibly be correct to make vav the offspring of 2 and 3, as these are the only male and female types that do not bear offspring. The Sefirot attributed to vav do follow 2 and 3, but to call them the offspring thereof is pure *post hoc ergo propter hoc* reasoning. (This is my feeble attempt at humor.)

The male half of the Name encompasses the forms before the Fall because the male or spinal column, Jachin, is still intact, whereas the female or front column has been broken off in order to allow the bearing of offspring. I have recently perceived, I think, what is going on here: because both columns are intact in Sefirot 1-3, only the male half of the Name reaches up *into* that 'supernal' realm. But this has implications that need to be pointed out. First of all, even though it is the male *half* that resonates with Sefirot 1-3, both male and female are involved in *invoking* the Name, thus giving her access to them as well (through said conjoining). Second, it implies that the Partzufim (minus their sexual misidentification) merely mark the upward extent of each half on the Tree, the female half extending as far up as the first form with broken front column (4), the male half extending all the way to the top, to the first form, with its unbroken male column. So the 'tiny' 1-2 and 3 wooing the larger 4-9 and 10 is actually just the tip of the iceberg, the part of the male half that extends upwards beyond the female half. I have put this awkwardly, but the reader can hopefully grasp what I mean. It also happens to be consistent with the average male being taller than the average female.

Aha! I just had an epiphany: the Partzufim may perhaps be telling us that even though the Name is divided into yod-heh and vav-heh, vav is Son *in the sense* that the male half *itself* extends *through* the female half to *reach* its (male) half. At least it is a way to picture Partzufim as something other than mere misdirection. And if you think about it, the female half resonating as far up as 4 and the male half resonating as far up as 1 is what identifies the seven manifested signs as 'doubles', being the signs that resonate with both halves.

The three pillars of Masonry are Wisdom, Strength, and Beauty, names right out of the Tree of Forms: the innocent male mode (Chokhmah, Wisdom), the procreative female mode (Gevurah, Power), and the mixed procreative mode, her offspring (Tiferet, Beauty). What this seems to convey is the male praying for the Wisdom to enable him to instill his Strength in the female, thus enabling her to instill her Beauty in the child (form, virgo, being on the female tetrad). (For desire fully expressed is power, and feeling fully expressed is beauty.)

This fits rather well what is conveyed by the Judaic tradition that a child conceived after an absence in which the man has remained 'male and female' (i.e. carried the feminine about within him as Shekhinah rather than conjoining with another) is a very holy and special one.[180] Indeed Percival stipulates that a year of abstinence is necessary for the conception of a child that is fully immune to disease.[181]

FOUR
Creation of Thoughts

Percival says any two consecutive signs of the microcosmic hexad can act conjointly on the intervening macrocosmic sign to produce a result in the macrocosm.[182] The particular case we humans notice is libra, where heh, the male organ scorpio, acts conjointly with qof, the womb virgo, on libra to give start to what *will* point straight down (when about to be born), a new body. What the Name suggests is its counterpart within (in the manifested) where scorpio (desire) and capricorn (Light of self-knowledge) act on intervening sagittary (thought) to create a thought: an object of desire mixed with Light of the Intelligence. Dalet's shift to the outer horizon signifies a thought centered on some object of nature, rather than directed towards self-knowledge (sagittary being the approach thereto). D the oak (Jove or thought) only marks dalet's (4's) and Jupiter's (4's) *numeric* heights by each thought's cycling about over to the nature side, in which process it passes (via the Throne world's unmanifested half) through the center of the Monad. Once on the nature side then, thoughts shape reality around their objects. Normal human thinking is obsessed with objects of nature, as the Buddha's teachings make very clear.

As that part of the noetic breath that is in the psychic atmosphere, vav points to the Light trapped in thoughts we send out into nature, where their objects are—Light imprisoned in nature waiting to be freed, as we Gnostics would say. Once freed and returned to the head, the Light is usually entrapped again in some new thought. The Great Work of alchemy entails *conserving* it, that is, *not* reissuing it in new thoughts (distortions of truth). Mem sofit must signify Light that has been freed and returned to the head—Light 'stored away for the righteous' as the *Zohar* calls it. It is knowledge, end result of learning. It is not automatic (as when reclaiming Light through food) but arises from accepting destiny cheerfully while fulfilling the responsibilities thereof.[183] Mem sofit is atop the year's heroic half, and the hero in Norse saga epitomizes cheerfulness and joviality in the face of unwished-for struggle he knows means his doom.[184]

The reordering of the simples—dividing them into the secular (upper outer), the chthonic (lower), and the sacerdotal (upper inner)—spells out the mechanism of it. Being where destiny first takes shape, in the unmanifested—thinker's domain, that of thoughts its doer has created— the upper-outer distributes the elements astrologically. The lower five signs have to do with the exteriorization of said thoughts and the doer's reaction to them: will reysh rebel from its destiny and desert its station, or remain steadfast and take what is coming to it and learn therefrom? If the doer's reaction to the exteriorization is such that it learns from it, it can balance the thought by completing its circle in the unmanifested *within*, where the elements are correctly distributed to their triads, dissolving the illusion.

Exteriorizations of thoughts (at libra, where lesser circles break through to the surface of greater ones) are in a very real sense the *q'lippot* or 'husks' Kabbalah speaks of: we see their shells or surfaces (physical results) but seldom perceive the thought-forms animating them; nor do we notice their cycling around in nature under the thinker's supervision—from life to life even—until they are balanced (dissolved as obstructions) and their trapped Light freed. Let us examine more closely the way in which Light is trapped in the first place. For this is the origin of the alternation in how planetary columns were 'flagged' (between valence of *number* and valence of *metal*).

Mem sofit's sound and its ±4 valence express the Monad's self-contained omnipresence (*mm*), by definition balanced: both mems are on the center-post. One translation of the passage in *SY* calling mem 'silent' has "MEM stands still."[185] When D, bearer of the valence (+2) of Jupiter's *number* (4), swings across—as thoughts carrying Light out into nature—from where it swept Jupiter's column on the intelligent side to where it sweeps Mercury's column on the nature side, it endows the latter with *metal* mercury's +2 valence. This must have dislodged Mercury's number, 8 (-2 valence), from that column to fly (as vapor) up as far as the center-post as fearn or samekh. And since mem itself is immovable (being all-encompassing), if 8's arrival at aries is to dislodge a ±4 valence from the center-post over to where it endows the roof of a column with a metal's valence, this ±4 valence must be lamedh or silicon, as indeed we see it is. This, then, brings about intermediate mem's reaching out via the sweep of its Cauldron-radius to re-label Jupiter's floor as well with tin's valence, which it does without having to be dislodged from the center-post. I would conclude D's swing over to the nature side carried the mercury column's floor, at least, with it; for the floor is ayin, the mental breath, whose origin must be the intelligent side.

A physical analogue to this immovable mem is the much-overlooked 'central frame'[186] of the universe: despite the Einsteinists' claim there is no such thing, whatever happens relative to it, it cannot 'go anywhere' *relative to itself*. Some of what has gone wrong in physics today can be traced to overlooking the fact that there *is* a privileged central frame, a necessity if the number of motions in the cosmos is finite (as opposed to numberless, which is an oxymoron).

Units of matter have their own goal in building out thoughts' structures into acts, objects, and events: to gain experience as their various functions in nature. Still, the result for *man* is to prod him with the consequences of his thinking. Nature seeks Upright Sentience *by* exteriorizing the thinking of conscious selves. Nature gets all its forms from us: it is this, not linear descent, that brings about that similarity between humans and animals the neo-Darwinists believe proves their (circular) theory.

The great error in biology in our day is that it sees every process as not only *built up from* but actually *determined by* its myriad lesser processes, these in turn by even *lesser* processes, and so on unto utter absurdity. Seriously: how can minute *sub*divisions of *constituent processes* that are subdivisions of *other* such processes (and so on up the chain of being) *determine* relatively stable forms such as living bodies? The answer is, they cannot.

Rupert Sheldrake has put forth (in at least two books)[187] criticism of the modern approach and postulated a field—the *morphogenetic* field—whereby forms of activity that have occurred in the past resonate with present activity to increase likelihood of *recurrence* of those forms. It does not claim to be the first such theory in biology (compare the 'creodes' postulated by C. H.

Waddington), but something must account for the 'ruts' life follows, from the intricate folding of protein molecules to the learning process itself. What is needed (and what Sheldrake's theory supplies) is a 'top-down' approach to explaining how life organizes itself: how activity patterns interact with the past's patterns to stabilize the processes of life. The only comment I wish to make is to emphasize—based on my experiences with memory and synchronicity—that the field affects and is affected by intelligent matter as well as nature matter.

A way to view it is this. Given our wheels, picture the present instant, progressing along merrily within its fourth wheel as if it were all there is (as materialists such as I was as a lad tend to view it), while in reality the third wheel is there imposing form *on* it, the second judging the third as it does this, and the first unifying the four to make it possible in the first place, all flying completely under (or rather over) the radar of those who consider only the present instant (gross physical matter). Such minds must be unaware of Plato's admonition that nothing can be known about the present instant (matter itself) other than what has durations passing *through* it.

The *Zohar* stipulates that when the second heh of the Name is lacking, there is only dalet, 'poverty'.[188] This is because thus truncated, the Name cuts off at vav, whose sign is dalet on the Cauldron. Most likely what is referenced here is thoughts held in nature and forced into repeated exteriorizations, their lessons unlearnt. Such 'poverty' is consistent with the missing second heh being the suit Money. Coins represent celestial rounds, and if the Knave is the 10th Sefirah, then it represents today, now. Exteriorization of a thought provides an opportunity to balance it, by treating it as one's Knave, meaning under one's 'orders'. So absence of the second heh must mean no Light reclaimed, the *true* poverty. What *tikkun* or 'restoration' *means*, this being Jewish Gnosticism, is the reclaiming or liberating of Light by the balancing and dissolving of thoughts, having learned from the exteriorizations, not rejected them as whims of the god Chance.

Resemblance of the Name to the process whereby our thoughts are generated then cycle through nature with their imprisoned Light is not a recommendation we create more and more thoughts and thus more and more of the karma or destiny they generate. Rather, it is an intimate reminder of the most fundamental duty governing the human world: to take care *what* thoughts we think and prioritize learning from the imprisoned Light, thereby liberating it and ultimately conserving it. And here is a somewhat encouraging quote from Percival: "It is not a misuse of Light to send it out into nature to maintain its higher forms as plants, trees, animals or rocks . . . it is returned and sooner or later [one] learns from it what it went through while out in nature. That Light will enlighten . . . show the stupendous wonders of plant life and the molecular and atomic marvels of organic and inorganic nature . . . affect destiny more quickly than any other power."[189] Is agriculture such non-misuse? My father grew up on a farm in the Midwest. (He and an older brother used to joust by tying ends of a rope around their waists and riding past each other to see who could un-horse the other.)

FIVE
The Power in the Name

Lurianic Kabbalah associated the letters of the Name with the four worlds, but in their natural order (the order of *Ofanim*), thus reversing the *middle two* from how Hermetic Kabbalah allocates elements to the Name, or from the 'mystery of the three mothers', or from how Tarot of Marseilles indicates which suit each letter of the Name hails from. It is comparable to describing the Sefirot of *Beri'ah* in a book called *Yetzirah*.

The astute Arthur M. Young, who wrote *The Reflexive Universe*—from which one can glean a great deal about the logic and dynamics of the Cauldron's seven stages of manifestation (I recommend it highly)[190]—managed in another work to *reverse* air and water as these relate to geometry, by making *angle* air and *line* water, thus crippling his view.[191] But in the Name, such reversal *may* have profound meaning, something we should at least explore. It would mean that while the Lurianic tradition is in part a cover-up, it also, like the reordering of simples, conveys something of value.

I understand it is a Buddhist concept that when you generate disharmony in the world it creates a tension that then seeks to right itself, to restore harmony and balance. This is another, perhaps more poetic and powerful way of describing the dynamics involved when a thought is created. With some thoughts, the disharmony may be minor; but in every case it involves some difference between how we perceive things and how they really are. So I have asked myself: is it possible that reversal of the order of air and water in the middle two letters of the Name could be a sort of intentional disharmony, whose tension is in fact part of its power?

The Lurianic scheme links Beri'ah, the thinker's world, to heh, scorpio the doer—of the form world—and Yetzirah, the doer's world, to vav, the Light trapped in thoughts that circulate about in the life world. It is a tension slightly reminiscent of what molds the periodic table, two steps pulling opposite one another, but instead of 1 and 2, it is 2 and 3. It is a tension inherent in the geometry of the round; for the Cauldron's air-level radii (leo and sagittary) intersect the Egg at unmanifested water, and the Cauldron's water-level radii (virgo and scorpio) at manifested air (figure 6, top).

This tension can only manifest in the Name as a result of the first heh being already—the instant it appears—united with yod, as Yah: they *interpenetrate* one another, yod at 2 bearing the bardic numeration third-to-last (19), heh at 3 bearing bardic numeration 2. *Together* they create a thought in intervening sagittary, thus immediately invoking the Beri'ah world, where the thought *resides*. Vav, then, represents the thought's cycling about in nature as it waits for the doer who created the thought to free the Light trapped in it, said Light being what preserves the character of the thought. Although it is maintained as a thought in the Throne world, it is the doer, in the form world, who must deal with it, learn from it, and eventually balance it, this last signified in this context by the final heh of the Name (without which, according to the *Zohar*, there is only dalet, 'poverty').

It is interesting that the traditional Jewish way of mating 'fathers' to mothers—yod to mem, heh to shin, and vav to alef—*would* corroborate the above application of worlds to letters if the mothers were associated with the correct worlds. They do not appear to be (judging from the elements assigned them in *SY*), but *we* may still associate them with the correct worlds. At least it offers an explanation of how the allocation may have originally come about.

Consider the pattern suggested by assignment of letters of the Name to human anatomy as it relates to the macrocosmic hexad. Yod the head extends down from 1, or aries the head—fire's source. Heh the shoulders is 3, gemini the shoulders—root of water, yet determined by the air radius of the Cauldron. In the manifested half, Sefirot drift along the arcs or months leading on from them: vav the torso starts at 4 or cancer, yet its implied origin at 9 or sagittary means it spans all six arcs of the manifested half, bound together (in the closed or circular zodiac) by the base of the fire triad, representing unity—manifesting as air, yet determined by the water level radii of the Cauldron. And the second heh signifies the loins by the arc leading back from it to libra—manifested earth. Or if thought of as the tenth Sefirah, perhaps this second heh follows the path of reysh, 'exiled' to the center of the wheel, from which it conveniently drops down into libra, its original station.

This means that, while the elements of the Cauldron are invoked in their natural order, fire-air-water-earth, the corresponding process in the Egg has them occur in the order fire-water-air-earth. This means that the rabbis' way of looking at it (worlds in their natural order) reflects the thinker's point of view—that of the Throne world, second by *its* reckoning—while the Tarot of Marseilles' way of parsing it reflects the doer's point of view—that of the Egg or form world, second by *its* reckoning. Does any of this reek of duality's rebellion against Unity?

Why would Kabbalistic tradition prefer the natural order, the way it appears to Sophia the Holy Spirit, while the order of the actual mechanics of it (fire-water-air-earth) is preserved by Hermetic tradition and by British Gnostic bards who designed the tarot? I would suggest this is because Hermetic tradition involved alchemy, a practical and one might argue *empirical* science.

Percival says the Name is that of the immortal body (our Adam Qadmon), whereas the name Adonai, אדני, is that of the ordinary human type. This latter reads like the Hebrew word for 'I', *ani*, with the outer horizon inserted between the initial alef and the pair nun-yod (originally reversed from the yod-nun of *ain*, 'no-thing'). But the final yod is actually a suffix added to the common Semitic term *adon*, 'lord'.

If the Name's divine creative power is that of two-columned Adam Qadmon, we humans can only invoke it as *pro*creative power. It takes two of us to make two columns: the Jachin in the male, from the original Jachin; and the Jachin in the female, from the original Boaz? whose breaking-off was in part *so* that it might form Jachin in the female? This last would imply that division into chaste types 2 and 3 was mere projection—a copy of the two-columned form—but upon transition to 4 and 5, breaking the front column necessitated 'stiffening' of Jachin in the female, at the expense of Boaz in the male. After all, if 2 and 3 are *not* fooled, then they rejoin.

Obviously, as two-columned Adam Qadmon the Name's two columns must be yod-heh and vav-heh: perhaps in Adam Qadmon, heh is more centered, being the doer or bridge-builder (where the coccyx is). After all, its arc of approach emerges *out* of libra (what links helium to its valence level). In us heh is off balance, leaving a hollow where the lower portion of the front column was. It is in this 'hollow' that the resulting child will develop (hence substitution of qof for heh in the Name outside of Bible-reading and prayers).

This pretty much exhausts what I at present know or even surmise concerning the Name, except for the sealing of the six directions, to which we now turn.

SIX
Sealing the Six Directions

The Sefirot signify transformation of *ain* (alef-yod-nun) into *ani* (alef-nun-yod); that is, of 'naught' into 'I'. If we take this as the template for sealing the six directions, it rules out the pattern in the Gra version,[192] where they are paired according to where vav is, as well as those Kaplan attributes[193] to the Ari, the *Zohar*, and the *Tikuney Zohar* (as well as the Long Version, a probable distortion of the Gra). The only other version he lists that is 'in the running' by this method, the Saadia, is like the Short Version's order I will list below (as a starting point) but with east and west reversed.

This is how I used to try and justify the list of combinations given in the Short Version. The first pair presented little difficulty: yod-heh-vav as *up*, yod-vav-heh as *down*, seemed to me to be because when heh or desire is *within* manifestation's limits, yod and vav, it will stand; but when *not* within those limits, things collapse. This holds true in the *Gra* version too, but the Gra has yod-heh-vav versus heh-yod-vav and thus veers away from the logic of *ain* into *ani*.

Next come east and west: heh-yod-vav versus heh-vav-yod. The quality this preserves that the Saadia version does not is that its letter permutations follow the order logically dictated by the Name: both the order in which they *begin* sequences, and which permutation of the other two occurs first. Heh does not in either case occur within limits of manifestation yod-vav, so this would be east and west to *fallen* Adam, 'below': east sealed by heh (desire) placing yod, east, ahead of vav, west; west sealed by heh (desire) placing vav, west, ahead of yod, east. It is true that the Saadia version's reversal of this makes the letters following heh actually *progress* in the direction being sealed, which explains how it may have come about (sailing pun intended). But reversing the order dictated by the Name deprives that scheme of the overall unity of the Short Version—yet ironically enough its east-west turns out to be correct (see below).

For south sealed by vav-yod-heh and north by vav-heh-yod (yod-heh-vav backwards) my reasoning was because north, being *up* on average for us, put heh back between manifestation's limits, whereas south, being *down*, did not. It also makes sense in that *south*, towards equator and ecliptic, is where celestial motions *are*—the vav or 'towards other' that is *Yah*, deity in its more *active* sense (male half of the Name)—and *north*, the pole, is where they are *not*—the vav or 'towards other' that is *not* Yah.

This was my reasoning, or rationalization, until I discovered the proper solution to the question of how to apply mothers to axes and doubles to their ends. I had surmised that voiced and unvoiced equivalents should be opposite faces of the 'cube of space', with reysh as the 'Holy Palace in the middle', where the axes meet. And I had surmised that each mother should be the axis on which its corresponding 'father' remained stationary in the initial position, the doubles attached to that axis being the two minds of the part of self evoked by that mother. That much I had right. But I still worried over number mismatches—like K and G bearing numbers that *SY* identified as south and north yet being on the east-west axis—and not certain which end of each axis was which in every case.

But I have seen the light: the solution is clear, and this is why. Having figured out once and for all how to place the doubles (part two, chapter 4), the mothers of course went with them: shin with D-T, alef with K-G, mem with P-B. And two permutations with corresponding stable introductory 'father' went with each of them, the 'fathers' being located on the Egg equivalents of the axes they represent: vav at D's cancer, heh at G's scorpio, and yod at B's capricorn. And vav, on the macrocosmic *side* of the Egg with ties to the macrocosmic *sign* of the self, is the up-down, or macrocosmic, axis. And analysis of *ayin* becoming *ani* shows that the second and third letters move *towards* where meaning ends up: *ayin*, 'nothing', ends in nun, N or negation (the sign one *back* from the start), while *ani*, 'I', ends in yod, sign of self-knowledge.   Therefore:

> Above was sealed with vav-heh-yod, yod being above heh.
> Below was sealed with vav-yod-heh, heh being below yod.
> East was sealed with heh-vav-yod, yod being east of vav.
> West was sealed with heh-yod-vav, vav being west of yod.
> South was sealed with yod-vav-heh, heh being south of vav.
> North was sealed with yod-heh-vav, vav being north of heh.

This scheme is in the opposite order from that of the Short Version, as if starting out from Malkut (10) and progressing *back up* the Tree, that is, outward across the stations or palaces of the Cauldron. What is it that is associated with climbing *back up* the Tree? Ah yes, the *tikkun*. I have concluded that the sealing of the six directions—which has a Gnostic, almost Solomon-like feel to it (who is reputed to have sealed demons up in jars)—is meant as the *means* of *tikkun*: the way to seal off all six directions from their characteristic distractions to allow concentration fully on restoration of the vessels, meaning rebuilding of Boaz. Starting from Malkut means starting out from the sign of self-knowledge, suggesting that to accomplish the Great Work one must be self-motivated.

Moreover, it shows in *actual practice* that 'doubling' of the manifested signs by both the male and female halves of the Name resonating that far. The male half resonating (if only when in conjunction with the female half) all the way through to the first three Sefirot is represented by yod and heh being first- and third-from-the-end, that is, from the tenth Sefirah, a reflection of the first through third Sefirot they stand for in the Name: placement there shows us they do not just stand for the first three but extend up through the broken vessels from the last three to *reach* the first three, sealing the six directions in the process.

I believe this pretty much exhausts what light I can shed on strictly Judaic traditions and stipulations, so let us turn now to various other strands of tradition that have some bearing on, or help to confirm, what has been said so far.

PART

FOUR

:

FURTHER

ALLIES

The Head's Predicament

Odd anyone could get heads to stick
on bodies such as these where the trick
is to appease the trapeze fabric
to where it thinks you share its rubric
that it's all molecules time's mules kick
not notions and nothing is epic.

There is no greater pain in the neck
than that round little ludicrous speck
making a body's life one spent wreck
by misdirecting it on some trek
after abstract facts it fain would check
expecting flesh to just genuflect.

Said bloated head needs a neck that's stout
to hold it up as it bobs about
boss to angels in its high hideout
princely perch till earth's lurch asserts clout
tells it how to hang and when to pout
leading it by hand into its snout.

*[In the traditional Welsh measure cyhydedd naw ban:
originally composed as satire aimed at a particularly
rude rival poet, it managed to drive him out of town!]*

ONE
Egyptian Hieroglyphics

Based on the clear idea presented herein of Egyptian equivalents to letters of the bardic alphabet (table 1), we can now form a picture of how ancient Egyptians most likely symbolized the structure of Cauldron and Egg in their own magic, for which they were quite renowned. It is an interesting picture indeed (see table 2).

Their three 'mother letters' were the Logos: *Egyptian vulture*, *quail chick*, and *owl*; or *'*, *w*, and *m*. Though they did hide its vowels behind related consonants (in this case a glottal stop and *w*), they evidently did not feel a need to equivocate by disguising or 'shushing' the middle term, as in other alphabets—almost as if Egypt *was* what is referred to as Saturn's 'Golden Age'. Of Greek alphabets, only Ionian and Delos and a few others included omega, as if attempting to repair the 'damage' done when Semites 'replaced' it with shin. These lack the sibilant san, from Semitic tzaddi, so perhaps their sigma stood at taurus, like the bethluisnion's willow month, S.

As to Hebrew substitution of bird signs for B and T, consider this from *tWG* (p. 224): "In his last Fable (277) Hyginus ['freedman of Emperor Augustus, Curator of Palatine Library, and friend of poet Ovid'] records: 1. that the Fates invented the seven letters: Alpha, (Omicron), Upsilon, Eta, Iota, Beta, and Tau. Or, alternatively, that Mercury invented them after watching the flight of cranes 'which make letters as they fly'." And in pages following, Graves discusses why *beta* and *tau* were singled out (to go with the vowels)—but we already know, do we not?

To get a sense of the Egyptian view of letters, let us look at the sequence of hieroglyphs implied by the bardic calendar. Separation into simples and doubles is also pertinent, judging from the resulting array of hieroglyphs. The outer Cauldron (from outer horizon to where one is seated) has four horizontal signs, in the sequence *hand*, *tongs*, *basket with handle*, *mouth*. I picture these on several levels, the simplest being: hand grasps tongs to lift contents of basket to feed mouth. Relating to the four senses: *hand* gestures for us to see; *tongs* can be a tuning fork; *basket* contains something to taste; *mouth* joins to that the sense of touch (Budge says Egyptians counted four senses, omitting smell[194]). The *hand* signifies one's reach, like oak; the *tongs* mean control, like holly (XI La Force); the *basket* holds what is gathered close (hazelnuts? almonds?); and the *mouth* is that through which medicine (as from elder) is administered (or whatever tree-substitute the Egyptians may have thought in terms of). The *tongs* were so-called by that great nineteenth-century scholar Isaac Taylor;[195] they are called 'tethering rope' by Gardiner.[196] (Both ensnare their prize.)

Moving past libra to the inner Cauldron, scorpio is the hieroglyph of an *alchemical oven*. Gardiner calls it 'stand with jar', but the 'jar' is a triangle pointing up (symbol for fire) and is *within* it, making it the alchemical oven oft pictured in medieval art: tapering towards the top, with flat roof and fire within. Alchemy blossomed in Ptolemaic Alexandria, and later it was one form through which Gnosticism escaped a complete expunging. Alchemy was apparently even named after Egypt (*khem*, the 'black land', which is probably where the term 'the black arts' originated). But its deep roots in smithcraft's inner mysteries long predate Alexandria.[197]

The two remaining hieroglyphs of the Cauldron obviously refer to the choice between returning back up the spine to the head or proceeding on down the legs to the feet, it having been decided in favor of the latter: *reed stool*, followed by *foot-and-ankle*. For if the Cauldron's curve follows the broken-and-extended zodiac down towards the ground, then sagittary (P) will be knee-high (a stool) and capricorn (B) would be at one's feet. They must have chosen these forms to remind us that with the Egg's broken-and-extended form, the Cauldron should follow it down (Prunikos?).

I would suggest the sign *serpent* (table 1a) is another symbol for scorpio and should be seated on the *alchemical oven* to represent the serpent power yoga locates here at the base of the spine, *serpent* also being a powerful symbol in certain branches of Gnosticism. These would be Egypt's counterpart of G's two runes, 'gift' (*alchemical oven*) and 'harvest' (*serpent*-ine dance).

Switching to the Egg, spring's first two months are tall narrow signs, the third miniscule: *wick of twisted flax*—found as late period *determinative* (ideogram) in a word meaning 'candle' (*t-k-'*)[198]—*fold of cloth*, and *sieve*. Summer's first two months are low flat signs and the third miniscule: *horned viper*, *forearm*, and *hillock*. A miniscule rounded *loaf* is libra, and self's three signs are *reed hut in field*, *one reed*, *two reeds*. Notice the two 'victories' at the end (ninth and tenth signs). There is echo of this all the way over in ancient Mexico, "where Quetzalcouatl is also called 'Ce acatl' = 1-Reed, and Tezcatlipoca 'Omacatl['] (Ome acatl) = 2-Reed."[199] Two low horizontal signs cap it off: *surface of water*, and *bolt* (having skipped *recumbent lion*, the Egyptians having had no L).

The *wick* of a candle is obviously highly appropriate for oxygen and for *up*. The *fold of cloth* for taurus is that in many wall paintings, held over the forearm, presumably for use when clearing one's throat. The space that separates things, gemini, is a *sieve*, which separates things. The *horned viper* reminds us to be like a horned viper when facing 'towards other', as you never know who or what you will meet (perhaps another horned viper); but more than that, its bite may have been associated with visions, this being the noetic breath vav; as a low flat sign, it extends straight out before one, being the sign that points straight ahead. The *forearm*, as mental breath and also as the sign standing for *life*, admonishes us to put thought into labor or activity thereby rendering it greater in accomplishment. The *hillock* is no problem: this was the time of year the Egyptians sought refuge on high ground from annual flooding of the Nile; for as tree-letter, it is the month of the apple, 'refuge of a hind' in bardic lore.

Egg's libra, *loaf*, obviously goes with *mouth*, Cauldron's libra. Then the *reed hut* of the doer, followed by the *one* and *two reeds* (as writing implements?) of thinker and knower. The *recumbent lion*, whose hieratic form became lamedh at aquarius—questioning sphinx, a test, or full moon in leo—was the hieroglyph that signified L in Ptolemaic Egypt and in Meroitic (see below), but in Egyptian it was the sound *rw*: L was missing from Egyptian (as in Japanese), but this hieroglyph was used in 'group writing' to transcribe the L in foreign names and words. That it references opposite sign leo is one indication, and the scales in trump VIII La Justice at aries another, that here in the third wheel the outward, active impulse of each radius is overpowered by its opposite, the reversed or inward (receptive) impulse. Another instance of referencing the opposite sign can be seen in the **hillock** for virgo, which is opposite the middle of the three signs standing for the last three *middot*, oriented as a hill-slope would be, that reference the three most common atom-types in earth's crust (see part one, chapter 15).

For Egyptians, the last two signs were probably **surface of water** (for aquarius, the water carrier) and **bolt**, both horizontal signs, the latter originally the voiced equivalent of **fold of cloth**, voiced because it approached tongue's tip aries from the voiced or active side. As the twelfth sign, it represented a return to aries—sealing up the round so to speak—perhaps actually pushed there later (by the insertion of **recumbent lion**?), as echoed by voiced 'second samekh' in Sabean (see chapter on Semitic letters, below), then later 'drying up' (becoming unvoiced) from contact (at aries) with the unvoiced passive side. (This last is speculation on my part.)

Conjunction of **loaf** and **mouth** brings up another topic: probable geodetic application of the bardic scheme. In Livio Catullo Stecchini's detailed appendix to Peter Tompkins' *Secrets of the Great Pyramid*, the high degree of sophistication of ancient Egyptian weights and measures is made clear. The Egyptian cubit was based on a degree of latitude, and they were well aware of the flattening at the poles, for which they had an accurate formula.[200] The location of the Greek oracular center of Delphi—the omphalos of Greece, sacred to the very god whose name spells out the tree-calendar (Apollo)—was based on a kindred tradition of careful measure, no doubt under Egyptian influence (during the Nubian twenty-fifth dynasty);[201] indeed the Greek cubit was slightly longer, as is a degree of latitude that far north. The Egyptian fascination with geodetic measure led to a mapping of the Dnieper, in what is now Russia, because they thought it a reflection of the Nile![202]

I found that if one carries this latter reasoning (Dnieper as reflection of the Nile) to its logical conclusion, it suggests an Egg with its hub at the center of Anatolia (Sardis in western Anatolia was such an 'omphalos' in later times, but too far west for our purpose) and its libra at the Great Pyramid (see chart 5). Indeed to Gnostics, Egypt symbolized the material world's corruptive influence, this most notably in the 'Hymn of the Pearl', where the 'prince' comes there from the east (where the self is) and thus follows the path of the Fall.[203] The Corn Spirit aries stands in the midst of the grasslands of the Dnieper bend (**wick of twisted flax**). Clockwise from there (zodiac in reverse), our **surface of water** is the Sea of Azov, our **recumbent lion** the mountains of the Caucasus (where they meet the Black Sea); **two reeds** would be the source of Tigris and Euphrates (not far from Ararat), **one reed** Upper Mesopotamia, and **reed hut** Moab.

Then at libra we find **loaf** for Lower Egypt (Egypt's bread basket) and **mouth** for Upper Egypt (the consumers)—the former on the inside, the latter on the outside, just where the *Bahir* places teyt and intermediate mem (standing in for reysh). Going down the Egg's other side, **fold of cloth** is near the mouths (throats) of the Danube, **sieve** at the mountains that act as a sieve to Greece (filtering out easy access by nomads of the steppe), **horned viper** at the west of Greece— Greek colonists going west being that viper, no doubt, for they sure had bite—**forearm** at the straits between Greece and Crete—where sailors perhaps had to pull hard on oars to keep from running aground—and *hillock* at the near shores of Libya near the Greek city of *Kyrene* (whence *Cyrenaica*)—which is *phonetically* close as well, the Greek *ky* (kappa upsilon) versus the bardic *qu* (koppa upsilon, koppa having been dropped from classical Greek).

With the Cauldron, it gets even more interesting in spots. Extending west from **mouth** (Egypt's consumers), **basket with handle** is the more distant coast of Libya (suggestive of sea trade perhaps, its sighting by Libyan sailors meaning sight of home), **tongs** the Tyrrhenian Sea— T's rune stood for the 'war' god Tyr, and a more war-torn sea in ancient times would be difficult to find—**hand** the mountainous source of both Rhine and Danube (north slope of the Alps), D being oak, tree of thunder god Thor and his goat (his totem, symbolic of mountain slopes).

On the other side, **alchemical oven** is the Syrian desert approaches to Mesopotamia— *gimel* means 'camel'—**reed stool** marks where the Caspian is pinched by southern Azerbaijan (and on its other side, western Turkmenistan), and **foot-and-ankle** signifies the Kirghiz-Kazak steppe, where Georges Dumézil and his French school of anthropologists put the motherland of the Indo-Europeans, that is, their birthplace (this being beth the birch).

Both Egg and Cauldron must have had, as indicated by P and B, a broken-and-extended version on the eastern or inner side. The first three on the Egg (**reed hut, one reed, two reeds**) are of interest: Gulf of Aqaba, the Hejaz, and Mecca (the rest listed in chart 5). Interesting, is it not, that Mecca should correspond, on the broken-and-extended zodiac, to that most sacred sign capricorn, the yod that begins the Name (though not the name corresponding to *Allah*, Hebrew *El*, singular of *Elohim*), whose place on the closed zodiac is 'near Ararat'. The corresponding alef-center would be roughly the third cataract, near the capital of Kush, which by the eighteenth dynasty formed the border with Nubia (Meroe is a bit south and east of it).

The three mothers as centers based on the circular zodiac are as follows. Alef the fir— the eagle-like **Egyptian vulture**—is at the center of Anatolia, which is mountainous terrain. The **quail chick** joins **wick of twisted flax** in the Dnieper bend (sounds about right). And **owl**, our mem sofit, stands beyond the eastern end of the Baltic Sea (which may have moved west since then), near Lake Ladoga, where Russia, Finland, and the Baltic countries more or less all meet.

Egyptian hieroglyphics constitute the oldest strata of bardic-related tradition I know of, though India has preserved certain teachings (such as the Trimurti) from a previous cycle, that is, with origins in the vicinity of 14,000 BCE, if my calculations are correct (based on Percival, since the half of the Great Year devoted to nature worship must have lasted from around 12,000 till the beginning of our era). Egypt almost certainly had its influence on the earliest sacred traditions of the West, early bronze age Scandinavians being an especially rich source of inscriptions, both in their own proto-Tifinag alphabet and in the early, consonants-only form of ogham, though proto-Tifinag appears perhaps to have been influenced more by Greeks (see below).

We can be sure Egypt had its effect on Semites, considering the story of Moses—not to mention the Hyksos. I would even suggest Semitic *adon*, 'lord', as in *Adonai*, might be related to the name Aton or Aten, pharaoh Akhenaten's name for the sun's disk, his cult being ancient Egyptians' only flirtation with monotheism. But what do I know.

TWO
Gilgamesh

Having recently read a translation of this fragmented epic in its Babylonian form,[204] I should point out some very interesting details that have survived the decay of the clay tablets on which it is inscribed. First of all, it evidences that bifurcation of bardic tradition between high or heroic and low or satiric Graves characterizes as oak king versus holly king (tanist), or waxing year versus waning year. The translation's introduction[205] speaks of its 'Apollonian phase' and its 'Dionysian phase': the former has heroes Gilgamesh and Enkidu slaying monsters, risking death to make names for themselves and win the 'immortality' of fame; the latter has Gilgamesh, after the death of his friend Enkidu, journeying to the 'abyss' in an eventually futile search for the antidote to death. There he learns about the great flood from its sole survivor, Utnapishtim.

Early on, the hero is said to be "two-thirds divine, one-third mortal."[206] Does this not sound familiar? Of the conscious self's three parts, only the doer underwent the Fall; thinker and knower are as they were, and since they are not fully embodied in the mortal body,[207] only the doer can be called mortal (cf. Arianism). This proportion of the divine in Gilgamesh is repeated in the second part, stipulated this time by 'scorpion woman',[208] scorpio *being* the ('mortal') doer.

Details in the second part stand out explicitly as artifacts of the lore of letters elucidated herein. As Gilgamesh sets off to seek the survivor of the great flood (and learn his secrets), he is confronted by 'scorpion man' and 'scorpion woman': this parallels the fact that as we progress onto the inner or active side of the wheel (here in the waning year or lower half of the Egg), the first sign encountered is scorpio. Soon after, he "picks up the Urnu-snakes"[209]—**serpent** being another of scorpio's symbols—and in doing so has "hindered the crossing"[210] (of the river of death, since scorpio *follows* libra or physical existence), or made it so none can cross ever again.

Furthermore, if you refer to table 2 (on distribution of the Egyptian hieroglyphs) you will note that the three simples descended from hieroglyphs involving reeds begin at scorpio: **reed hut**, **one reed** (**reed stool** on the Cauldron), and **two reeds**—the three signs of the conscious self. Just so, not long after his encounter with scorpion man and scorpion woman, Gilgamesh is told by Utnapishtim how the god Ea, to evade the gods' agreement (p. 229) not to warn humans of the flood, speaks of it to a *wall of reeds* (of Egyptians' **reed hut**?), behind which Utnapishtim listens.[211] Indeed the translators point out (p. 243) that Ea's sign is the goat-fish, which puts him precisely at sign capricorn (**two reeds**): does Ea represent the knower or Father? And just before Utnapishtim reveals this, he says, "I will uncover for you, Gilgamesh, a hidden thing, / tell you a secret of the gods."[212] We are now in a position to see just how deep a secret it was. (Rumi used the reed or reed-pipe as a symbol of the mystic's longing for god.)[213]

Finally, note that the *-mesh* in the hero's name has been translated 'rowan' and associated in a Mesopotamian text *twice* with aquarius![214]

THREE
Meroitic Alphabet (Nubia)

I will wager most of you are unaware Nubia is reputed to have sent Christian knights to the Crusades (source of the medieval legend of the *black knight?*). Saladin dispatched a punitive expedition against the Nubian realm of Makuria, though it had to be recalled. (It was conquered soon after for Islam by the Mamelukes of Egypt.) Earlier, in the Ptolemaic era, a thriving culture with its capital at Meroe used an alphabet I find very interesting. I sense in it much from bardic tradition, with a bit of Osiris and Geb worship thrown in for good measure. If you will consult table 7, you will see this alphabet that caught my eye years ago. It appears to be the complete bardic sequence, including vowels, strongly influenced by the Ptolemaic Greeks yet conforming more closely to the bardic scheme than the *classical* Greek alphabet did.

The very first consonant (in the bardic sequence) is intriguing. It pictures an animal that in some renderings looks quite passable as a ***boibalis***: the *roebuck fawn*, or *antelope bull-calf*, as Graves translates it in the archaic Greek hymn he reconstructed out of the Boibel Loth names of bardic letters in Irish lore (see table 4). I take this hymn as a relic of Orphism. The only other crossover here is "I flow away" for R, which in the Meroitic is a hieroglyph that may picture an ***aquifer*** (based on Egyptian) or a ***coffin***, *both* of which fit "I flow away.".

Many points of interest. Alef, hub of the zodiac of the seated torso, is a ***seated person***. Bardic Aa—Hebrew teyt—appears to be two letters, syllabic in nature, standing for *to* and *te*: ***horn***, and ***reed shelter***. This corresponds to the fire breath (see below for an analysis). The air breath, E, is the Egyptian ideogram for ***feather***. Vowel U (*w*) is a ***lasso*** to rope the antelope bull-calf with, as if they knew B was *five* and U fifth-from-the-end. The death tree yew (I) is ***person w/ arm raised*** (standing), derived from the cry of lamentation (our 'o', see table 7). Yod is our familiar ***two reeds*** (note that here I and Ii are *i* and *y*, not *z* and *y*). The most puzzling vowel is O, as mental breath; but it is, after all, the ***ox's head***.

It has just dawned on me while writing this that they seemingly envisioned pillars Boaz and Jachin, or outer and inner, as bull-like versus reed-like. For teyt—*to* and *te*—as boundary between outer and inner, has a bull's ***horn*** for the one, and the ***reed shelter*** whose hieratic form became Semitic heh for the other. The U that points without is the ***lasso*** that snares the ***boibalis*** (antelope bull-calf), and the O following it on the round is the ***ox's head***; whereas the Ii pointing within is ***two reeds***. Preceding *it* on the round is the standing ***person w/ arm raised*** that replaced the sign for ***one reed*** (zayin) because it occurred in the word of lamentation alongside it: this is our yew or I, pillar Jachin. And Boaz, B, is the ***boibalis*** itself. How interesting.

The Cauldron is amazing. D, Osiris's ***djed eye*** (according to Gardiner), represents our eye on the horizon—which it even looks like, taking the curve under it as the Cauldron's cross section. This was the eye Horus gave his deceased father to sustain him in the afterlife; and the Meroitic letter probably got its sound from the initial. It is also called the *wedjat* eye, that is, *djed* (pillar or spine of Osiris) with the prefix *w*, the Egyptian counterpart of omega, obliquely referencing D's sign but on the Egg (through vav). Next is an unmistakable reference to hearing: a ***priest in bird mask*** seen from above, with arms stretched forward *or* lines connecting ears to the source of a sound. This is a modification of ***tongs*** in the source Egyptian (which Gardiner identifies as ***loop of rope***). K (*kh*) is ***narrow-necked jar***, another symbol for 'what is gathered close' (virgo), to go with the hazelnut Epictetus's fable (see chapter 7 below) places *in* said jar, which when grasped by the boy could not be extracted without his unclenching the fist holding it. In Egyptian, it was ***basket with handle***: these two shapes, narrow-necked jar versus shallow bowl, figure in a fable of Æsop's, the Wolf and the Crane. The R we have already dealt with. G (*k*) appears to be the hieroglyph of the ***Geb goose*** (whose initial was often unvoiced): Geb was the earth god, so that works well for G being the sign controlling the earth triad (sign of the doer). He was also the father of snakes, a link to the ***serpent*** hieroglyph doubling G in Egypt, as well as to ivy's (and scorpio's) serpentine nature. P is the Egyptian ***reed stool***. And B we have already dealt with.

The L and N follow Ptolemaic Egyptian, as well as the hieratic sources of Semitic. The Ng, which *may* stand at aries like the Ng-equivalent samekh (*ñ* in Lycian), is a plant (perhaps ***sedge***) associated with Upper Egypt.[215] The simple letter at taurus, ***woven strands*** or ***enclosure***, is puzzling but may have to do with the curtailing or corralling of motion, the meaning of taurus being motion itself. The ***opened mouth*** at gemini may symbolize 'hot air' (no-thing, The Fool). M and S are the same signs that Semitic adapted from Egyptian hieratic: ***owl***, and ***lotus pool***.

It is interesting that inhabitants of Ethiopia, farther south, received bardic tradition via the south Semitic alphabet (see next chapter), from which their early alphabet and letter order clearly derive; while inhabitants of Nubia—in a slightly later epoch it would appear—fashioned their own system, with vowels, albeit using Egyptian signs, yet based squarely on a kindred current of tradition, one which links all the alphabets treated herein as of quasi-bardic origin. I do not mean to imply, of course, that it all originated with Celts! merely that the letter-tradition *we* see most clearly through its Celtic and Judaic strands touched many peoples in antiquity. Who knows just where it originated, if not in the last great civilization (destroyed over ten thousand years ago by massive inundations). Both classical and Celtic traditions seem to point to very early (perhaps even pre-Mycenaean) Greek origin. I am inclined to think it of extreme antiquity: perhaps Plato was right and Greece was a thriving concern in the era of the destruction of the last civilization, in which case a shared Greco-Atlantean origin would perhaps be plausible.

Not all alphabets with only one version of peh rejected the Corn Spirit: the ogham tree-alphabet has fearn the alder up at or near aries and ngetal the reed at sagittary. But the one peh-equivalent in Meroitic and Egyptian shows itself tied to sagittary, since it follows the broken-and-extended zodiac down to knee-high. An important lesson we may take from Meroitic is that here a branch of bardic tradition that rejected the Corn Spirit heresy apparently associated itself especially with Geb and with the story of his son Osiris.

FOUR
Ugaritic and South Semitic

One link in the chain connecting the Celtic tree-calendar to Semitic tradition can be seen in the following quote: "Compare also the 'epitheton' of Ugaritic Baal, *alíyn*, and its possible derivation from Hebrew 'allôn ('êlôn), Oak, Therebynth, holy tree, and allânati as name of the fourth month, i.e., the month of Tammuz."[216] Tammuz is the month of the summer solstice.

I have developed theories about most of the shapes in the Ugaritic cuneiform, it being a mystery what the linear letters it is patterned on (if any) may have looked like. But I will not bore you with that here (see appendix). I wish to simply point out a certain symmetry I noticed deriving from its letter order (see chart 2), because it bolsters my case as to which *Sabean* letters correspond to which Hebrew letters in terms of place on the zodiac and physiological attribution.

It is my contention the letter pairs that are in Hebrew fifth and eight from both beginning and end were each reversed as to physiological placement and thus zodiac sign in the Sabean alef-beyt, which I take as the standard version of south Semitic. It is clear to me that this is so, for I know what parts of the body the letters stand for, and the shapes make it obvious. And it is no problem phonetically, the phonetic values being close. But quickly before I present the rest of my case, consider the Ugaritic. It has some extra letters sprinkled in from what Hebrew has, the same more or less as in south Semitic save for a couple of extra 'alefs' in addition to the initial one, alefs that instead of the initial one's "ah" are sounded "eh / ih" and "oh / oo" respectively. These two are tacked on *after* tav, then capped off with a sibilant related to shin, or possibly to samekh: its form in south Semitic shows two shins back to back, a shape also reminiscent of the old samekh's corresponding hieroglyph (oddly enough a shape identical to *late* runic Ng).

I am proposing we look at Ugaritic *minus* the last three seemingly tacked-on characters and note that even though it has five extra characters interspersed into it (not counting the three extra after tav at the end), the pattern of the four letters is still symmetrical. But they are now sixth and ninth from both beginning and end, instead of fifth and eighth. That is all I brought it up for, this otherwise charming (if alphabets happen to fascinate you, as they do me) Ugaritic cuneiform alphabet of northern Lebanon from the third quarter of the second millennium BCE.

The above concerns a purely phonetic consideration, a re-classification of otherwise close sounds; so reversing each pair is a minor adjustment that does *not* make nonsense of the phonetic structure. The shapes easily justify the moves. The sibilants are the most obvious. In chart 3 (we are in south Semitic letter-order now), they are the penultimate letter overall and the fourth-to-last letter of the first half. We know these, respectively, as samekh and tzaddi, head and neck (aries and taurus): obviously the head is *there* on the one, *not* there on the other (which shows the stub of the neck after beheading).

The other two are the first and third letters. The first clearly shows arms being raised in the air—for cheyt the shoulders—while the third is a comb, like heh, except the handle emerges from its spine perpendicularly, rather than extending it at one end. Put in vernacular terms, it is more of an *afro* type of comb (forgive this old hippy his perhaps outdated terminology). There is also a second cheyt: the fourteenth character shows arms raised in the air from a *sitting* position.

In fact almost all the shapes in the Sabean alphabet are easily explainable in bardic terms. I will just mention those that are different from north Semitic. Since beyt means 'house', it is a flat-roofed dwelling.   L pictures the eaves of a (slanted) roof, as in runic. These last two are combined in a ligature for Baal (*dwelling* plus *eaves*) to express a second, harder form of ayin, perhaps from its being the preferred middle sound in the Sabean pronunciation of the god's name (often spelled *Ba'al*)? Some knowledgeable linguist can hopefully confirm or deny this.

Bernal[217] contends that the B-shaped mem in south Semitic was the *original* M, but to me the old Hebrew shape, a mother grasping us to her bosom, too closely expresses its core meaning to be derivative (other than from the hieratic for *owl* itself of course). Qof is fruit on its branch. Vav is a melon halved, symbolizing the breasts (since sometimes found shaped like a lazy-8), or cleavage perhaps. Reysh is an opened mouth seen from the side (R's hieroglyph was a mouth). Kaf signifies 'under one roof', another symbol for what is gathered close.

The alternate shin, though reminiscent of Egyptian samekh-equivalent **wick of twisted flax**, is probably just two *shin*s back to back. Since old Semitic peh pictures that part of beyt that is *under* the rim of the helmet (or priest's mitre), my guess is that this peh pictures an earring. Alef is obvious: dwelling B but with smoke spiraling out, signifying it is the spirit that *inhabits* the dwelling, not the raw shell itself; but the two are obviously linked, as the first vowel and first consonant (in both tree-alphabet and Greek). Voiced and unvoiced teyts could be rooftops seen from above, as if from that executive jet we see the hamlet from in that old version of XXI Le Monde, or else they picture boxes stacked side by side or one atop the other, the latter requiring one lift up one of them, which entails a grunt, so that is the voiced one (how I keep track of it).

The D in the shape of an axe is easy; for in table 4 you will see that for D it has 'cleave wood'; and another line of Taliesin's that Graves associates with oak in *tWG* is "I have been a tree stump in a shovel."[218] The zayin I take for an hourglass, perhaps related to the fact that our Z picturing a cold front also probably hearkened from seafarers: if anyone back then used an hourglass it would have been seafarers, for they require an accurate measure of time to reckon longitude. The second D is the bier of the hero. That yod showing a 'head on a pike' is perhaps rather the head of a child (or sperm with a tail, had they microscopes), just as yod in the Name is said to picture the head (meaning of offspring, as opposed to aries on the Egg, which in Sabean shows the head atop the shoulders). The second T shows the chain of responsibility binding us to others via conscience. The second form of samekh there beside the first could be one seated in a chair, or half a samekh, or it could be an animal (or even a flower, when the chair part is curved); but I opt for the chair (to parallel the seated form of cheyt).

It should be noted that in Sabean the letters that have two forms are: shin, its two doubles dalet and tav, and the four signs of the macrocosmic hexad that are on the macrocosmic or nature side of the Egg.

FIVE
Tifinag and Numidian

Next we turn to a tale which I really enjoy telling and which the academics who police Wikipedia will not allow to be told there—I know, because I have tried. The discoveries of the founder of the American Epigraphic Society, Barry Fell—without doubt the greatest epigrapher of the twentieth century—including a multitude of Old World inscriptions found from North and South America to Polynesia, are black-balled by academia for one reason (aside from their fear of facing the truth): his Ph.D. was not in epigraphy but in marine biology, the subject he taught at Harvard. I know this is the only reason because I have read where he made mincemeat of his critics in rebuttals in his periodical the *Epigraphic Society Occasional Papers*, which I used to have on a DVD until fire destroyed it (and half my notes on Jung and others) over a decade ago. Barry Fell could have *taught* epigraphy in most universities, but he had much more important work to do, and it is the results of that work which now Wikipedia readers, and those seeking information from other sources (mainly scholarly), are not allowed, by the high-handed attitude of academia, to even be made aware of, unless they happen onto one or more of his three books on epigraphy (listed in the bibliography), or works of those like myself who are impressed by results, not academic acceptance.

The North Atlantic goes through phases when it is much warmer than at other times. The Viking Age was one of these, followed by a so-called mini-ice-age that cut off much of the trade the warm period sparked. Another warm spell was in the early Scandinavian Bronze Age. This was a period recorded in many rock carvings from the region showing ships were an important part of that culture. Two modes of writing are used in these inscriptions: early Scandinavian Tifinag (see table 5), and an ancient form of ogham without vowels known as *ogam consaine*. In the latter, instead of the third tier of consonants being expressed with strokes *slanting* across the line so that the vowels could use strokes that were straight across (or sometimes just dots), the vowels were omitted, allowing the third group of consonants to have their strokes straight across. Thus the old Semitic samekh was the *ogam consaine* Ng (found in Lycian with the sound ñ).

Around 1700 BCE, a seafaring prince named Woden-lithi left elaborate inscriptions near modern day Peterborough, Canada, with religious and calendar instructions for a colony he left there to trade with the native population for the vast tonnages of copper mined on the north shore of Lake Superior.[219] Most of that copper evidently went to fuel the northern European Bronze Age, since there was no appreciable Bronze Age in North America. Whatever linguistic scholars may claim to know, the Low German dialect these colonists spoke and the gods they revered were quite similar to those of the Viking Age—Woden, Freyr, and so on—although Loki may have been known at the time more for his craftiness than his malevolence.

I connect many Germanic gods to Celtic ones—Loki to Lugh, Fro to Vran or Bran, Thor and Tiw to Gallic Taranis and Teutates, Woden (*Guodan* to Longobards and in Westphalia)[220] to

Gwydion ap Don, and Frigga (lest she be confused with Fro's sister Freya) to Brighid. With this discovery that the Germanic gods go clear back to the early second millennium BCE, it is unclear who got them from whom; or both may be the long-preserved heritage of the beaker culture, the gods of the indigenous peoples of western and central Europe (my view).

Many earmarks of the bardic corpus can be traced in early Tifinag, but that is not the only reason it is interesting: it is also interesting because of where it ended up, that is, amongst the ancient Berbers and modern Tuaregs of North Africa. How it got there is this. In roughly 1200 BCE, Egypt was beset by a confederation of marauders called by historians the Sea Peoples. The Egyptian bas relief of the battle (won by the Egyptians) shows some of them had horned helmets, suggesting Nordic tribes of some sort. Soon after, many of them settled in nearby Libya, later enlisting in the Egyptian navy, and later yet forming a dynasty. The Libyo-Egyptian language inscribed in a Libyan alphabet quite close to, yet different from, Tifinag—the Numidian—ended up being spread all over the world, including Polynesia. Fell's attempt to identify the traces of it he had found in his native New Zealand was what led him to many of his discoveries.

What was the story? The Berbers are a fairer skinned people than the surrounding Arabs, and it is probable they, and their kindred Tuaregs to the south, include distant descendants of those marauders: it was the ancient Berbers who used Tifinag. What amuses me (in a bitter sort of way) is that Wikipedia tells us that that alphabet used by Egyptian sailors (a use not even on its radar), which became known as the Libyan or Numidian alphabet, was the *source* of Tifinag. No, Tifinag in its *Scandinavian* form predated Libyan by half a millennium. And in tracing the changes from the one to the other, it is key that whereas Tifinag had (still has) the letter that is the sun symbol (circle with central dot) for S, early spring's willow month, the Libyan alphabet it spawned moved this symbol back all the way to the letter B, to the birch month with which the year begins, this because, being now well south of the Arctic Circle, it no longer had need of saving the symbol for later in the year to await the sun's coming out of its Arctic sleep.

It is clear Tifinag expressed the tree calendar. Let us follow the shapes, and Barry Fell's projected names reconstructed *from* those shapes (table 5). The Sun Hero when first born needs shielding: B, *bukla*, 'shield, buckler'. He is educated, taught to classify things: L, *liki*, 'like, equal'. Then (in tree-calendar order, as in table 6) he distinguishes himself from others of his kind and embarks on his life's work: N, *naddr*, 'nail', one of the two 'like' things but by itself now, indicative also of a spear-shaft or other handle made of ash. He then embarks on his heroic voyage: F, *far*, 'ferry', for alder's resistance to moisture meant it was used early on for boats.[221] Then he steps into the spotlight: S, *sol*, 'sun'. There he faces his doom, written in the stars: H, *Hestamerki*, 'Pegasus'. So he (as waxing year, sacrificed at summer solstice) exits through the door into manifestation: D, *dyrr*, 'door', which can also double (by its shape) as his dolmen or tomb. He is succeeded by the holly king, his slayer or tanist: T, *tagg*, 'barbed arrow'. Hence a cairn is raised for the slain hero: K, *kuml*, 'cairn, heap'. Then come the ins and outs of time: M, *mán*, 'moon'. And this necessitates a roof's shelter, in preparation for winter: G, *ghomr*, 'roof beams'. Therefore its thatch is repaired: Ng, *gneipa*, 'bent', referring to reed, whose flexibility made it the subject of a fable by Aesop (see chapter 7, below). Thus we have come full circle: R, *hringr*, 'ring'.

I cannot say for sure, but I have speculated that the equivalents of bardic Kk and Ss may have been *par*, 'pair' (as in choice?), for interrogative consonant Q, under Greek influence, as the Greek interrogative consonant became pi—at various times in various regions, no doubt— and *rifa*, 'to split' (as in strife), for blackthorn's Ss, this paralleling the later Germanic *z* ending, usually transcribed as *R*. Notice both of these reference duality, as befits letters that double other letters.

The vowels are sketchy, but theta-equivalent (Aa) *thili*, 'planks, partition', is suggestive of the deck of a ship, from which palms in exotic lands would be seen. And the yod-equivalent (Ii), *Yorsa*, 'Cassiopeia', is quite amazing: one form it took in North Africa shows the golden sickle druids used in harvesting oak-mistletoe! The two weights for *waettir*, 'weights', might suggest a couple (U the heather, vav being Hebrew 'and'), if my speculation is correct and they reversed O and U on the fingers (see below). And *zaun*, 'railing, fence', for the death tree yew— also under Greek influence? (i.e. from whatever was zeta's proto-Mycenaean equivalent?)—may simply mean the end of the line, the edge. (See below as to why it does not represent straif.)

Several points need to be remarked. The *rune* S was also named 'sun', you will recall, but shaped like a lightning's zigzag, as was the later Numidian (and Greek) version: polarity between mother letters M and S as 'moon' and 'sun' seems quite natural, given *SY*'s placement of them at 'belly' and 'head' (water and fire) and *mayim* meaning 'seas' in Hebrew. Hebrew D is *also* named 'door'. The T became a cross (+) or X shape in Libya, but in *runic* it was also an arrow (albeit pointing up). And the cairn for K is obviously just another way of symbolizing what is gathered close—a stack of nuts, perhaps? The Numidian form may picture a passage grave, whose main purpose was to mark a direction on the horizon, cairns having had a similar role. I love how the ancestor of our *ellipsis*—the three dots, Q—shows apples *not yet* gathered, while K shows them (or nuts) gathered into a pile.

The throat or tzaddi-equivalent is *very* obvious in North African Tifinag: it unmistakably shows a torc, which is worn at the throat. I am dissatisfied with the hourglass that is tzaddi's equivalent in Numidian; it could represent *time untilled*, which is what attracts La Mère du Bois (forest's vanguard in reclaiming untilled land), yet this same shape is found for zayin in south Semitic. It is one of those loose ends over which I lose sleep. Yet here it is similar to an angular form of the torc letter in North African Tifinag, a shape that reminds me of something I was told by a friend of Irish ancestry: she said a properly made torc had a reputation for strangling a liar! Having once pictured it, I cannot help but see that angular form now as a person pictured from above grasping at his or her throat trying to keep from being strangled by it: bleak humor?

A couple more things before we move on. Vowels in North Africa included *all* ogham vowels (or rather consonant equivalents thereof), the first four *in ogham form* with second and third reversed, the fifth like the cross-stroke by which we mark fifth when doing a simple tally.

And there is an intricate rearrangement having to do once again, it appears, with our Corn Spirit 'heresy'. I saved alder for last because it is so delicious. Fearn the alder's great resistance to moisture meant it was used in boats, so in Scandinavia it was a boat or ship: *far*, 'ferry'. But in North Africa it took a shape that looks like the map symbol for a bridge, signifying no doubt one with alder pilings. But the schism producing the later *Numidian* alphabet evidently involved abandonment of the Corn Spirit; for F the alder is gone from that alphabet. Instead we find the famous cauldron Bran invaded Ireland to retrieve, and in an interesting context. To sort out the forms of *g* in North African Tifinag, I have assimilated the erect male member (the vertical line straddled by two dots at its base) to the Greek style gamma of Numidian, which depicts the erect male member from the side—G being scorpio, after all—and put the other *g*, a cauldron, in place of ogham Ng (in North African Tifinag). It then becomes a simple thing to hypothesize that later the Numidian alphabet replaced that Ng with P, as in the bethluisnion! but kept the *character* for Ng, a cauldron, to stand for the new sound. My *guess* is that then, to fill the space of the missing F, a sibilant was chosen—to be on tongue's tip and thus conform to the more orthodox approach of Hebrew—namely the half-circle with dot in the middle I have listed beside Numidian sigma.

It makes sense when you think about it. It was that alphabet on the right that ended up being inscribed all over the world, wherever those hearty sailors roved, so perhaps they had less reason to revere the Corn Spirit than those who stayed behind to eventually become the Tuaregs we know today—once a formidable force that actually brought down the Mali Empire (they took Timbuktu and Oualata in the 1430s). Not all who used the Numidian alphabet went to sea, of course; the Numidians of North Africa were at first allies and finally foes of Carthage during its generations-long struggle with Rome (during whose Hannibal-in-Italy phase Archimedes was slain in Syracuse). With regard to those who *did* go to sea, is it possible that the term *Maori*—in New Zealand, where Barry Fell first discovered inscriptions later discovered to be Numidian, which he sometimes called *Maurian*—is related to the term *Moor*? Remember the strange fact of a Polynesian *kahuna*—term I think akin to Hebrew *kohen*, 'priest'—that was found in North Africa? And as I believe I mentioned, those Egypto-Libyan sailors reached North America from both directions, even establishing a culture on our southwestern plateau, as clearly evidenced by inscriptions and by linguistic traces it left in the Zuñi tongue.

SIX

Greece, Anatolia, and the West

The Greeks must have had a thriving bardic tradition before they had an openly inscribed set of letters (considered Phoenician in origin, hence our word *phonetics*), as is fairly clear from the Homeric epics, considered to be transcriptions of verbal performance by a *rhapsodist*. The interesting thing to me is that just as later Greek drama was divided into high tragedy and low comedy, one Homeric epic is high or heroic, comparable to tragedy, while the other is satiric, comparable to low comedy, with a little comedy of manners thrown in I guess you might say.

This is not generally recognized, I think, but the two epics are quite opposite in character. In the *Iliad* it is the deaths of heroes that constitute the theme, occurring in the old way nobility fought, conveyed to the 'front' in chariots. My strong sense is that it was originally an Anatolian heroic epic of the (heroic) death of Hector, his farewell to his wife being the highpoint of the story to anyone with sensitivity greater than that of an ox. But it was later reworked by some Achacan hick of a 'Homer' into: gee, that Achaean, Achilles, sure was formidable, and gee, that Trojan, Hector, sure was a coward, a propagandistic reworking as obvious to me as the fact that Hercules *slaying* the lion was not the original form of tarot trump XI La Force.

The *Odyssey*, or Trickster's voyage home, on the other hand is running satire of extremes of hospitality versus lack thereof, coupled with Trickster's love life. It includes transformation of his crew into pigs, and ends with a volley of barbs. In bardic tradition amongst Celtic tribes, satire was the 'other cheek' that got turned towards an inhospitable chief or other disreputable person by a poet: it was the poet's *weapon*. Hence the theme of hospitality or lack thereof that runs through this epic.

Since they have the figure Dionysus in common with Orphism, being performed during his festival, the tragedy and comedy of later dramatic tradition may have been a continuation of the bardic mysteries surrounding Orpheus (and how could his have been mysteries of any other kind, considering he was the greatest singer-poet of all time, capable of charming even beasts), whose severed head even prophesied, as did that of Bran the Blessed. It is not difficult to link *Orph-* by metathesis (reversal of consonants) to *Fro* and the root *vron* it shares with *Bran*. That makes the possibly Orphic (or at any rate early) reconstructed Greek 'hymn' of table 4 quite intriguing, a precious window on pre-Sophoclean Hellenic lore. Certainly the god Phanes of Orphic cosmogony, born of the Word Egg, embodies the mysteries expounded herein in being described as female in front and male behind,[222] just as female column Boaz, broken off at the sternum, is the front column and Jachin, the male column, our backbone.

Considering primacy of the vowels in correctly placing bardic letters on the Egg, it is hard for me to think of the original Greek alphabet, whose age is not firmly established anyway, as *derivative* of the Semitic. I am willing to concede its characters' shapes derived therefrom but feel there must have been a much older oral tradition to which those characters simply adhered.

After all, however low an opinion modern academics may have of the intellect of the ancients, it is not difficult to distinguish vowel sounds along with those of consonants. For crying out loud, any scop (pronounced 'shope') of the 'primitive' Germanic tribes routinely alliterated vowels, and with the 'primitive' Finns, the vowels to be alliterated had to *match*.[223]

I cannot rule out that the complete bardo-Judeo-scientific scheme expounded herein was put together by some extraordinary mind of the pre-classical age, but the most plausible scenario is preservation by unbroken oral tradition from sciences predating the end of the last Ice Age. That *tools* were mostly primitive during that long interim does not mean *minds* were.

One current that I see is the recurring concealment of vowels. The fact that early ogham, *ogam consaine*, omitted its vowels and made do with fifteen letters tells me something was afoot. When Tifinag seemed to adopt ogham vowel-equivalents once it reached North Africa (some of which had been used before in the north), *even then* it used thinly disguised consonants, as in the Egyptian and Semitic. In the latter (a derivative of hieratic) as in Egyptian itself (that hoary old institution), the vowels, while clear in terms of placement on the Egg, were already disguised as consonants. I am convinced of a strong taboo against the vowels (the breaths) from the earliest times, not rescinded till the age of the Greeks, with their outspoken humanism and rationalism, to be followed later by the Irish Celts, who were strongly influenced by them.

A brief note on theta or teyt: how it came to be a crossed circle if its hieratic precursor was that of the semicircle hieroglyph standing for *loaf*. The crossed circle is like the Egyptian ideogram meaning 'place' (a crossroads), and indeed that is the symbolic meaning of the palm: location, location, location. But it could originally have come about, perhaps even humorously, from a shift in the shape of a loaf in Semitic culture from a half-round Egyptian *loaf* to the pita-shaped flatbread of Palestine (quartered into pizza slices). Another possibly humorous touch is alteration of ayin from the hieratic of the *forearm* hieroglyph (see table 1) into our spokeless circle or *moving* wheel O: feather-like tails at either end of a horizontal stroke slanted off on opposite sides, which made it look like it was spinning, hence they spun it.

I have gathered a few of the alphabets of the Greeks and their related strata of letters for the reader's perusal—tables 9 and 10—and will only make a few remarks on them in passing. (The various Greek, Italic, and Anatolian characters were redrawn by me mostly from tables printed in Bernal and in the edition of the Britannica I first learned out of, that of the early 50s.)

Greek T-square tau, as conscience, means what is 'on the square' (a 'square deal'); tav as *crossroads* (T's Semitic precursor) broadens this into the idea of *public* shame. One wonders if it was in Crete that they got the idea to turn the Semitic ox, alef, nose up (A), as if looking down on it; for in Crete men *and women* used to vault over them (bulls, that is). One must agree with Bernal that the Greek beta did not derive from Phoenician beyt, the latter a helmet or the high priest's mitre, the former a pregnant torso in profile. Both fit the underlying symbolic meaning, if from different angles. Bernal traces beta[224] (and linguistically he seems to be on solid ground) to south-Semitic mem, which is identical. If he is right, it is still later in origin than mem's north Semitic form showing a mother clasping us to her bosom, which I take to be its earliest form: it is easy to see how this arose from a hieratic version of the *owl* hieroglyph. It may, as he said, be a harder case to argue that over time the stem closed over the w-shaped part (to form the south Semitic mem) than that it slid out of sync with it (to form north Semitic mem). But perhaps that is not what happened: perhaps the pregnant-torso shape (south Semitic mem) was conjured up on its own, based on the lips, and Greek beta then derived from that.

Some Italic sets in table 9 are among the oldest types. I would like to draw attention to the variant of Messapic and Roman A with two parallel branches—like fir's rune (ᚠ), to which it may be related—and the Roman E consisting of two parallel posts, which may have evolved into runic E (ᛗ). Also, there is the Attic crooked iota: north Semitic yod has always looked to me first and foremost like someone drawing a line in the dirt with a stick clutched in both hands (see table 3), perhaps because of a Celtic taboo on any more permanent inscribing of letter-forms, Celts being mercenaries hired by the Semitic Carthaginians to fight against the Greeks and later the Romans. I imagine therefore that that Attic crooked iota pictures a hand drawing a line on a chalkboard with a piece of chalk, later simplified to just the line itself. Finally, let me point to the Etruscan tzaddi-equivalent shaped like the Numidian one (an hourglass), but on its side.

In table 10, the alphabet on the right has some claim to being related to Etruscan in its origin, and it shares with the latter the figure-8 form standing for the *f* sound. (It is interesting that 8 happens to be its bardic number, though this is long before adoption and standardization of Arabic numerals.) It is plausible that Etruscans came from the Lydian region: they seem to be the Tyrrhenians (after whom that sea is named) or Tyrsenians—perhaps the Teresh, who were one of the Sea Peoples. What few comments I have on Lydian are inserted into the table.

It is the Lycian alphabet I find the more interesting of the two. The first two characters look to me like the pine and the fir, the two trees associated with alef in bardic lore. The theta looks like it is meant to convey the idea of touch (libra's sense), being where the two sides of the Egg touch. The doubled K of Q *looks* like two Ks back to back. The X shape for the sound *m*-with-a-tilde happens to be roughly the shape of ogham M, while *ñ* is *ogam consaine* Ng. And towards the end are two letters that appear to be the *tops* of pine and fir: indeed both these trees are present in mountainous, sea-bound Anatolia. And at the end a puzzling thing: it appears to have both the western and eastern versions of chi—cross and trident, respectively. Perhaps they just packed them in to be useful, sort of like the Elder Futhark packing in both P and Ng.

SEVEN
My Beloved Æsop

In my earlier attempt at this monograph, I just opened a paperback Æsop and commented on fable after fable that had clear relevance to the bardic corpus. Since then I acquired (and later discovered my good fortune) the Loeb Classical Library's *Babrius and Phaedrus*, translated by B. E. Perry.[225] It was only much later that I realized it contained the so-called 'Perry index' of Æsopian fables, a nearly complete list of fables tradition has attributed to Æsop. Since I consider him my first and greatest teacher (after my parents), I made a full study of them and catalogued them: *politics* and *human nature* were the two biggest categories. The two that will be key to us are *bardic* and *Hermetic* (numbers in parentheses are those of the Perry index).

There are a whole host related to tree-letters. I will start with one that escaped Perry's net but is a genuine oldie (accredited to Epictetus), the Boy and the Filberts: he reaches in a narrow necked jar (Meroitic K) and grabs a filbert (hazel) but then cannot get his fist out—the name of letter *kaf* means the palm or curved part of the hand, *yod* (letter preceding it). The Fir and the Bramble (304) has the former boasting it is tall and well-proportioned, grows straight, neighbor to the clouds, main pillar of a house, keel of a ship; whereupon bramble talks of the axes that are forever cleaving firs and says it prefers being the humble bramble. One Perry gives as the *Oaks and Zeus* (302) I first heard (more correctly I think) as a man asking the *ash* for its wood, which ash gives only to then be set upon by axes with ash handles: this relates directly to trump XIII (forest's grim reaper). The Oak and the Reed (70) has the former, battered down by a massive storm and washed downriver, marvel to find the reed—Ng, which occupies D's original post— still standing, told it is because they are flexible and bow meekly to the powerful.   This relates directly to the Scandinavian Tifinag letter Ng (ngetal the reed): Barry Fell suggests (table 5) it bore the name *gneipa*, 'bent', fitting name considering Æsop's tale. The preceding Scandinavian Tifinag letter G, *ghomr* or 'roof beams', strongly suggests the reed Ng following as thatch.

One of the more telling ones is the Fox and the Grapes (15), for it measures the height of mem sofit: height the fox cannot quite jump—where he tried to leap up and grab some grapes but could not and says, "They were probably sour anyway." Another one that escaped Perry's net is the Hedge and the Vineyard (got from Estrange of 1714, *Fables of Æsop*), where a foolish heir cut down a hedge around the vineyard he inherits because it bore no grapes, with predictable results: "I, the Guardian of Boundaries" (see table 4). And have I not also heard the expression 'good fences make good neighbors'?

Of those that have to do with particular signs and their animal representation, the most important is perhaps the Stag and the Oxen (492), where the stag hides from hunters in an ox stall (he is successful only for a time): this represents the fact that in northern Europe the stag replaced the bull as sign taurus, as shown on a rock carving from Peterborough, Canada.[226] And the rune for tzaddi is 'elk'. Take the Stag, the Horse, and Man (269a, mentioned in Aristotle's

Art of Rhetoric), where the horse is at war with the stag and enlists man's help only to later be unable to rid itself of man's bridle: 'horse' and 'elk' are the diameter scorpio-taurus in runes, that arrow for 2 that flipped around to point down (to express helium's inertness). The same tale was told with boar in place of stag, but that would shift it to aries (see below), as if the tale were trying to connect the two signs ruled by Mars. There are two (85 and 694) where a boar or pig gets in among sheep (with different results): this suggests the link between the boar and aries (the ram). Attribution of the line "I am a boar" from the ancient Song of Amergin (chapter XII in *tWG*) is at stake: Graves assigns it to G (scorpio); yet the boar is Fro's totem (man seemingly having learned to plow from watching the boar root up the ground with his snout), and Fro is Bran the alder (fearn). In fact, in that same Bronze Age rock carving referenced above showing elk for taurus, the figure for aries, identified as a bear by Fell and accompanied by the Tifinag letters [B?] R N[227] as in Bruin (the B is obscured), looks more like a boar to me—thinner ears, and what looks like a little teat but I interpret as a tuft of hair (which many boars have). I doubt that a bear would symbolize aries (though they do 'root out' beehives with their snouts). The (consonants-only) primitive Germanic root for *boar* is B R.

There is one fable that puts 'father' yod together with the proper mother letter: the owl (437a, or swallow, 39) warns her fellow birds about mistletoe on oaks (a druid fable?), whence will come the birdlime that will ensnare them. The owl is the hieroglyph of mem, and mistletoe is yod. The Cicada and the Owl (507) has owl silence the cicada's racket so he can rest during the day—'mum's the word'.

There is an interesting fable called the Fox and the Crane (426), one I remember well from childhood, in which wolf invites crane to a dinner of thin soup served in a shallow bowl, which the crane can get little of, so crane invites fox to a dinner served in a narrow-necked vessel fox cannot even get into. This illustrates the contrast between Egyptian and Meroitic kaf: the shallow **basket with handle** and the **narrow-necked jar**. Then there is the Goose that laid the Golden Egg (87), which selfishness killed for its contents (to no profit), which would seem to point to the Geb goose in Meroitic, at Cauldron's scorpio (desire). Then there is the fable (456) Galen relays about the Fool and the Sieve he wished to mend but did not know where to plug it and where not! It is interesting that this puts the unnumbered trump (The Fool) together with its hieroglyph, from whose hieratic form came Semitic cheyt (table 1): this suggests H's association with The Fool is as old as this fable, for inventors of the Tarot of Marseilles would hardly have been familiar with the original hieroglyph letter cheyt evolved from.

By far the most jaw-dropping tale from my point of view is the one at the top of my list of Hermetic fables, the Lion and Three Bulls (372). Can you guess? Three bulls stick close together as they graze and so cannot be overcome by the hungry lion; hence he sows dissent with crafty words, undermining their unity until he is able one by one to devour them. It is the tale of volatile mercury and its vapors: leo's column gobbling up taurus's two adjacent columns' upper halves. The revenge for this seems to be one (481) about the old lion abused (for past wrongs) by a boar (aries, the Corn Spirit), a bull (taurus), and an ass—gemini? based both on its powerful shoulders' heft and on traditional association of *ass* with *fool* even though asses are really rather smart? It is the ass's kick that proves fatal. The Lion in the Farmer's Yard (144) seems to have left this work unfinished: he locks the lion in his farmyard, but it destroys all his sheep (ram aries) then his cattle (taurus) till finally the fearful farmer lets him out—into gemini, space?

It is clear from the Tarot of Marseilles who the recurring character of fox-trickster is: he is I Le Bateleur (alef). The Fox and the Goat in the Well (9) is my second favorite: fox falls in a well and is trapped; thirsty goat arrives, inquires about water in well; fox sings its praises; goat jumps in; fox climbs on horns and gets out. This is obvious reference to the Fall and to capricorn as the sign of the self-knowledge the doer seeks. Finally, the Two Wallets (266), which is my third favorite and the one with the most telling moral: the titan Prometheus when he fashioned us hung two wallets on each of us, the one in front full of others' faults, and one in back full of our own (the larger). This is why we easily see others' faults but have a hard time seeing our own. Too true. Indeed it is behind us—straight back from what is ahead or *out*ward—that self, and thus responsibility, is to be found.

Many other fables reward the astute reader. But I shall leave exploration of them *to* the reader, for now.

EIGHT
The Tarot of Marseilles

The occultists like to speak of 'Major and Minor Arcana', the former being the trumps, the latter the four suits. But the actual organization of the Tarot of Marseilles is into three parts: trumps, court cards, and pips (ordinary numbered cards of each suit). In fact, these stem from the three mothers. Alef (ailm) gives birth to the twenty-two letters of the alef-beyt, the trumps. Shin (saille) is numbered 16 in bardic tradition and thus spawns the sixteen court cards, meaning the Name, or what rules nature (divine creative power). Mem (muin) is 40 in Hebrew and thus spawns the 40 pips, which measure our progress onto the intelligent side. Trumps have names *and* numbers (rank); court cards only names; pips only numbers.

The letters or trumps most intimately involve doer alef or its stand-in, the body-mind. The Name (in four worlds) and Tree (in four worlds) relate respectively to thinker and knower, hence to feeling and desire respectively, their substitutes in humans. The thinker is the part that marshals destiny (our roles) involving nature's four elements; Sefirot signify reflection *on* those elements, evoking mind (intelligent side), pure numbers being abstract (though quite real).

That occultists' interpretation of the trumps themselves is flawed should be clear from how seamlessly and accurately bardic numbering of letters identifies what their trumps must be (table 11). Trumps even illustrate the chemical atom-types the letters stand for in the Kabbalistic scheme (table 12). But do, please, at least give the Hermetic camp credit for grasping that there had to have been a relationship *from the start* between tarot and Kabbalah, for the simple reason that tarot's three domains mirror flawlessly the three domains of the Kabbalah.

I have wondered whether some 'Kabbalah' might have entered into the seemingly earlier phenomenon of ordinary playing cards, which contained two of these three domains. There is an indication cards came from the Mamelukes. It is not inconceivable that esoteric lore preserved in the Muslim world (by Sufis?) informed their structure. Cards probably entered Europe through Spain (the Moors) via the close cultural ties dating from the Troubadour era. A Provençal origin of tarot is thus much more likely than an Italian one. The Mameluke cards were produced under Muslim overlordship and thus lacked human likenesses; they just had the three court titles King, Deputy, Second Deputy (with suit symbols only)—similar to the officers of the Masonic Lodge (Master, Senior Warden, Junior Warden). Note that *three* added to ten pips suggests the three remaining *middot* after the ten Sefirot. Suits seem to have originated in the earlier Chinese cards, brought west by Mongols (the Chinese also had their alchemists, namely the Taoists).

In the Tarot of Marseilles, it is interesting how the aces of the suits of Clubs and Swords echo the theme of Jachin-Boaz as fire and air (shown by the King of Clubs and Queen of Swords generating the two pillars): in the Ace of Clubs, the right hand holding it enters the card from a cloud on the right, while in the Ace of Swords, the right hand holding it enters the card *through* a cloud on the left, the sword's point being thrust through the crown at the top. The Ace of Cups has a cup that looks like a palace with seven spires, thus linking it to the *Hekhalot* ('Palaces'), and since these are associated with the Cauldron or Throne world, it reminds us that the Tree of Forms *begins* at the center of that world. The Ace of Coins is just one big yellow (gold) coin.

For those who do not own a deck of these indispensible cards—the trumps of my own deck were lost in a fire (oh wow, I just replaced my deck with a newer one and Grimaud has altered the English translation of La Papesse to 'The High Priestess'! yich!)—I should briefly describe the court cards, then point out relevant details in the trumps. The King of Clubs is obviously (by his epaulettes) a general. That of Swords is a bit more effeminate and holds a small scepter in his left hand (and large sword in his right). That of Cups is a bit of a dandy (an alcoholic?). These first three have crowns and wide brimmed hats, though in Cups the brim is more like huge mouse ears. The King of Money does not have a crown but has an intact wide-brimmed hat, looks like a rich merchant, and is seated outdoors. All four kings carry their suit symbol in their right hand and are looking just to our right (Unity). The first two are beardless; the third and fourth have two-pronged white beards. Interestingly, to reinforce swords' duality its King has the masks of tragedy and comedy on his shoulders, instead of epaulettes: tragedy on his right shoulder, comedy on his left (as if from the point of view of the Master in the east, the waxing year to the right, the waning to the left). To emphasize clubs being the kings' proper suit, the King of Clubs wears red shoes, the other three blue.

The queens again all bear their suit symbols in their right hand. The Queen of Swords' sleek sword has a red blade, marking Swords as the queen's proper suit (since she has *used* hers). One of the errors of versions other than the Grimaud is a proliferation of red blades! The Queen of Cups—whose cup is lidded (spherical)—has a small sword in her left hand, that of Coins a medium sized scepter in her left hand. That of Clubs is looking to our right (like all four kings), the other three to our left, that of Coins actually in profile. All wear crowns, though in Coins it looks more like a fashionable headdress; and long robes, blue with red capes except in Swords, where it is red with a blue cape. The faces are: in Swords, serious as hell; in Clubs, slightly embarrassed; in Cups, someone who drinks; and in Coins, sharp featured. All but that of Coins (who has blue hair) have long white hair, that of Clubs *very* long. There is a bit of canopy over the throne in Cups, reminiscent of La Papesse (heh, whose suit is cups). The throne in Swords is reminiscent of that in La Justice (who has an even larger sword in her right hand). The Queen of Coins appears to stand in front of her chair; the rest are seated.

The white-haired, white-shoed Knight of Clubs rides a beige-caparisoned white horse, wears a broad-brimmed hat like Le Bateleur, and carries his club in his left hand: the horse faces to our left but both its and the knight's heads are turned decisively back the other way (to our right). The dark-blue-haired Knight of Swords, riding a red-and-gold caparisoned beige horse whose front feet are in the air, gallops to our left with his (white) sword in his left hand, angled forward: he has on what looks like a yellow cap of some sort (reysh-shaped) and has a mask for an epaulette on his left shoulder. This mask suggests that the heh that goes with the Knights is in the male half of the Name, since the King (yod) of Swords has two masks, one on each shoulder. The white-haired Knight of Cups rides a prancing beige horse towards our left, front right hoof raised high: he wears a yellow cape and holds a chalice with shallow, cylindrical cup with red interior and stem in (on) his right palm, as if offering it as a gift. The white-haired Knight of Money wears a cap, has a small club in his right hand leaning on his right shoulder, rides a beige horse towards our right (left front hoof raised), and most notably is looking at his suit symbol suspended in air ahead of him! to tell us that we have not yet gotten to the heh whose suit this is (second heh of Name).

The Knave of Clubs is seen in profile facing to our right wearing a red cap and dressed quite aristocratically: his large (shoulder height), dark-colored club rests upright with its thick end on the ground, his left hand at its top, his right farther down on it. The Knave of Swords stands facing us looking downward to our left wearing a broad-brimmed hat and aristocratically dressed, his large yellow sword in his left hand leaning towards his head, his right hand on his red scabbard—since he is the heh that goes with the Queen of Swords and her red sword. The Knave of Cups has frazzled white hair and is walking to our left, having obviously *stolen* the hourglass-shaped chalice he carries in his right hand, the lid held in his left: he is the only knave dressed more or less like a serving class person. The Knave of Coins has his card title printed along the side of the card, not the bottom like the other court cards: he faces us, sharply dressed with broad-brimmed hat, left hand resting on his gold (yellow) belt, holding one coin (about the size of his face) face-high with his right hand, eying it, with another similar coin near his feet directly below the first (about ankle height). His hat has its brim on the side of the coin shorter than on the other side, probably just so as not to collide with the upraised coin.

Wherever I have not specified the color of clothing, it is red and blue. One of the striking things about the twelve simples amongst trumps (described below) is that the six macrocosmic signs (and them only) are all normal (large) figures dressed in red and blue *with the exception of libra*, whose red-and-blue-draped figure is offset one to the right, that is, to scorpio, obviously following the offsetting to the right (within) of the lowest letter of the Name, the heh, to hint that though in Adam Qadmon it would surely be balanced (at libra), as we mortals perceive the Name it is out of balance (like us).

Some quick comments on trumps. The Fool tells us specifically where his sign is on the Egg; for his mantle or collar has five (dark blue) balls hanging from it, where the stick holding his belongings crosses his shoulders are two more (white), from which his mantle hangs, and an eighth ball—this one red—is suspended by his curly hat or hair above the shoulder to our left, this being where gemini *is* on the round (on the left just above the seven manifested signs). He carries a walking stick in his right hand, and a dog paws the pouch hanging from his waist. The Magician (Le Bateleur) wears a broad-brimmed hat like the kings do, a small ball in his right hand, a nine-inch wand upraised in his left; his left leg obscures one of the legs of his table (the one standing for the vowels, no doubt, since he *is* one), which has cups, balls, knives, and a purse on it. In addition to the intimate scene above La Papesse (mentioned earlier), the headdress is rather phallic or rocket-like (a rounded mitre)—perhaps in anticipation of later occultists going by Hebrew numbering, where beyt the mitre (in Semitic) is 2, not 5 (Le Pape). In addition to the shield-eagle's feathers extending beyond their shield to embrace The Empress about the middle, the strap around her neck and the one around her chest are connected by a short vertical strap and together form an image quite like the ancient letter zayin. The Emperor has a beryl on his chest, a shield eagle at his feet, is helmed for war (seen in profile facing to our left), and bears in his right hand a sceptre with a ball on the end, surmounted by a cross—the Empress has a longer one (with ball and cross) in her left hand, resting on her lap. The Pope has the twin doorposts behind him, holds a staff topped with *ogam consaine* Ng in his left hand (letter-month of previous sign in ogham), extends the first two fingers of his right hand in blessing, and has a white beard and shirt sleeves, as befits white-barked birch; the two children appear tonsured, the one on the left with round hat hanging at left shoulder, mother's arm extending across the back of the one on the right, her hand between them. The Lover's legs and feet are bare, robed sweetheart on his left (both are blond), robed cleric with dark blue hair—who could well be the Queen of Coins—on his right; Cupid, above, aims at his left shoulder (or heart?) from white circle with multicolored rays. The Chariot is canopied, four-posted, its two wheels shown perpendicular to the direction it faces, with two horses (one red, one blue), 'S.M' on the chariot front, yellow-haired driver crowned, with sceptre in right hand, mask on each shoulder, and red epaulette hanging down from the mask on his left (since he is part of the waning year). Light-haired Justice has a yellow-pillared throne, large yellow sword held vertical in the right hand, yellow scales held in her left hand, yellow (including crown) radiantly outlining her head and two small concentric yellow circles where her third eye should be: she is red robed and blue caped, like the Queen of Swords, and *not* blindfolded. The Hermit is light haired, robed, with pointy hood draped down his back, walking to our left with lantern raised in right hand, curved yellow walking stick in left, which I interpret as the hint of a urine stream (kaf being kidneys and kaf sofit the bladder). The Wheel of Fortune is six-spoked, with stand and crank, with a dark blue yellow-crowned red-winged sphinx presiding on top, a vested rabbit (or rodent with big ears) climbing up the right side, and a skirted monkey descending on the left: all three have tails.

XI Force is a blue-robed red-caped yellow-sleeved woman with broad-brimmed hat and hint of a crown (yellow spikes) holding open a lion's jaws. The Hanged Man has two tree trunks with six red buds each holding up a dark horizontal from which he hangs by the left foot with the right crossed behind it, arms akimbo, dark hair flying downwards, blue jerkin with yellow skirt with two crescents on it (bulge upward), red tights, red sleeves, obviously dancing a jig upside down. Trump XIII shows the flesh-colored skeleton with dark-outlined head facing to our right wielding red-bladed, yellow-handled scythe like an oar, severed heads of crowned king at bottom right and queen (sans crown) at bottom left, the latter trampled by Death's left foot, with severed hands and feet scattered about. Temperance is blue-haired (five-petaled red flower in middle), blue-and-red-robed, yellow girded, with wings obviously held on by the yellow cloth across the front of her neck, pouring two parallel wavy white lines—aquarius symbol—from blue vase in left hand to red vase in right. Le Diable with clawed feet in blue tights held up by a red crescent-shaped 'belt', standing on red anvil, flesh-colored from waist up but with lines across chest, right breast a full circle, left an incomplete one, yellow haired with antlers and dark blue bat wings, white rod held vertical in left hand, right hand waving, towers over naked, red-haired male and female (male on our right) hominids with antlers, horns, and tails, tethered by collars to the red anvil. La Maison Dieu shows a cannonball trailed by red and yellow flames heading for a partly yellow crown askew on top of a (flesh-colored?) tower with two small (testicular) blue windows surmounted by a taller (phallic) blue window, with multicolored dots everywhere and the twins falling to the ground, one in front, and one behind (head and right arm showing). The Star shows a naked, blue-haired woman kneeling on her left knee and pouring from two red vessels, from the one in her left hand onto the ground, from the one in her right hand into a pond, amid yellow rolling terrain with dark flower (?) on our right and a small dark tree with dark bird perched in it on our left: over her are seven stars in a cup arrangement around a larger eighth one. The Moon shows two flesh-colored hyena- or rodent-like dogs barking at droplets in the air that descend from a dark blue orb with multi-colored rays between two yellow towers in broken yellow terrain with dark blue pool in foreground inhabited by dark blue lobster-like crustacean. The Sun shows two lightly collared, yellow-haired, dark-blue-girded boys at play (wrestling) before yellow wall topped in red under yellow sun with sixteen multicolored rays and many black lines emanating from it and droplets of sweat (obviously) flying all about. Le Jugement pictures Judgment Day: red-sleeved archangel with trumpet (bearing white flag with yellow cross) held up to a white crescent around its throat (rather than to its mouth), with flesh-colored hair, head-wings, wings, and white halo: the archangel is perched (shown from chest up) behind smoke and pikes of battle, a naked couple below (seen from waist up), with child facing them (seen from buttocks up) emerging from a dark rectangle (coffin) in broken yellow terrain. And The World shows a naked female (though the breasts look pasted on) dancer on her right leg with left folded behind, draped in square-Hebrew shaped flesh-colored kaf with small wand in left hand and something indiscernible in her right, surrounded by yellow-, red-, and blue-wreathed vertical lozenge, with red-winged blue-robed red-haloed angel on cloud at upper left (outside lozenge), flesh-colored winged bull at lower left, yellow white-haloed winged lion at lower right, and blue-winged red-haloed yellow eagle on cloud at upper right.

The pips (except for the aces, described above) have dark-blue tipped-and-bound crossed (X-like) yellow staves; curved dark-blue crossed-at-both-ends semi-circular scimitars (the odd numbers having a straight sword in the middle); yellow goblets with red interiors; round gold (yellow) coins; with flower designs filling the spaces in Cups and Money. This may be less exciting than the images found on pips of the more popular decks, but in this, the *original* (and only authentic) tarot, the pips are meant to be abstract, as they represent knower mem.

Important warning. There is an attractive looking deck out there, the Jodorowsky, to which a fourth color, green, has been added. I know of no evidence that there was any green in the original; and more importantly, the Jodorowsky makes *multiple* obvious errors of coloration, such as downplaying yellow on the Corn Spirit's La Justice and adding several red swords into the mix (besides the Queen of Swords, where it belongs). So just as the Crowley deck is nice art but useless as a deck of tarot, the Jodorowsky unfortunately falls far short of the high standards and authenticity of the Grimaud.

NINE
The Future of Science (commentary)

How to make Pseudo-Science your Standard Model

Assume no mind exists at the origin or root of things
nothing but nature bits banging about without purpose
      as if science simply meant
      the opposite of religion
assume that even lacking any emotion or cognition
matter so detests itself it flees in all directions
      this based on redshift
      of light from far-off galaxies
interpreted as Doppler shift from stars' retreat asunder
even though the alternative that the light loses energy
      interacting with the intervening
      plasma is more logical
assume from this flying-apart that the cosmos had a beginning
      with the basic picture skewed
      it is hard to think otherwise
even if such a beginning will completely contradict
the conservation laws on which science itself rests,
      a return to superstition
      with grown humans thinking
all matter started out crammed within a single point—
      even though there isn't any
      'within' *to* a point—
and by the old notion that attracted opposite charges
will neutralize the effect of an electric field at a distance,
assume the only force on any grand scale is gravity—
      ignoring plasma physics
      whose laws predict otherwise
since stars are electric discharges shaped by magnetic z-pinch
arrayed all in filaments their motions quite explainable—
      yet gravity *can* 'explain' things
      if we only invent *dark matter*
which since undetectable can be said to be anywhere
      needed to make the math work

> and if the math still misses what's observed invent *inflation*
> a supernatural increase in the rate of the expansion
> and then add in *dark energy* . . .
> now all that's required is to figure out the origin
> of mind in a universe where no supposed ingredient
> is conscious it exists

Near as I can tell, theoretical physics has been going backwards (becoming less and less empirically sound) for most of the years I have been alive, this though the previous decades had seen quite substantial progress. Technology advances, and individual fields here and there (such as plasma physics) profit by this, but by and large in universities it is not what works but what is acceptable to the mob—the entrenched interests—that is allowed to be taught. So cosmologists have ignored the recent advances in plasma physics, fixated as they are on the Einsteinian theory of gravitation, even though they admit 99.999% of all visible matter is plasma (a gas of charged particles). The Einsteinian (Riemannian) tensor calculus was *extremely* difficult to learn—as I found out when running down its first logical misstep (forming an *affine connection* by applying Euclidean and 'non-Euclidean' partial derivatives to a 'non-Euclidean' space, where Euclidean partial derivatives are undefined)—hence stiff resistance to having to 'retool' by learning how plasma actually behaves. Thus gross ignorance is the sole reason for theorizing existence of ten times as much (undetectable) 'dark matter', which they have evidently decided is *not* plasma and will therefore 'outvote' it or something. They remain willfully unaware that plasma physics can readily explain by electromagnetism both intra-galactic motion and formation and distribution of stars.[228]

Einstein himself was a scientist of the old school (despite errors) and would be appalled today at the eclipse of empiricism. I feel forced to reject his take on relativity, having seen it demonstrated that one need not assume 'curved space-time' and the egalitarianism of reference frames to derive the critical relations that 'prove' it,[229] such as $e = mc^2$ or the advance of the perihelion of Mercury. Hence I am not forced to reject absolute simultaneity, which allows me to define Asiyah, the smallest of Ezekiel's four wheels (symbolizing physical matter itself), as 'the present instant': there are other *kinds* of time, but physical time (not to be confused with pulse) is quite Newtonian. Einstein's stature as a scientist is very high in my book in spite of that; for two of his 1905 papers, added to Planck's discovery of 1900, constitute the tripod on which the edifice of a sound quantum mechanics rests!

The whole of today's cosmology is a house of cards, based on unfounded assumptions. It assumes the Hubble redshift is caused by galaxies' receding velocity, which has led the current model to the absurdity of all matter having begun 'contained' in a single point, all conservation laws suddenly having *leaped* into being at some instant in the past, with nothing, not even time, before that. Common sense alone tells us this is ridiculous. Other than the Doppler shifts caused by motion within galaxies or galactic clusters, the light's loss of energy with distance must have another cause, such as interaction with the sparse plasma between source and telescope (as in the

Plasma Redshift Cosmology mentioned earlier). Cosmologists ignore intrinsic redshift: the 'anomaly' of quasars arises from overestimating distance in the first place (based on redshift); for observation shows that they emanate out of mature galaxies of much lesser redshift.[230]

If you would like to see just how crazy modern physics has become, read Brian Greene's 1999 book *The Elegant Universe*.[231] If he thinks such ultra-complexity for ultra-complexity's sake is 'elegant', he must have a mind utterly incapable of comprehending Picasso! nor does he realize that motions being (*as he admits*) smeared out over 'an infinite number of locations' (as necessitated by a 'two dimensional' *string*) is a contradiction in terms.

Bring into the general mix the embarrassment physics must have felt, over a half-century ago, after a couple of centuries of pooh-poohing the mere notion of four elements, when they finally discovered to their immense chagrin that matter really does come in four distinct types of elementary particle, or, dare one say, what the philosophers of the age prior to chemists called *elements*. (And if you have read this book you know I do not in the least belittle the periodic table of *chemical* 'elements'.) That *quark* theory was a body-fake to cover up discovery of four elementary particle types is patently obvious once you realize it is based on a 'force' that cannot be overcome by a greater force (and therefore is not a force): the 'force' of *quark-confinement* is obviously the simple (or not so simple) fact that the point-like articulations within mesons and baryons are *parts* of those particles; that is, motions bound together by local interconnectedness. They were originally called *partons* and should still be so called. (I have explained, earlier in this book, why the term *hadron* is farcical.)

Turning to biological sciences, in which I am less steeped, some of our accomplishments in those fields today I find impressive: functions of various parts of the brain, intricate activities within cells, areas our incredible technology allows us to explore in near magical detail. But the whole approach to an overview is hung up on the idea that mind is a byproduct of brain, not vice versa. Really? You are going to try to build a logical world-view on the idea that involvement of mind with physical nature is just a *fluke*? I once held such views and know how tenuous they are, how easily knocked down. *That* is the real house of cards behind the modernist world-view. I am especially saddened as well to see many of the empirical advances in analytical psychology forged by the Jungian school in danger of falling by the wayside, because of condemnation, I am led to understand, of Jung's alleged affairs with patients. It has seemingly become eclipsed by the current faith in drugs: note the multiple mass killings that have resulted from use of drugs on troubled youths without understanding the side effects!

My father, who raised me as an atheist materialist, would still spar with me intellectually after I turned Gnostic. The sticking point with him seemed to be, "How can one mind" (meaning one God) "have determined all this?" to which I would invariably reply (seemingly without any affect), "Why are you fixated on there being only *one*?" (His upbringing was monotheistic.)

Odd as it may sound, upon invention of the microscope the empirical development of medicine over two millenniums was discarded in favor of the microbe, thus crippling modern medicine's ability to deal with most *chronic* ailments.[232] Arthritis was quite curable in former centuries: humoric medicine (notorious for its leeches and ineffectual against infectious disease) dealt with it quite effectively. Today, the old methods still *work* but are little *known*. Fear of lawsuits no doubt inhibits more widespread use, the method's rationale being no longer fully understood. (The humoric treatment, called *exanthematic*, involves surface 'counter-irritation' coupled with a blood-cleansing agent taken internally.)

Judging from the inside of Disney Hall here in Los Angeles, I do think that *acoustics* has made tremendous strides in recent decades. I chalk this down to its being in essence a *practical* science—what is usually referred to as *technological progress*.

I do not think much progress will be made in the theoretical sciences until something is done about the bottleneck of the 'peer review' system. New ideas are squelched by peer pressure and fear of having to retool. Nor will life sciences reach higher ground till atheistic materialism ceases to be the state religion. I understand the disrepute theology earned for itself in the past; still, the chief advances in science over the centuries were typically inspired by that theology, however flawed. Isaac Newton was a practicing alchemist, as well as a *devout Christian* (as was Leibniz). And the central thrust of Judaism has always been to probe, to question, to argue, to study, *not* simply to accept by rote.

Biology should leave open the exact form involvement of mind takes until or unless it can be given an empirical basis. *Intelligent design*—or as I like to think of it, descent of the less efficient from the more efficient, that is, devolution by error rather than evolution by 'chance'— should at least be *allowed to be taught* and *considered*, for truth will never come to those who close themselves off from dissent. Mind is an integral part of the cosmos: that there can be no evolution without involution, without mind's active involvement, should be self-evident.

Scientific education has become so politicized (in the sense of running cover for outdated models) that I imagine it will be quite some time before we begin once more to see any progress comparable to the age of Galileo and Newton, or of Faraday and Maxwell, or of Planck, Einstein, de Broglie, Bohr, Heisenberg, and Schrödinger. It would require *humility* on the part of those versed in what has been unearthed so far and thus put in charge of educating those who will be responsible for that future progress. Remember, in the late nineteenth century the notion got bandied about that science had neared its apex, that soon there would be nothing left to discover: reflect for a moment on how wrong that notion turned out to be.

We have glimpsed how much deeper into the mysteries of interplay of mind and matter science *could* probe from the astute integration of seemingly disparate disciplines embodied in the preceding pages. I shall expect science to have progressed at least part of the way along that road when I am again washed up on these shores of existence: if said expectation is met, perhaps I will not, next time round, cry for hours each day for weeks on end as I did this time, acting the part of that little devil in trump XV with real Thespian gusto (having inherited the required genes from my father the actor and Shakespeare aficionado). If not, heaven help my future parents!

APPENDIX
The Forms of the Ugaritic Cuneiform Alphabet

I have discovered, I think, some aspects of the rationale behind the forms used in this alphabet (chart 2) suggested by the bardic corpus outlined in this book and its insights into the meanings of individual letters. It is written from left to right, so the wedges when horizontal are arrows pointing in the direction one writes. This cinches the meaning of the first form, that of initial alef (➤): it is two horizontal wedges in succession and thus clearly signifies motive power *in* that direction—*continuation* of motion—considering its form in Sabean shows the spirit that *inhabits* a dwelling. Alef is the doer; the ox; motivator or continuer of action.

Beyt (𐎁) and dalet (𐎄) are best taken in tandem; for the former signifies the dwelling *within* (inner half of Cauldron)—the inner temple—the latter its extension *without* (outer half of Cauldron)—the outer temple—here *added to* the inner. Gimel (𐎂) is a single upright wedge and may stand for the erect member—as in Berber Tifinag (and Numidian, Greek, and Sabean)—it being Cauldron's scorpio (but more on it later). Of the two (𐎅 and 𐎆) that correspond to heh, whose place one of them occupies: the second one is our 'comb', E, the first one the same but seen edge on. Vav (➤) is obviously a breast, the extra wedge at its tip being either its nipple or milk pouring forth from it. Zayin (𐎇), whose name in Hebrew meant 'sword' or 'sharp weapon', is much like ancient Hebrew zayin and pictures a sword, pommel upward.

The next two are somewhat tricky: cheyt (𐎈), by placement, and teyt (𐎉). The first differs from the second in having a small shaft-less arrow pointing to the bottom of its central staff: my interpretation of this (which could well be wrong) is that since they are shoulders and loins, respectively, the little arrow pointing to the bottom of the former's staff indicates there is more to come below so to speak, so that the cross formed by the rest of it marks the complex of the shoulders; whereas in the second form there is no 'more to come below', so that the cross marks the lower structure, the loins. That larger shaft-less arrow (pointing left) both have at the right end of the horizontal must indicate that in each we are dealing with a structure penned in on both sides, rather than some dynamic involving movement to the right.

The meaning of the yod (𐎊) came to me right away: it appears to picture treetops, hence the place where one looks to find the mistletoe or loranthus square Hebrew yod (י) signifies. The kaf (➤) is fairly obvious: it is the cupped hand square Hebrew kaf (כ) is said to picture (which is the meaning of its name). Shin (𐎌) is straightforward enough: the ***lotus pool***, or the crown (ש) of square Hebrew, but also a bow with two arrows, reminding us of shin's relationship to sagittary the archer. The lamedh (𐎍) stumps me, unless it pictures dalet (𐎄) minus its floor, since it resides at the point on the Egg where the Cauldron-radius of dalet at its original station intersects it. The mem (𐎎) can be read in one of two ways: as pointing to the head of the erect member, where sensation is centered—since mem is in one sense the ecstasy resident *at* libra in fallen Adam—or, the more likely, as pointing to the top of Uprightness Itself (Adam Qadmon), where mem sofit resides. What I have to say regarding tzaddi (and gimel) below lends strength to the latter of these two interpretations.

The second dalet (⟨∕)—a bow and arrow—resembles Latin D and points to D's original station (of the Cauldron), sagittary the archer. Nun (⊶) hearkens back to its hieroglyph, ***surface of water***. Tzaddi (Π) must stand for strife between two ten-fingereds. It is interesting to note that bardic 10 (one ten-fingered) is a single upright (Ι), while bardic 20 (two ten-fingereds) is two uprights (Π). The letter corresponding to samekh (Ψ), whose place it holds, pictures the head (or a tulip?). The other samekh-equivalent (⊨⟨), which is voiced, shows an animal on its side (with horns), a product of the hunt: this suggests it represented the *return* to aries (from the voiced or active side), thus completing the cycle (end of the road for the poor animal). Ayin (⟨) is a bit like the sign used to indicate it phonetically: taken in tandem with the Ugaritic qof (⊣), it is apparent that the large shaft-less arrow pointing left here stands for the complete round— pictured as a return back the way we came—and thus is unadorned in the case of ayin but has a stem attached in the case of qof the apple. This interpretation just occurred to me, and I rather like it.

The peh (⊨) is similar to Nordic Tifinag *p* (Q?)—*par*, 'pair'—and even to Latin F or digamma; but it may, rather, simply signify speech as that which projects forward *on two levels*: as sound, and as thought. Based on R's form in Sabean (an open mouth in profile), reysh (⊳) obviously pictures an open mouth, the two wedges on upper and lower jaw being the teeth. The two tavs (⟨ and ⊢) I take as picturing, respectively, an arrowhead seeking the heart—of an upright ten-fingered being, being bardic 11—and either a *stoppage* of alef's progress (of two successive arrows) or an arrow in flight. The second form of ayin (⟨) points to leo being one thirty-degree angle below straight out. It also suggests looking at a thing from more than one angle (triangulation), or two paths crossing, or perhaps the more esoteric meaning of *where two thoughts intersect*, which is what precipitates thoughts' *exteriorization*, meaning physical reality.

After the final tav come what I consider added-on letters. The alef with *e* or *i* (⊨) is a permutation of heh (our E). The alef with *o* or *u* (Ⅲ) may be a permutation of dalet, the same sign as U or vav, but on the Cauldron. The last letter (⁞Ι⁞), an *s* sound, seems reminiscent of the two-shins-back-to-back form of the second shin in Sabean; or else it may relate to old Hebrew samekh (*ogam consaine* Ng).

Not a bad start.

Select Bibliography

Beckmann, Petr, *Einstein Plus Two* (Boulder, CO: Golem Press, 1987).

Boman, Thorleif, *Hebrew Thought Compared with Greek* (New York: Norton Library, 1970).

Book of Formation (Sepher Yetzirah): The Letters of Our Father Abraham (Los Angeles: Work of the Chariot, 1970).

Bothezat, George de, *Back to Newton: A Challenge to Einstein's Theory of Relativity* (New York: G. E. Stechert and Co., 1936).

Budge, Sir E. A. Wallis, *Egyptian Grammar: Easy Lessons in Egyptian Hieroglyphics* (New York: Dover Publications, 1976).

Cremo, Michael A., and Thompson, Richard L., *Forbidden Archeology: The Hidden History of the Human Race* (Los Angeles: Bhaktivedanta Book Publishing, 1996).

Dan, Joseph, ed., Kiener, Ronald C., tr., *The Early Kabbalah* (New York: Paulist Press, 1986).

Daniels, Peter T., and Bright, William, eds., *The World's Writing Systems* (New York: Oxford University Press, 1996).

Davidson, B., *The Analytical Hebrew and Chaldee Lexicon: Consisting of An Alphabetical Arrangement of Every Word and Inflection Contained in the Old Testament Scriptures, Precisely as They Occur in the Sacred Text, with a Grammatical Analysis of Each Word, and Lexicographical Illustration of the Meanings* (London: Samuel Bagster & Sons, 1966).

Dobbs, Betty Jo Teeter, *The Foundations of Newton's Alchemy, or "The Hunting of the Greene Lyon"* (New York: Cambridge University Press, 1975).

Doresse, Jean, *The Secret Books of the Egyptian Gnostics: An Introduction to the Gnostic Coptic manuscripts discovered at Chenoboskian* (Rochester, VT: Inner Traditions, 1986).

Dunn, Christopher, *The Giza Power Plant: Technologies of Ancient Egypt* (Rochester, VT: Bear & Company, 1998).

Easwaran, Eknath, tr. and intro., *The Dhammapada* (Petaluma, CA: Nilgiri Press, 1986).

Ellis, Peter Berresford, *The Druids* (Grand Rapids, MI: William B. Eerdmans, 1994).

Evola, Julius, *The Metaphysics of Sex* (New York: Inner Traditions, 1983).

Fell, Barry, *America B.C.: Ancient Settlers in the New World* (New York: Quadrangle, 1976).

Fell, Barry, *Bronze Age America* (Boston: Little, Brown & Company, 1976).

Fell, Barry, *Saga America* (New York: Times Books, 1983).

Fernando, Antony, with Swidler, Leonard, *Buddhism Made Plain: An Introduction for Christians and Jews* (Maryknoll, NY: Orbis Books, 1985).

Frazer, Sir James George, *The Golden Bough: A Study in Magic and Religion*, one volume abridged (New York: The Macmillan Co., 1947).

Gardiner, Sir Alan, *Egyptian Grammar: Being an Introduction to the Study of Hieroglyphs*, third edition (Oxford: Griffith Institute, Ashmolean Museum, 1957).

Graves, Robert, *The White Goddess: A Historical Grammar of Poetic Myth*, first American, amended and enlarged edition (New York: Farrar, Straus & Giroux, 1966).

Grimm, Jacob, *Teutonic Mythology* (in four volumes), translated from fourth edition with notes and appendix by James Steven Stallybrass (New York: Dover Publications, 1966),

Hancock, Graham, *Fingerprints of the Gods* (New York: Random House, 1995).

Harner, Michael, *The Way of the Shaman: A Guide to Power and Healing* (New York: Bantam Books, 1982).

Ithel, J. Williams ab, ed., *The Barddas of Iolo Morganwg: A Collection of Original Documents, Illustrative of the Theology, Wisdom, and Usages of the Bardo-Druidic System of the Isle of Britain* (Boston: WeiserBooks, 2004).

Jensen, Hans, *Sign, Symbol and Script: An Account of Man's Efforts to Write* (New York: G. P. Putnam's Sons, 1969).

Joad, C. E. M., *Guide to Philosophy* (New York: Random House, ca. 1935).

Jonas, Hans, *The Gnostic Religion: The Message of the Alien God and the Beginnings of Christianity* (Boston: Beacon Press, 1963).

Jung, C. J., *Alchemical Studies* (New York: Princeton University Press, 1968).

Jung, C. J., *Psychology and Alchemy* (Princeton, NJ: Princeton University Press, 1968).

Kaplan, Aryeh, *Sefer Yetzirah: The Book of Creation* (York Beach, ME: Samuel Weiser, 1990).

Kaplan, Aryeh, tr., intro., and commentary, *The Bahir: Illumination* (Boston: WeiserBooks, 1979).

Kaplan, Stuart R., *The Encyclopedia of Tarot* (Stamford, CT: U.S. Games Systems, 1986), vol. II.

Lerner, Eric J., *The Big Bang Never Happened* (New York: Vintage Books, 1992).

Littleton, C. Scott, *The New Comparative Mythology: An Anthropological Assessment of the Theories of Georges Dumézil* (Berkeley: University of California Press, 1973),

Long, Max Freedom, *The Huna Code in Religions: The Influence of the Huna Tradition on Modern Faith* (Marina del Rey, CA: DeVorss & Co., 1965).

Murray, Gilbert, *The Five Stages of Greek Religion* (Gordon City, NY: Doubleday, 1951).

Patai, Raphael, *The Hebrew Goddess*, third enlarged edition (Detroit: Wayne State University, 1990).

Patai, Raphael, *The Jewish Alchemists: A History and Source Book* (Princeton, NJ: Princeton University Press, 1994).

Paterson, Jacqueline Memory, *Tree Wisdom* (San Francisco: Thorsons [*An Imprint of* Harper Collins], 1996).

Percival, Harold W., *Thinking and Destiny* (Dallas: The Word Foundation, Inc., 1974 [orig. 1946]).

Percival, Harold Waldwin, *Masonry and Its Symbols: In the Light of Thinking and Destiny* (New York: The Word Publishing Company, 1952).

Rees, Alwyn, and Rees, Brinley, *Celtic Heritage: Ancient Tradition in Ireland and Wales* (New York: Thames & Hudson, 1961).

Rougemont, Denis de, *Love in the Western World* (Garden City, NY: Doubleday, 1957).

Santillana, Giorgio de, and Dechend, Hertha von, *Hamlet's Mill* (Boston: David R. Godine, 1992).

Scholem, Gershom, *Alchemy and Kabbalah* (Putnam, CT: Spring Publications, 2006).

Scholem, Gershom, *Kabbalah* (New York: Meridian, 1978).

Scholem, Gershom, *Major Trends in Jewish Mysticism* (New York: Schocken Books, 1974).

Scholem, Gershom, *Origins of the Kabbalah* (Jewish Publication Society Princeton University Press, 1987).

Scholem, Gershom, sel. and ed., *Zohar: The Book of Splendor (Basic Readings from the Kabbalah)* (New York: Schocken Books, 1963).

Sheldrake, Rupert, *A New Science of Life: The Hypothesis of Formative Causation* (Los Angeles: J. P. Tarcher, 1981).

Sheldrake, Rupert, *The Presence of the Past: Morphic Resonance and the Habits of Nature* (New York: Times Books, 1988).

Sperling, Harry, and Simon, Maurice, tr., *The Zohar* (London: Soncino Press, 1934).

Stecchini, Livio Catullo, appendix (pp. 287-382) to Tompkins, Peter, *Secrets of the Great Pyramid* (New York: Harper Collophon Books, 1978), entitled 'Notes on the Relation of Ancient Measures to the Great Pyramid'.

Taylor, Isaac, *The Alphabet: An Account of the Origin and Development of Letters* (London: K. Paul, Trench & Company, 1883).

The Epigraphic Society Occasional Publications and Papers (Arlington, MA: [archives of the] Dawson Library, 1975*ff*).

Tomas, Andrew, *We Are Not the First* (London: Souvineer Press, 1971).

Wehr, M. Russell, and Richards, James A. Jr., *Physics of the Atom* (Palo Alto, CA: Addison-Wesley Publishing Co., 1967).

Young, Arthur M., *The Reflexive Universe: Evolution of Consciousness* (Lake Oswego, OR: Robert Briggs Associates, 1976

FIGURES

&

TABLES

AND FIVE CHARTS

THE MONAD:

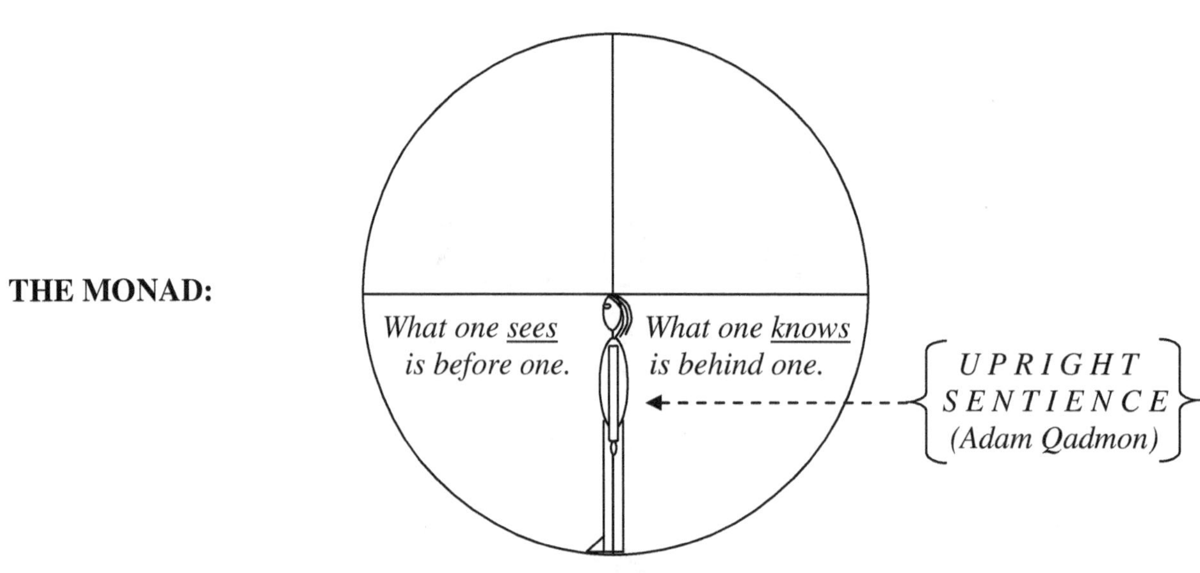

THE SEFIROT
DESCRIBED BY THE BOOK *BAHIR* (12TH-CENTURY PROVENCE)

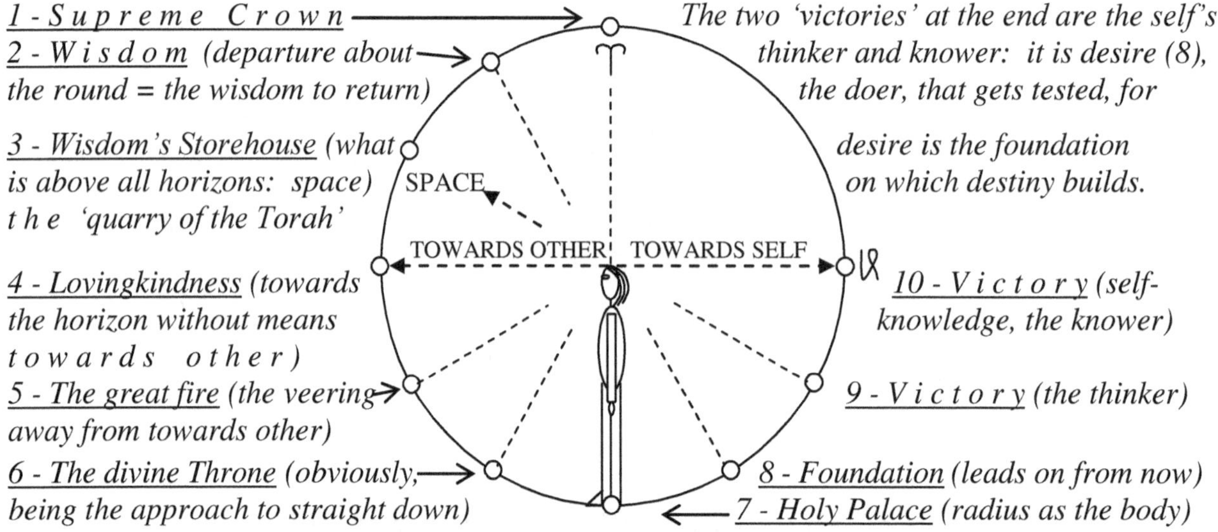

The Monad and the Sefirot (*Radiant Brow*)

FIGURE 1

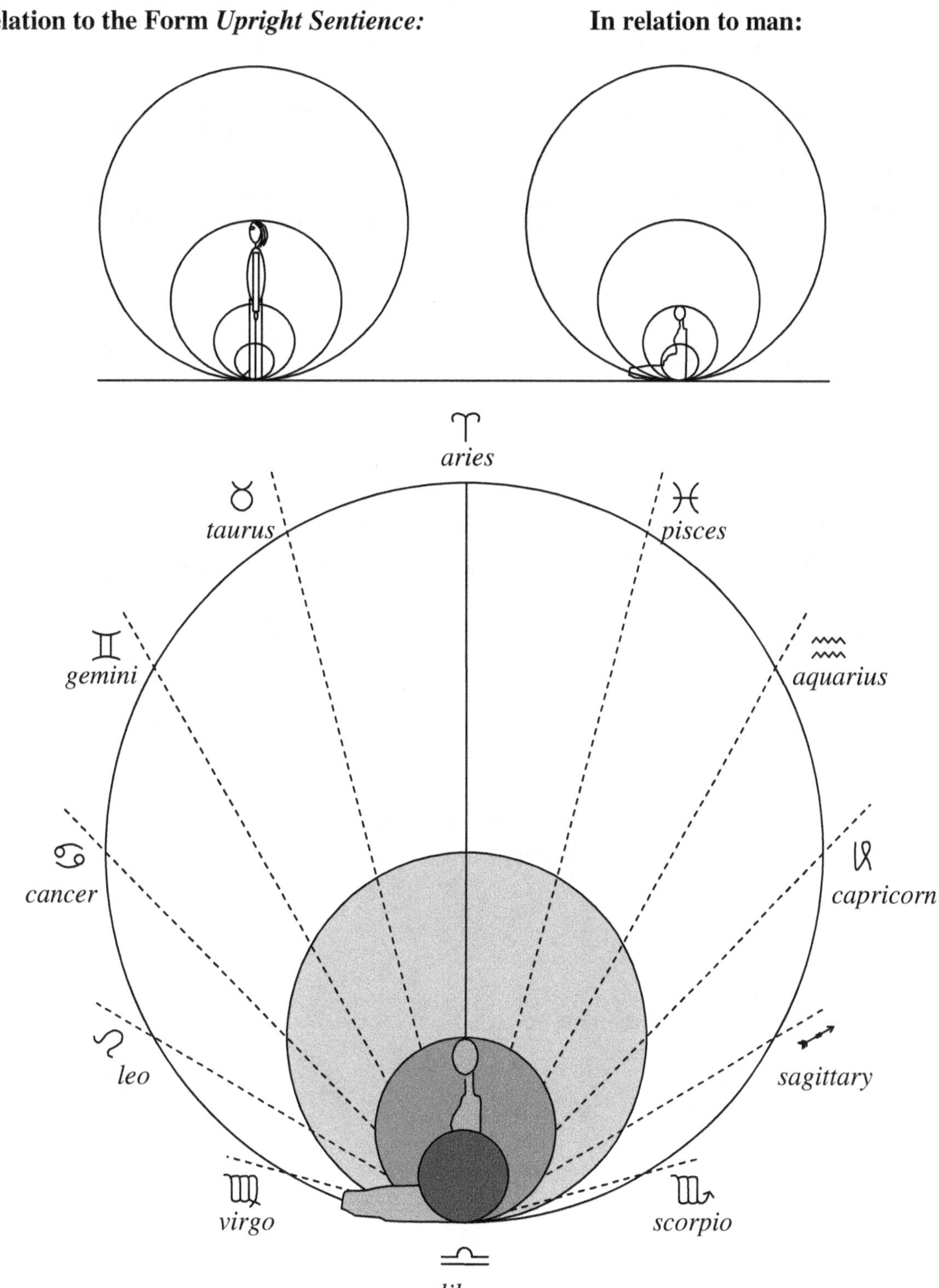

Ezekiel's Wheels

FIGURE 2

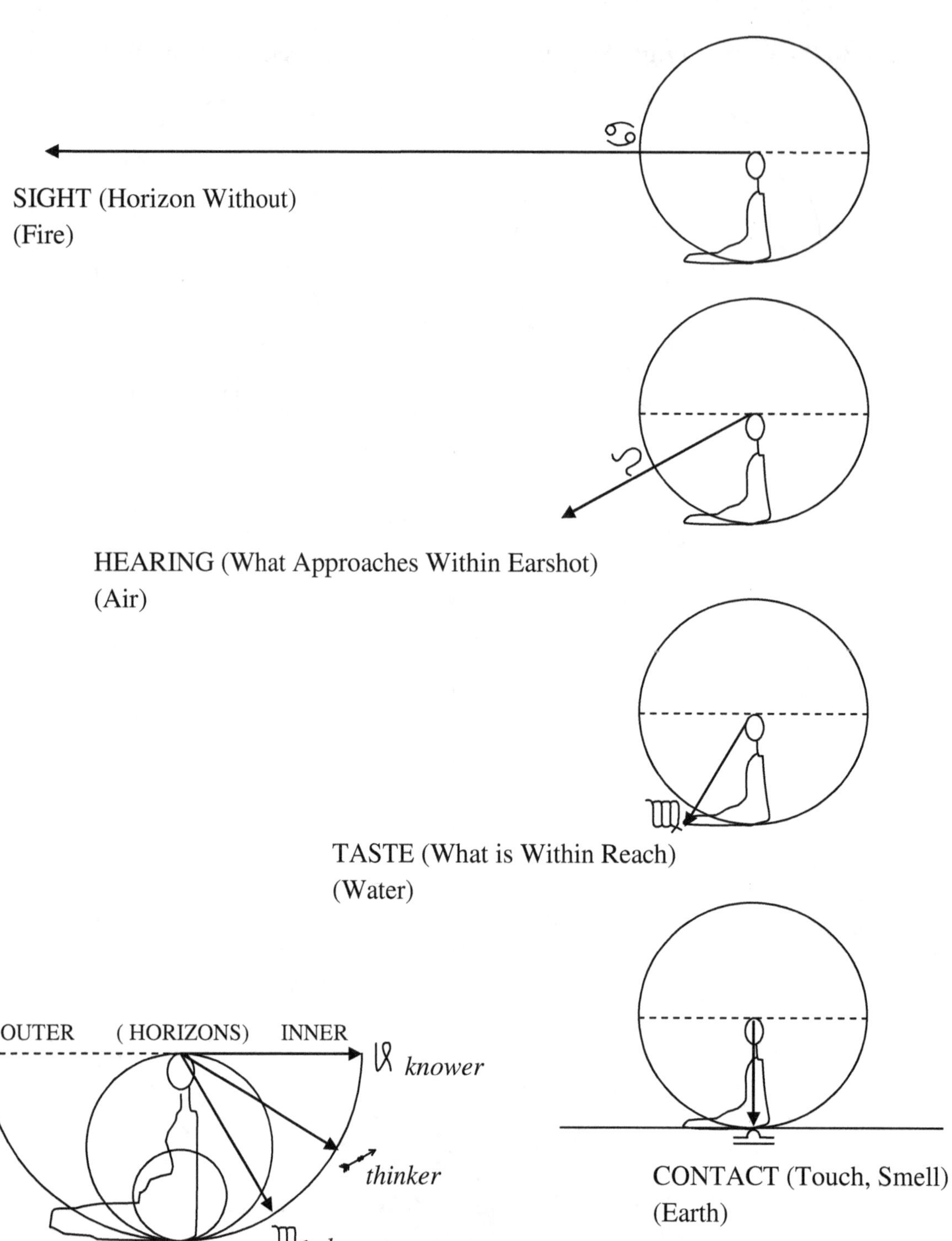

Cauldron as Elements and Self

FIGURE 3

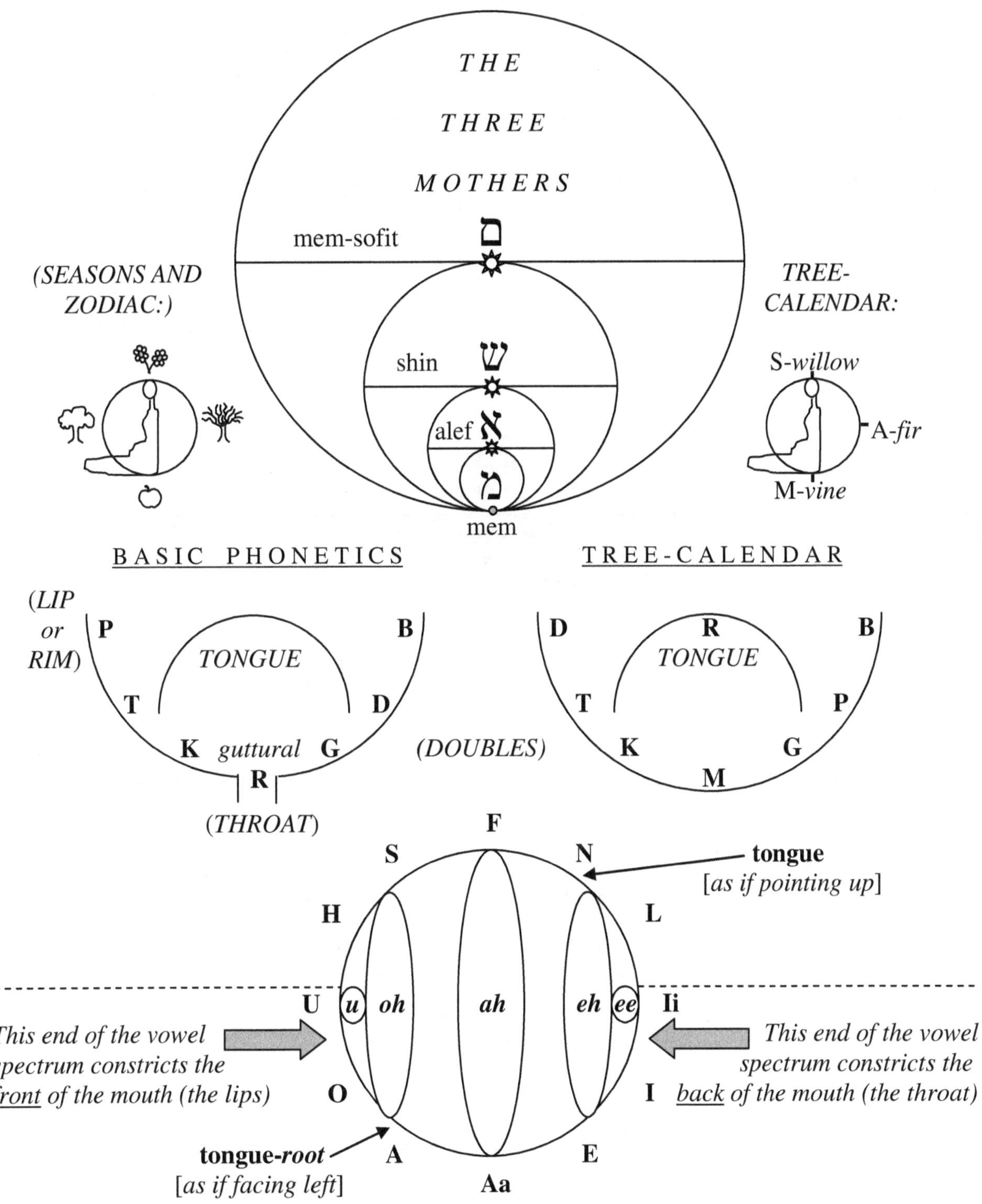

Phonetic Structure of the Bardic Alphabet

FIGURE 4

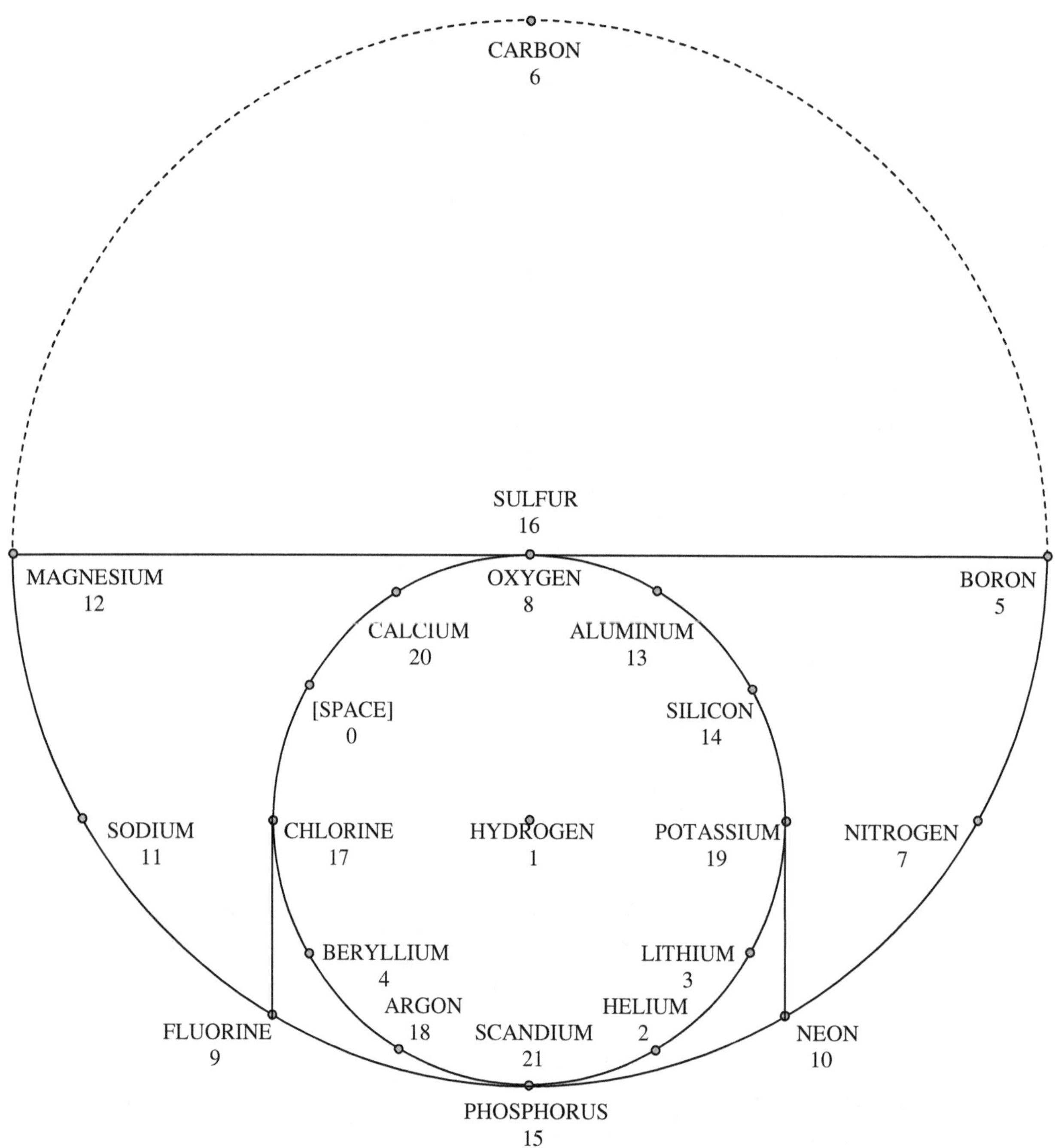

Bardic Numeration as Atom-Types

FIGURE 5

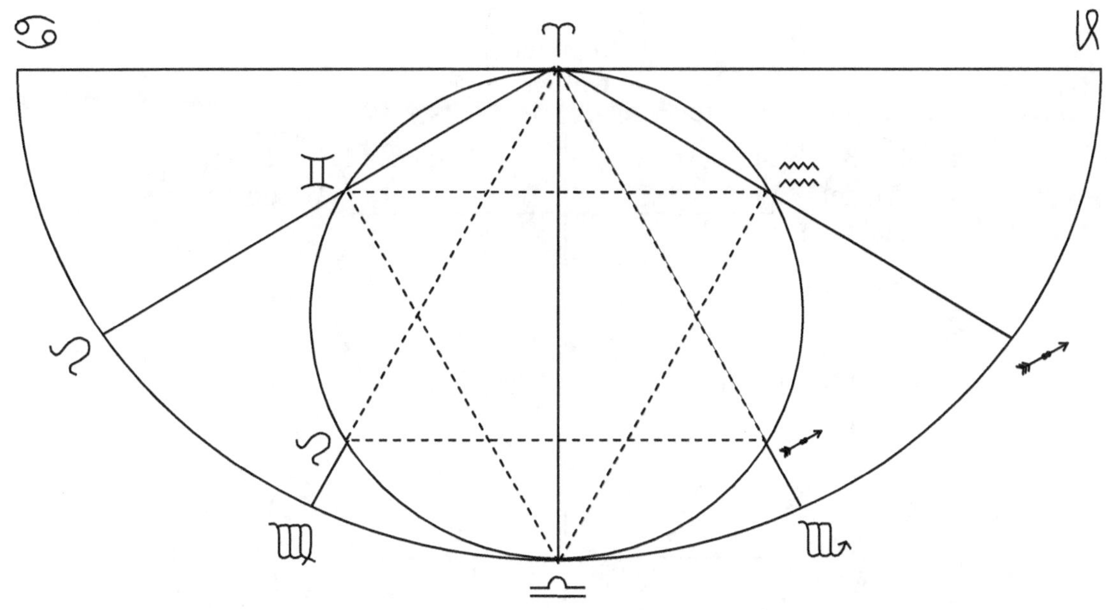

*The signs of the macrocosmic hexad are fixed by the radii
of the manifested half of the greater world it rests in.*

Symmetry of the

Water and

Fire Triads:

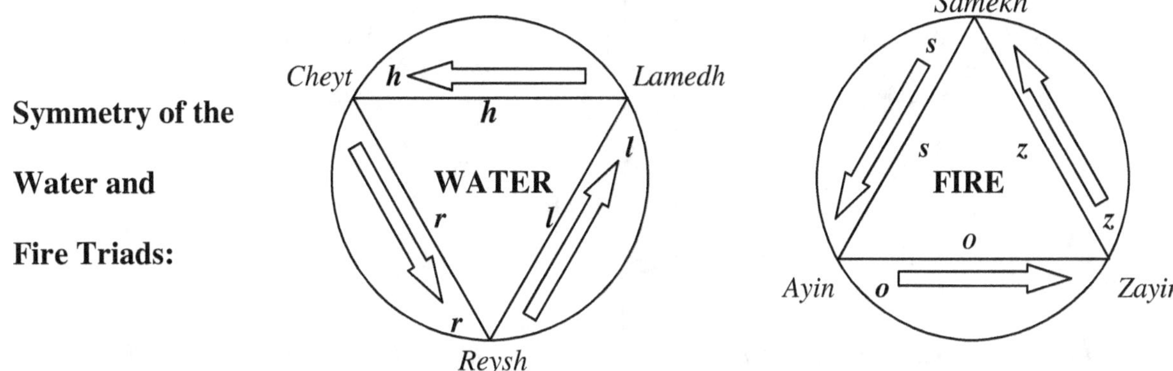

The Macrocosmic Hexad

FIGURE 6

159

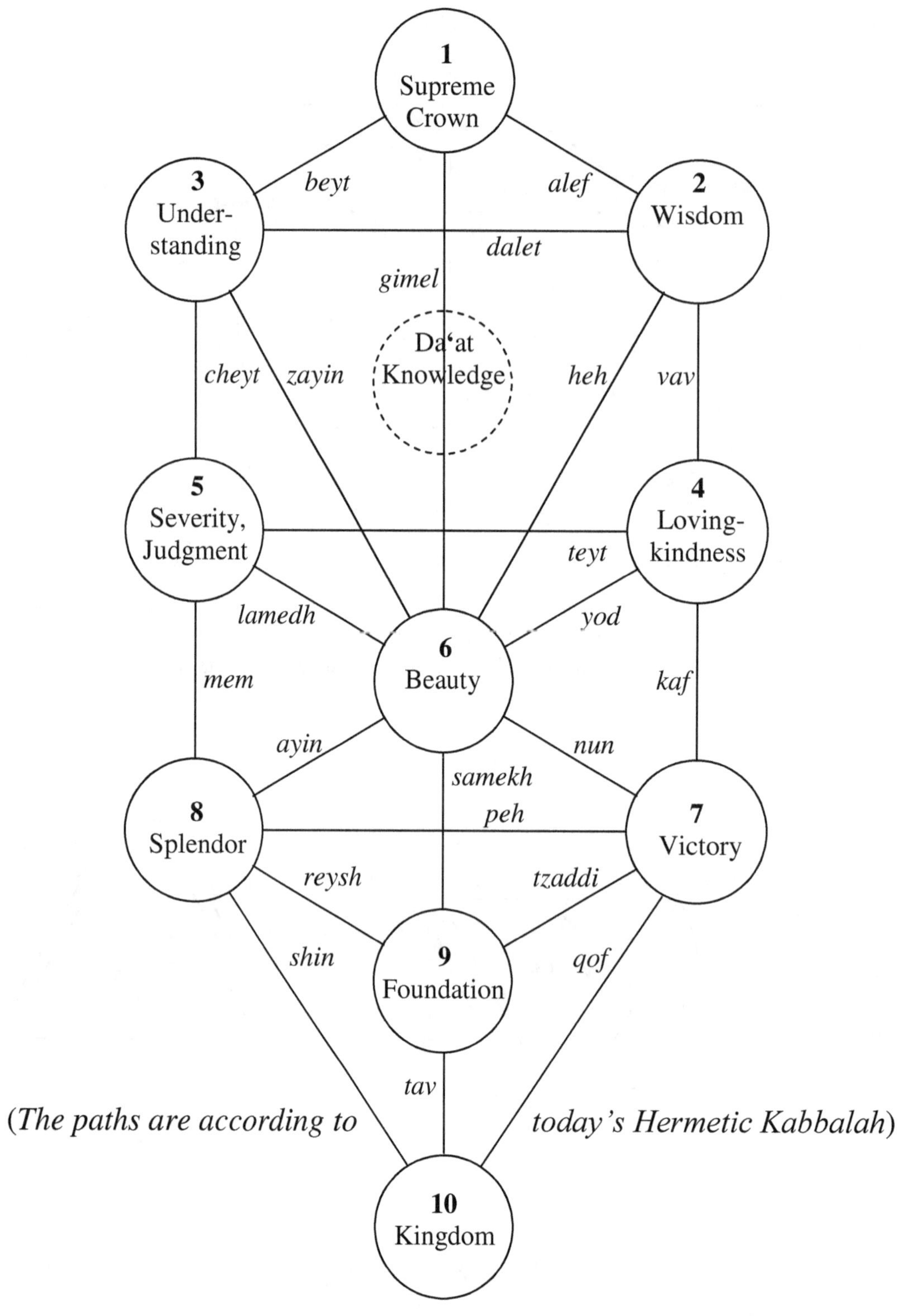

Paths on the Triadic Tree

FIGURE 7

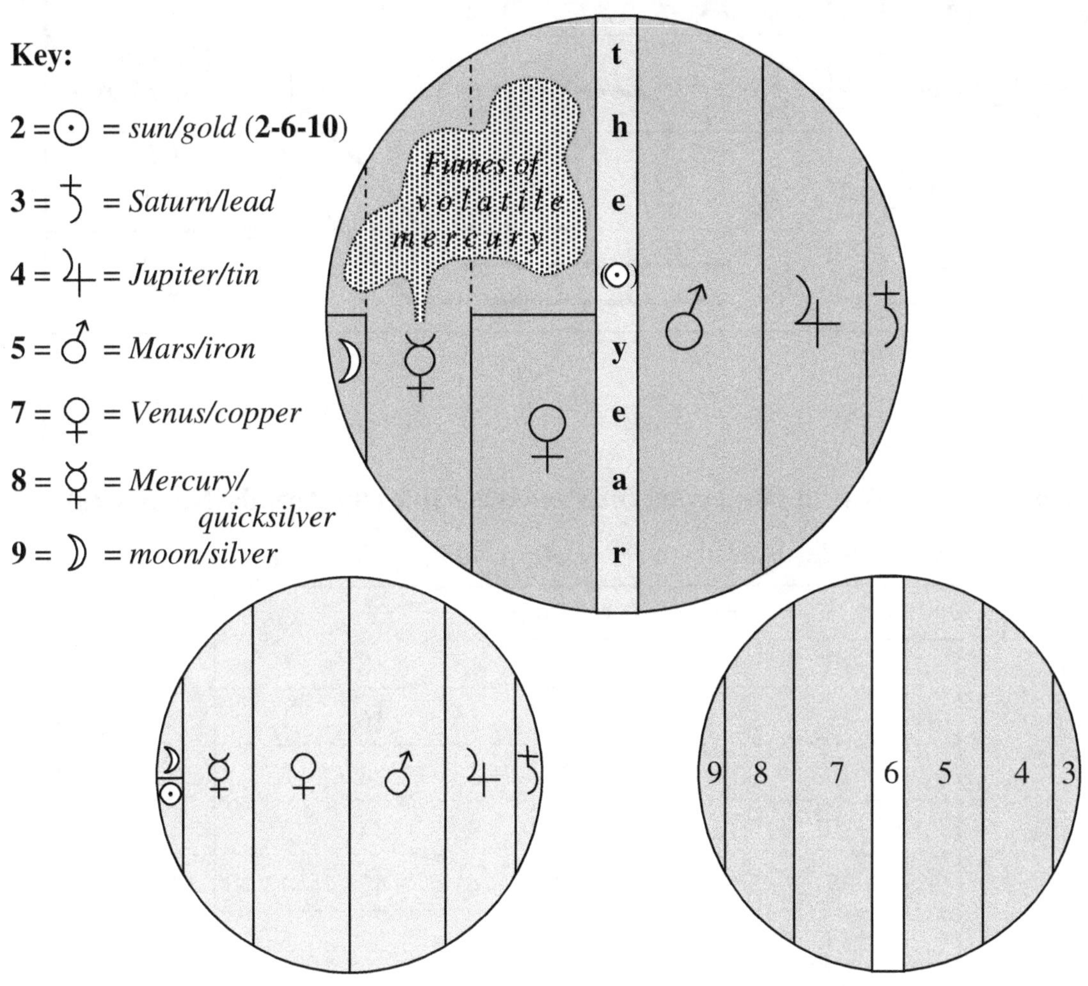

Planetary rulership in astrology
A sign is ruled by the column the round just traversed to get there. But silver's column is divided, as the silvered mirror in which gold is reflected—just as the moon shines by the sun's reflected light.

The Seven Pillars of Wisdom
The numbers correctly applied to the columns of planetary metals, key to the pattern involving valence which letters' numbers reveal; as atomic *numbers, their valences are -1-2-3±4+3+2+1.*

Planetary Columns in the Hermetic Vessel

FIGURE 8

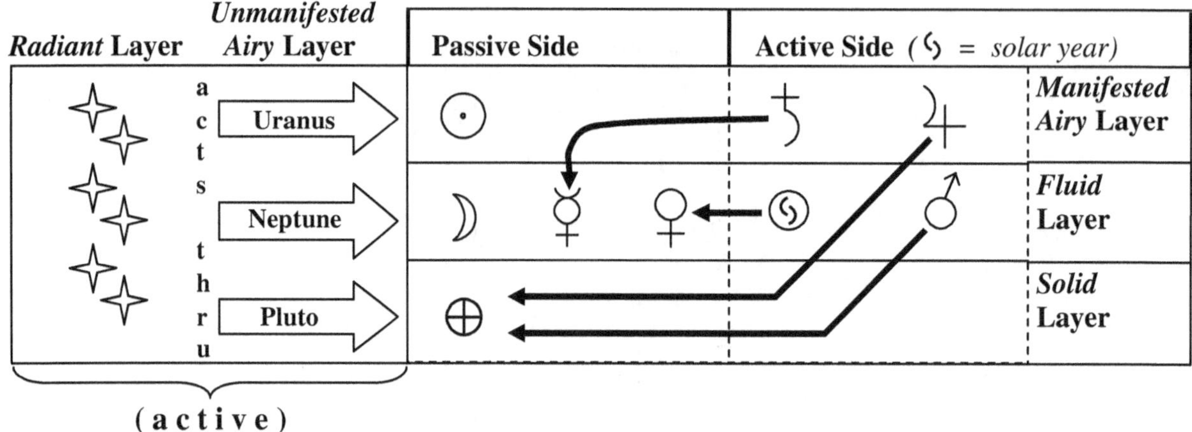

Older, More Correct Way of Displaying the Periodic Table (By Periods, Not Series)

Columns:	±0	+1	+2	+3	±4	−3	−2(+6)	−1	(+8)
	Inert	1				h y d r o g e n		1	
○ = *active*	2	3	4	5	6	7	8	9	
planetary metals	10	11	12	13	14	15	16	17	
	18	19	20	21	22	23	24	25	26 27 28
☐ = *passive*		29	30	31	32	33	34	35	
planetary metals	36	37	38	39	40	41	42	43	44 45 46
		47	48	49	50	51	52	53	
▱ = *rare*	54	55	56	57-71	72	73	74	75	76 77 78
earth		79	80	81	82	83	84	85	
metals	86	87	88	89-103	[etc.]				

Numbers in chart are atomic *numbers (how many protons in nucleus) of chemical 'elements' (the atom-types): +1, +2, etc. along top refer to* valence *electrons, whether 'extra' (beyond nearest stable 'shell') and available for bonding, or number of electrons* lacking *to* complete *such shell.*

Planetary Functions, and the Periodic Table

FIGURE 9

Elements are arranged about the round as the Zohar *has them, taking north as up—since it* is, *on average, for humans. But the* rationale *arises from the innate structure of the tree-alphabet when marshaled according to division into mothers, doubles, and simples and given the numbers the bards called them by.* Harold W. Percival *has stipulated that heat is a combination of* pyrogen *and* aerogen, *which is to say the fiery and airy, magnetism a combination of* fluogen *and* geogen, *which is to say the watery and earthy. The rest correspond as shown, I believe.*

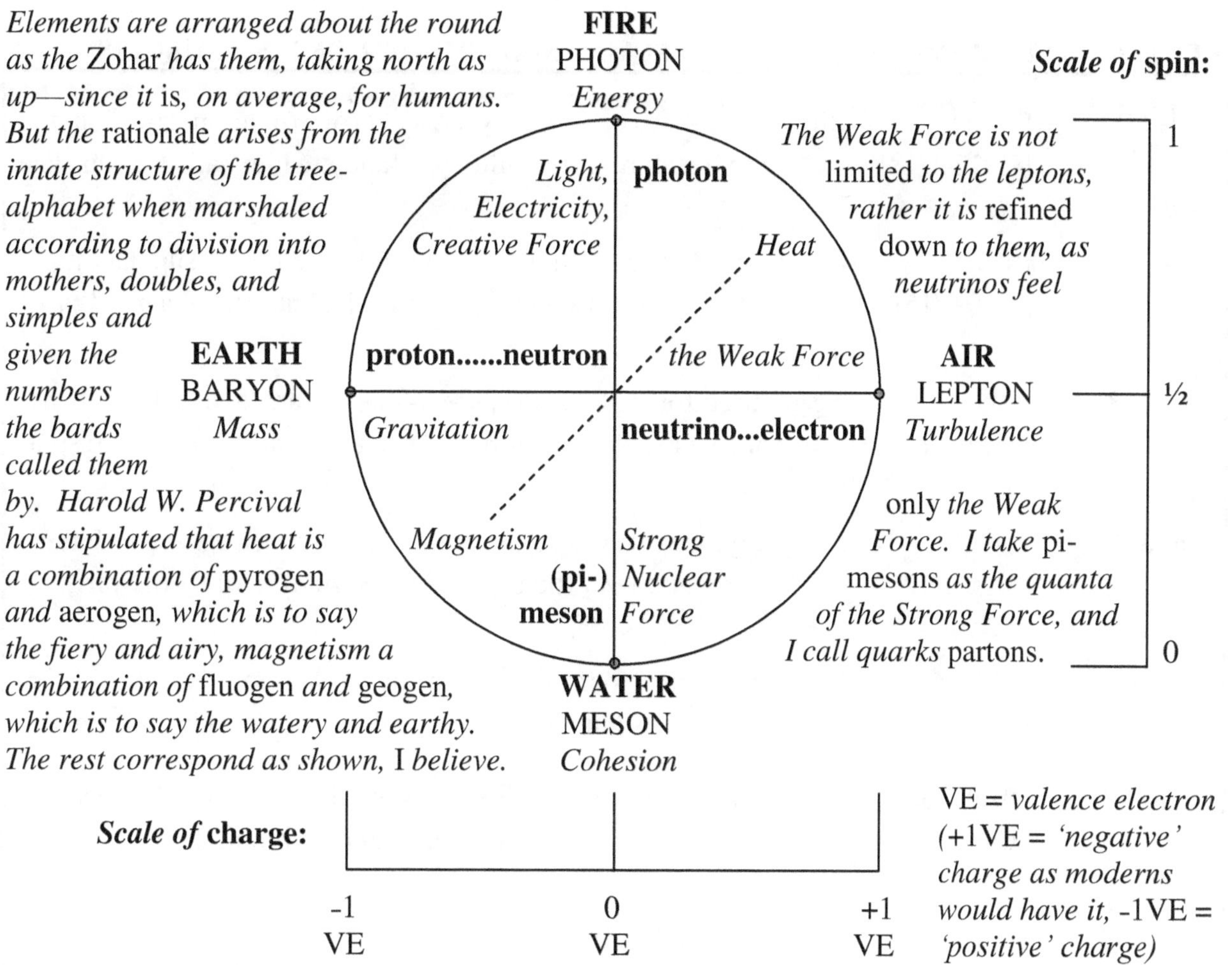

The Four Particle-Types and the Forces of Physics

FIGURE 10

TABLE ZERO: PRIMARY KEY, IRISH TREE-LETTERS

LETTER	TREE [MONTH]	PRESUMED MAIN THRUST OF ITS SYMBOLISM
Beth (5)	Birch [12/22-1/18]	<u>Bi</u>rth of sun-hero or waxing year, *start* (of growth in day's length): small stature + flexibility = infancy; white bark = clean slate.
Luis (14)	Rowan [1/19-2/15]	<u>L</u>earning: shelters young of species that eventually supplant it; rowan whips used to tame bewitched horses; aka *quicken*.
Nion (13)	Ash [2/16-3/15]	<u>N</u>eed: used for tool handles, spear-shafts, oars, axe handles; bane of forests; Norse *world-tree* because where humans grasp it.
Fearn (8)	Alder [3/16-4/12]	<u>F</u>ecundity: tree of Celtic Saturn, *Bran* or *Vran*, cognate with the Germanic *vron* (boar-god *Fro*); *sprouting* of Corn Spirit.
Saille (16)	Willow [4/13-5/10]	<u>S</u>pringing-forth: fount-like shape suggests spring's ebullience, or tears (Jews hung their harps sadly on its boughs in Babylon).
and **Straif [20]**	Blackthorn [*same*]	<u>S</u>trife (surely cognate): called La Mère du Bois ('The Mother of the Wood'), forest's vanguard in reclaiming untilled land.
Huath (0)	Hawthorn [5/11-6/7]	<u>H</u>edge (blocks/separates): aka *may*, its thorns defend snowy white blossoms some say bear a strong scent of female sexuality.
Duir (12)	Oak [6/8-7/5]	<u>D</u>oorway into manifestation: en*dur*ance, reach, compass, domain, horizon; heroic waxing year's *sacrifice* at summer solstice.
Tinne (11)	Holly [7/6-8/2]	<u>T</u>rust: upon hero's death, the *folk* (Ir. *tuatha*) must step up; only *discipline* can transform many *small* pricks into one *big* one.
Coll (9)	Hazel [8/3-8/30]	<u>C</u>oncentration: Fionn Mac Cumhail got his poetic gift (inspiration, *awen*) from salmon fed by the 'Nine Hazels of Poetic Art'.
and **Quert [18]**	Apple [*same*]	<u>Q</u>uest, what bears fruit: *Book of Ballymote*'s 'refuge of a hind'; Myrddin Wylt sang of its shelter to his friend, a wild piglet.

TABLE ZERO (Cont.)

LETTER	TREE [MONTH]	PRESUMED MAIN THRUST OF ITS SYMBOLISM
Muin (6)	Vine [8/31-9/27]	<u>Mu</u>nificence: harvest celebration; sweetness ('mm') of grape and interconnectedness of vine; *wine* meant *love* in Sufi poetry.
Gort (10)	Ivy [9/28-10/25]	<u>G</u>allivanting: serpent-like wandering, seeking, symbol of desire; M & G = yoga's serpent-power coiled up at base of spine.
Peith (7) *or* **Ngetal**, Reed [10/26-11/22]	Whitten	<u>P</u>rophecy: Welsh *peithynen*, divining by maxims on wheel spokes, (ink made from the dried berries) <u>In</u>genuity: thatch, writing, measure; bends, unlike oak (Æsop).
Ruis (15)	Elder [11/23-12/20]	<u>R</u>ide, journey, departure: wood of Irish witches' magic horses; *brings devil into house* (i.e. burns poorly); Elder Mother.

- -

LETTER	TREE [MONTH]	PRESUMED MAIN THRUST OF ITS SYMBOLISM
(Ailm) [21]* *and*	Palm	<u>Al</u>location, location, location, location; *phoenix* (born of fire); sunlit tropical climes, sea travel; laurels; present instant.
Ailm (1)	Fir (or Pine)	<u>Al</u>titude: what levitates, is lofty (fir limits *lateral* growth, redirects to the very top); *yuletide, new moon* (year or moon *arising*).
Onn (4)	Furze (Gorse)	<u>On</u>set (spring's): yellow-flowered; in spring old prickles are burnt off so new sprouts might feed sheep; *spring, waxing moon.*
Ura [17]	Heather	<u>Ur</u>ge (summer's): 17 meant *of age;* like *heath, ura* meant 'earth'; 'earth'; bed of lovers' trysts; draws bees; *summer, full moon.*
Eadhe (2)	Aspen	<u>E</u>mpathy (autumn's): quivering aspen shimmers at slightest breeze and thus stands for the winds of *autumn; waning moon.*
Idho (3) *and*	Yew	<u>I</u>mpact (winter's): long-lived churchyard emblem of death-rebirth; wood of longbows; and of poison; hence *winter, old moon.*
(Gr.Ixias)[19]	Mistletoe	<u>In</u>violate (cut off w/ sheets beneath); *Yule* (solstice), *dark of moon.*

*Numbers in brackets **[17-]** kept secret (not given) in Irish tradition, but easily ferreted-out.*

NOTE: Letter-names in *parentheses* Graves gave as probable secret letters: Aa (which he linked to Ω), and Ii or Y [*White Goddess*, Ch. 14]; square-Hebrew *yod* is suspended in air like mistletoe or loranthus.

TABLE 1: THE EGYPTIAN AND SEMITIC LETTERS

THREE MOTHERS & SEVEN DOUBLES

Hieroglyphic	Substitutions	Hieratic Form	North Semitic	Square Hebrew	Sign, or Element & Anatomical Placement	South Semitic: Sabean	Thamudic
					[Original station in brackets]		
3 (ꜣ)				א	△ sympathetic nerves		
(w) (sh)				שׁ	△ cerebrospinal nerves	(s²)	
m				מ ם	▽ the blood		
d				ד	lungs (*l. eye*)	ḏ	ḍ
ṯ			t	ת	heart (*r. eye*)	ṯ	
k				כ ך	kidneys (*r. ear*)		
r				ר	gonads (*mouth*)		
g				ג	adrenals (*l. nostril*)		
p				ף פ	pituitary (*r. nostril*)		
b				ב	pineal (*l. ear*)		

THE TWELVE SIMPLES

Hieroglyphic	Substitutions	Hieratic Form	North Semitic	Square Hebrew	Sign, or Element & Anatomical Placement	South Semitic: Sabean	Thamudic
ḥ			s (s³)		head	ṣ, ẓ	
s			ṣ		neck, throat	(s¹, s³)	
ḫ			ch		shoulders	ḥ, ḫ	
f			(v, w)		breasts	(w)	
'					heart 'chakra'	(ġ)	
q					womb (prostate)		
t			ṭ		loins, crotch	(ḍ)	ḏ
h					organ of nakedness	(ḥ)	
ï			z		lower spine; thighs		
y					mid-spine; knees		
rw			l		back of shoulders; ankles		
n					back of neck; feet		

TABLE 1a, *ADDENDA*: TEYT + LEFTOVERS

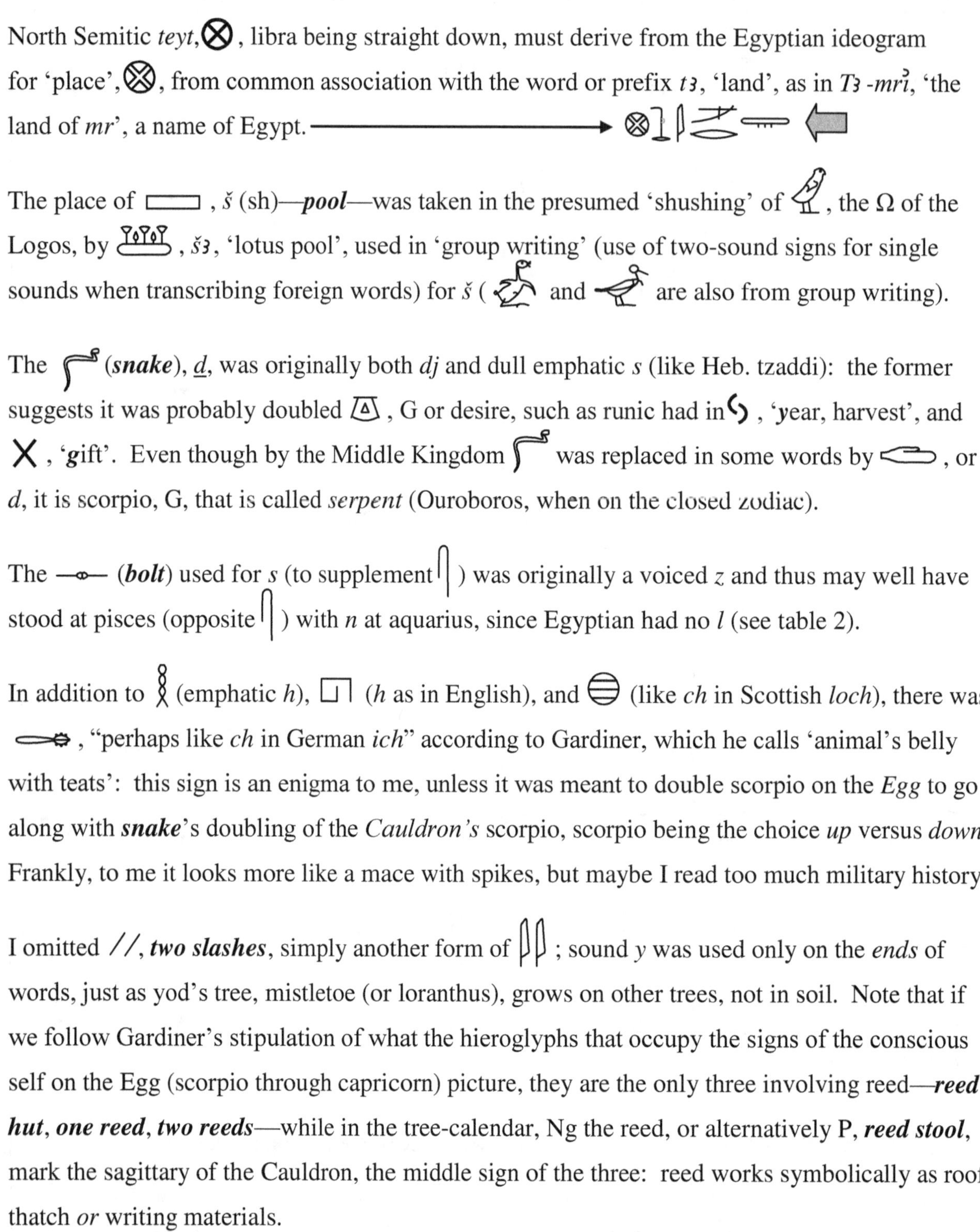

North Semitic *teyt*, ⊗ , libra being straight down, must derive from the Egyptian ideogram for 'place', ⊗ , from common association with the word or prefix *t3*, 'land', as in *T3 -mrỉ*, 'the land of *mr*', a name of Egypt. ⟶

The place of ▭ , *š* (sh)—***pool***—was taken in the presumed 'shushing' of , the Ω of the Logos, by , *š3*, 'lotus pool', used in 'group writing' (use of two-sound signs for single sounds when transcribing foreign words) for *š* (and are also from group writing).

The (***snake***), *ḏ*, was originally both *dj* and dull emphatic *s* (like Heb. tzaddi): the former suggests it was probably doubled , G or desire, such as runic had in , 'year, harvest', and X , '***gift***'. Even though by the Middle Kingdom was replaced in some words by , or *d*, it is scorpio, G, that is called *serpent* (Ouroboros, when on the closed zodiac).

The (***bolt***) used for *s* (to supplement) was originally a voiced *z* and thus may well have stood at pisces (opposite) with *n* at aquarius, since Egyptian had no *l* (see table 2).

In addition to (emphatic *h*), (*h* as in English), and (like *ch* in Scottish *loch*), there was , "perhaps like *ch* in German *ich*" according to Gardiner, which he calls 'animal's belly with teats': this sign is an enigma to me, unless it was meant to double scorpio on the *Egg* to go along with ***snake***'s doubling of the *Cauldron's* scorpio, scorpio being the choice *up* versus *down*. Frankly, to me it looks more like a mace with spikes, but maybe I read too much military history.

I omitted *//*, ***two slashes***, simply another form of ; sound *y* was used only on the *ends* of words, just as yod's tree, mistletoe (or loranthus), grows on other trees, not in soil. Note that if we follow Gardiner's stipulation of what the hieroglyphs that occupy the signs of the conscious self on the Egg (scorpio through capricorn) picture, they are the only three involving reed—***reed hut, one reed, two reeds***—while in the tree-calendar, Ng the reed, or alternatively P, ***reed stool***, mark the sagittary of the Cauldron, the middle sign of the three: reed works symbolically as roof thatch *or* writing materials.

TABLE 2: AN INSIGHT INTO *EGYPTIAN* MAGIC?

Hieroglyph	What it Represented	(Counterparts in Hebrew, Greek)		What it Probably Symbolized
3 (ꜣ)	Egyptian vulture	א	A	Tool using bird, rises while circling.
w	quail chick	[שׁ]	[Σ]Ω	Renewal, growth.
m	owl	מ	M	Silent flight.
d	hand	ד	Δ	One's reach (gesturing with hand).
ṯ	tongs	ת	T	One's control (fueling alchemical oven).
k	basket with handle	כ	K	What is gathered close (fruit or nuts).
r	mouth	ר	P	What is taken in (consumed).
g	alchemical oven	ג	Γ[X]	The transmuting of desire.
p	reed stool	פ	Π	What supports one's weight seated.
b	foot and ankle	ב	B	What supports one's weight standing.
ḥ	wick of twisted flax	ס	Ξ	What sticks out at top of candle (flame).
s	folded cloth	צ	[Ψ]	Draped on forearm (for clearing of throat).
ḫ	sieve	ח	H	What filters or separates.
f	horned viper	ו	Y	What extends out ahead.
ꜥ	forearm	ע	O	What greets, offers, pulls, works.
q	hill slope	ק	[Φ]	Womb-like swelling, refuge from Nile flood.
t	round loaf	ט	Θ	What sustains.
h	reed shelter in field	ה	E	What refreshes.
ỉ	flowering reed	ד	Z	Writing, preserving record of.
y	two reed-flowers	׳	I	Checking or confirming record of.
n	surface of water	[נ]	[N]	What stirs or reflects.
z	bolt	[ ]	[ ]	What seals things up, finishes.

TABLE 3: WHAT THE SEMITIC SHAPES CONVEY

Canaanite	What it pictures	Sabean	What it pictures
ʾ	Head of ox; fire triad.		Dwelling with fire in hearth; hand-mill?
š	Molar, bare breasts.	ś	Zigzag, lightning bolt.
			Woven strands; 2 zigzags back to back.
m	Mother gathering to bosom.		Closed lips, pregnant torso (Ethiop.).
d	A jib (which swings about).		Axe; bow with arrowhead.
		d	*End of road* for hero: his bed or bier.
t	Crossroads; one's mark.		One's mark (one's bond).
		t	Chain (oath) binding two individuals.
k	Flower? hazel wand? brush? cupped hand?		What is 'under one roof'.
r	Stick horse.		Opened mouth from side.
g	Pyramid in sand? camel hump?		Erect phallus seen from side; gibbet?
p	Ear; bottom half of *beyt*.		Vaginal opening, or mayhap an earring.
b	High priest's mitre, or helmet.		Interior of dwelling.
s	Spine with vertebrae.	s̠	Head on shoulders (Ethiop. ,).
		z̠	Animal; person in chair.
ṣ	Standard in midst of battle.	s	Neck with head *missing*.
ḥ	Stacked crates.	h	Arms raised *standing* (inverted).
		ḫ	Arms raised *seated* (inverted).
w	Breast pouring forth milk.		A melon halved.
ʿ	Wheel *in motion*.		The round or *circulatio*.
		ġ	+ 1 = *Bel* (*Baʿal*).
q	Fruit with stem, or being cut.		Fruit on branch.
ṭ	Wheel *stopped*; slice of pita?	t d	Roof from above? stacked crates?
h	A comb.	h	A comb.
z	Column; cold front; swan. (Swans *winter* in Near East.)	z	Hourglass.
y	Drawing line in dirt with stick.		Head of child? seed with root?
l	Left nostril; shepherd's crook.		Eaves of roof.
n	Hand lifted (greeting, farewell).		Hand raised (or minus left wall).

TABLE 4: O'FLAHERTY'S BOIBEL LOTH (ORPHIC?)

Letter > Name	From Riddles in *Hanes Taliesin*	Graves's Archaic Greek Equivalents	Orphic Significance? (Graves's Translation as Hymn)
BOIBEL	Babel	BOIBALION	I, the Roebuck fawn, (or Antelope-bull calf)
LOTH	Lot's wife	LŌTO-	On the Lotus
FORANN	Vran	FORĀMENON	Ferried,
SALIA	Salome	SALOÖMAI	Lurch to and fro,
NEIAGADON	Ne-esthan	NE-ĀGATON	New-born.
UIRIA	Hur	ŪRIOS	I, the Guardian of Boundaries, (or the Benignant One)
DAIBHAITH	David	DAVIZŌ	Cleave wood.
TEILMON	Taliesin	TELĀMŌN or TLĀMŌN	I, the suffering one,
CAOI	Kai	CAIOMAI	Am consumed by fire,
CAILEP	Caleb	CALYPTOMAI	Vanish.
MOIRIA	Moriah	MOIRAŌ	I distribute,
GATH	Hu Gadarn	GĀTHEŌ	I rejoice.
NGOIMAR	Gomer	GNŌRIMOS	I, the famous one,
IDRA	Idris	IDRYOMAI	Establish.

(*I   r e p l a c e s   **Z**— p e r h a p s   t o   p o i n t   t o   z e t a = b a r d i c   **I** ?*)

Letter > Name	From Riddles in *Hanes Taliesin*	Graves's Archaic Greek Equivalents	Orphic Significance? (Graves's Translation as Hymn)
RIUBEN [?*originally:*]	Rhea	(RYMBONAŌ) RHEŌ	(I swing about again.) I flow away.

T H E   V O W E L S

Letter > Name	From Riddles in *Hanes Taliesin*	Graves's Archaic Greek Equivalents	Orphic Significance? (Graves's Translation as Hymn)
ACAB	Acab (Jacob)	ACHAIVA	The Spinner (*a title of Demeter*)
OSE	Jose(ph)	OSSA	Fame
URA	Uriel	URANIA	Queen of Heaven
ESU	Jesus	(H)ESUCHIA	Repose (*Graves: was H dropped to honor Gallic woodcutter god Esus?*)
JAICHIM	Jachin	IACHEMA	Shrieking, *or* Hissing

TABLE 5: TIFINAG & NUMIDIAN, IN *OGHAM* ORDER

Ogham	Nordic Tifinag & Name [after Fell]	Berber Tifinag	Comments	Numidian
B	*bukla*, shield, buckler		Year needs shielding at birth; birth of *sun* in Numidian.	
L	∘ ∘ *or* ‖ *liki*, like, equal	‖	Learning to classify like things.	
F	*far*, ferry	(& x̄ z̄?)	F-alder is *water-resistant* wood, used for *bridge* pilings.	?
S	⊙ *sol*, sun	⊙	*Runic* S had the form ⌇ or ⌇ yet was called **sōwilō*, 'sun'.	
N	*naddr*, nail		N-ash, wood of spear-shafts, oars, and tool handles.	
H	∘ ∘ / ∘ ∘ *Hestemerki*, Pegasus	∘ ∘ / ∘ ∘	Space separates (as does the *hefted shield* in Numidian).	
D	∧⊓ *dyrr*, door	∧ (& ♯ ž?)	D-oak, wood of doors, the doorway into manifestation.	
T	*tagg*, barbed arrow	+	One *aims* for the heart (heart = crossroads).	t
K	*kuml*, cairn, heap		Gathered close, to mark point on horizon (like *passage grave* ?).	
Q	*par*, pair	∘ ∘ ∘	Q, apple (fallen fruit).	‖‖
M	*mán*, moon	⊐	Heb. *mayim* signifies 'seas'.	
G	∘ ∘ ∘ *ghomr*, roof beams	ǧ	*Support* for thatch Ng (Gr. γγ) the reed; changed to erect phallus.	
Ng	*gneipa*, bent	g	Ng-reed, Aesop's example of what *bends* to survive.	p
Z	Z……………[S s - b l a c k t h o r n … (L a M è r e d u B o i s)]	š	Torc (neck,); hourglass = time, as encroachment of wild?	s
R	*hringr*, ring (& *rifa*, to split)	○	Year come full circle, in need of recharge (a new central dot).	○
Aa (Θ)	⊔ th *thili*, planks, partition (u n i t y)	⊔ ḍ, t	Dental consonant everywhere except Graves's projected 22-letter bethluisnion.	∃,
A	∘ (u n i t y)	∘	[Alef (alpha)]	∘
O	⊠ *or* ☰ *waettir*, weights	w	*Surely was no* y, *related to Gr.* υ, *but instead an* ayin-like ǧ, *with it & reversed to place* , *on forefinger, &* , *on middle finger?*	=
U	…………………………………	ǧ(y?)		≡
E	…………………………………	h	[Heh (epsilon)] (*This* comb has *four* teeth.)	≡
I	⊢ tz *zaun*, railing, fence (or perhaps for Z, above?)	z *or* j	'Missing link' between zayin / zeta and bardic I?	dz *or* z
Ii	y *Yorsa*, Cassiopeia		Mistletoe-harvest's gold sickle!	Z

172

TABLE 6: SAME LETTERS IN *TREE-CALENDAR* ORDER

Nordic Tifinag / Berber	(Libyan) Numidian	Tree-Letter	Month *or* Season
b		s^2 *beth*, birch (ב)	22 Dec. - 18 Jan. (*all 'in' capricorn*)
l		*luis*, rowan (ל)	19 Jan. - 15 Feb. (*11/12 'in' aquarius*)
n		*nion*, ash (נ)	16 Feb. - 15 March (*5/6 'in' pisces*)
f	[(& ž?)	s^2 *fearn*, alder (פ or ף)	16 March - 12 April (*3/4 'in' aries*)
s	?	š *saille*, willow (ש)	13 April - 10 May (*2/3 'in' taurus*)
(?) r	š	s [*straif*, blackthorn] (צ)	''
[A terminal R sounded *z* is how rune Y (see table 8) is oft identified.]			
h		*huath*, hawthorn (ח)	11 May - 7 June (*7/12 'in' gemini*)
d	(& ž?)	*duir*, oak (ד)	8 June - 5 July (*1/2 'in' cancer*)
t		ṭ *tinne*, holly (ת)	6 July - 2 Aug. (*5/12 'in' leo*)
k		*coll*, hazel (כ)	3 Aug. - 30 Aug. (*1/3 'in' virgo*)
(?) p	q	[*quert*, apple] (ק)	''
[Lat. Q = Gr. P (interrogative initial), just as there were Q-Celts and P-Celts.]			
m		*muin*, vine (מ)	31 Aug. - 27 Sept. (*1/4 'in' libra*)
gh	ǧ	*gort*, ivy (ג)	28 Sept. - 25 Oct. (*1/6 'in' scorpio*)
gn	g	p *ngetal*, reed (ס) **or**	26 Oct. - 22 Nov.
[cf. Ethiop. samekh (see table 3)]		*peith*, water elder (פ)	(*1/12 'in' sagittary*)
hr	r	*ruis*, elder (ר)	23 Nov. - 20 Dec.
[The *hr* is invariably *initial*, rather than terminal.]			[all *after sagittary*]
th	d, ṭ	[*ailm*, palm] (ט)	physical location
		(*unseasonal warmth*	*seen from deck of ship?*)
	'	*ailm*, silver fir (א)	yuletide; new moon
w		*onn*, furze (gorse) (ע)	spring; waxing moon
	ġ	*ura*, heather (ו)	summer; full moon
	h	*eadhe*, aspen (ה)	fall; waning moon
tz	z / j	dz, z *idho*, yew (ז)	winter; old moon
y		[Gr. *ixias*, mistletoe] (י)	~21 Dec.; dark of the moon

TABLE 7: MEROITIC (NUBIA), IN OGHAM ORDER

Ogham	Meroitic Hieroglyph	Its Signification	Comments
B		**Bull or Boibalis**	B = Boibel < Boibalion = 'roebuck fawn' or 'antelope bull-calf'.
L		**Recumbent lion**	*The Ptolemaic form*
F	*or* (p)	**Reed stool**	*The Ptolemaic form*
S	(š, s)	**Lotus pool**	*From Egyptian group-writing*
N		**Surface of water**	*The Ptolemaic form* ($\sim$)
H	(kh, ḫ)	**Opened mouth**	Signifies hot air (*ha*), empty space?
D		**Eye of Horus**	Eye on the horizon (Cauldron's rim).
T	*or*	**Bird-priest (~ tongs)**	*Egyptian letter* T ($\sim$)
		(seen from above, with lines linking ears to sound's source)	
K	(kh, ḫ)	**Small-necked jar**	What is *gathered close* (cf. ⁖, ʰ, Ɔ).
Q	Δ *or*	**Hill-slope**	*The Ptolemaic form*
		(Q-apple = 'refuge of hind'; hill-slope = refuge from Nile flood)	
M		**Owl**	*The Ptolemaic form*
G	(k)	*Gb*-goose	*Geb* was the Egyptian earth god.
Ng	(ñ)	**Plant of Upper Egypt** *Sedge?*	Links Cauldron to the broken-and-extended zodiac via geodetic model, as w/ Egyp. P (*reed stool*) & B (*foot*)?
Z(Ss)	(s)	**Woven strands, enclosure?**	D_2 (Thamudic *d*, Berber Tifinağ *ẕ*)?
R	*or*	**Aquifer (coffin?)**	Water associated with death, like R-elder.
(Θ[Aa])	(to/tê) / (te)	**Horn / reed hut**	Links teyt to Ugaritic-like double alef.
A		**Seated person**	Alef is zodiac of seated torso.
O	(o/ê)	**Head of ox**	The *motor's* motivation.
U	(w)	**Lasso**	*The Ptolemaic form*
		(U, numbered 17, 5th-to-last, lassos bull B, 5: birch = heath *pregnant*.)	
E		**Feather**	Fitting, for the air breath.
I		**Man w/ arm raised**	Egyptian *ỉ*, 'O', was spelt:
(Y[Ii])	(y)	**Two reed-flowers**	*The Ptolemaic form*

TABLE 8: THE ELDER FUTHARK (GERMANIC RUNES)

Name	Meaning	Shape	What It Pictures	Tree
fehu (f/v)	cattle [wealth]		Stalk of grain, symbol of Corn Spirit.	*alder*
ūruz (u)	aurochs, manly strength		Aurochs (drinking) horn upended.	*heather*
þurisaz (th)	giant		Giant's girth.	*oak*
ansuz (a)	god		Fir tree.	*fir*
raiðō (r)	ride, journey		Shaman-priest in animal headdress.	*elder*
kenaz (k) (or *kanō*	torch skiff)		Poet's opened mouth: salmon of wisdom goes in, poetry comes out.	*hazel*
gebō (g)	gift		(Silhouette of) tripod of cauldron?	*ivy₁*
wunjō (w)	joy		Fruit on branch (or half on knife).	*apple*
hagalaz (h)	hail		Section of fence (hawthorn = hedge).	*hawthorn*
nauðiz (n)	need, necessity		Needfire; oar through side of ship.	*ash*
īsa (i)	ice		Icicle.	*mistletoe*
jēra (y)	year, harvest		Linked arms of harvest dance.	*ivy₂*
eihwaz (e/i)	yew tree		Border between cold air and warm.	*yew*
perþ- (p)	?		Rune-cup throwing divinatory dice.	*whitten*
algiz (z) or *alhiz*	defense, protection elk		Eagle's-eye view of elk.	*blackthorn*
sōwilō (s)	sun (Latin *sol*)		Lightning bolt, or hanging bough.	*willow*
tīwaz (t)	the god Tiw (Tyr)		Spear or arrow pointing upward.	*holly*
ƀairkana- (b)	birch twig		Pregnant torso (birch = birth).	*birch*
ehwaz (e)	horse (L. *equus*)		Horse's underside (*motion's* breeze).	*aspen*
mannaz (m)	man, human		Two *wunjōs* kissing.	*vine*
laguz (l)	water (Eng. *lake*)		Eaves of roof.	*rowan*
inguz (ng)	the god or hero Ing		(O.Eng.) A knot (woven strands).	*reed/broom*
ōþila,-ala (o)	heritage, inheritance		Hood of one's teacher.	*furze*
dagaz (d)	day		Hourglass on its side = present instant.	*palm*

Note: and (*f* and *p* turned sideways) suggest Greek *pi* and *omega*, numbered in Greek 80 and 800, the numbers of *peh* and *feh-sofit* (*peh*'s final form) in Hebrew. Hmm.

TABLE 9: SOME ITALIC & GREEK ALPHABETS

	Italic:			Greek:			
	Etruscan	Messapic	Latin	Chalcidic	Formello	Samos	Attica
a	ᗅ	ᗅᐱ	ᗅᐱᗅ	ᗅᗅ	ᗅ	ᗅ	ᗷᗈ
b	ᗸᗷ	B	ᗷB	B	ᗷ	ᗷ	ᗷ
g	ᗈᗈ	Γ	ᗈC	Cᐱ	ᗈ	Τ	ᐱ
d	◁	DΔ	ᗡD	ᗡDΔ	D	◁	Δ
e	ᗄᗄᗄ	ᗄE	EΙΙ	ᗄᗄE	ᗄ	ᗄᗄ	ᗄᗄᗄ
v	Ⅎ	ᗄ	FΙᐟ	Ⅽ	ᗄ	Ⅎ	
z	I	IⅎF	[G (g)]		‡ (z)		I
h	ᗷᗷᗷ	ᗷᗷH	H	ᗷ	ᗷ		ᗷ
th	⊗⊙	⊕O		⊗⊕	⊕		⊕
i	Ι	Ι	Ι	Ι	Ι	Ι	ᗄᗄ
k	ᛕ	ᛕ	K	K	ᛕ	ᛕ	K
l	ᒐ	ᐱ	ᒐL	ᒐᐱ	ᒐ	ᒐ	ᒐᒐ
m	ᛗᛗ	ᛗM	M	M	ᛗ	ᛗ	ᛗᛗ
n	ᛁᛝ	ᛝN	N	ᛝ	ᛝ		ᛝ
s/sc	⊞	+× (x)		+	⊞	Ⅲ	
o	O	OⒹ◇	O	O	⊙	O	Oᒐᒐᒐᒐᒐᒐᒐᒐᒐᒐᒐᒐ
p	ᒐᒐ	ᒐᒐᒐ	ᒐᒐ	ᒐᒐ	ᒐ	ᒐ	ᒐᒐ
š	ᛩM	ᒐ			M		
q	�	999Φ	ᛰᛰ	ᛰ	ᛰ	Φ	ᛰ
r	ᛪᛩ	ᛈᛈR	ᛈᛈR	ᛡᛈᛈᛈ	ᛈ	◁	ᛈᛈᛡ
s	ᛪᛪ	ᛪᛪSC	ᛪS	ᛪᛪᛪ	ᛪ		ᛪᛪ
t	ᛐ	ᛐᛐ	ᛐ	ᛐ	ᛐ		ᛐ
u	ᛉᛐᛐ		ᛐᛐ	ᛉᛐ	ᛉ	ᛉ	ᛉᛐ
ph	Φ	[× (x)]	Φ		[+ (x)]	Φ	ΦΦ
kh	ᛉᛉ	×	kh ᛉ	ph Φ	kh ×ᛡ		×+
f	8	ᴣ ᛉᛐᛉ	[Υ (y)] *Added*	kh ᛉ	ps ᛉᛡ		
		t(th) Ψ	[Z (z)] *later.*	kh ᛉ	ō Ω		

TABLE 10: TWO ANATOLIAN ALPHABETS

Lycian (from Southern Anatolia)	Lydian (from Northwestern Anatolia)
a [glyph] ⇐ Cf. Chalcidic [glyph] (table 9): pine?	a [glyph]
e [glyph] ⇐ From Thamudic [glyph] via [glyph]? fir?	b [glyph]
b [glyph] (second being lower case *b*?)	d [glyph] ⇐ Greek Δ minus base?
β [glyph] ⇐ No doubt related to *m*, below.	e [glyph] ⇐ Related to epsilon, surely.
g [glyph] ⇐ Cf. *Samos* form (table 9).	v [glyph] ⇐ (Greek *digamma*.)
d [glyph]	i [glyph]
i [glyph]	ı [glyph]
w [glyph]	k [glyph]
z [glyph]	l [glyph]
θ [glyph] ⇐ (Inner and outer *meet* at libra.)	m [glyph]
j [glyph]	n [glyph]
c [glyph]	o [glyph]
q [glyph]	r [glyph]
l [glyph]	s [glyph] ⇐ Zeta? (cf. Messapic *z*, table 9).
m [glyph]	ś [glyph]
n [glyph]	t [glyph]
m̃ [glyph] ⇐ From *ogam consaine* M?	u [glyph]
ñ [glyph] ⇐ **This is *ogam consaine* Ng!**	f [glyph] ⇐ Also in Etruscan (see table 9).
u [glyph]	p [glyph] ⇐ I have no clue.
p [glyph]	ã [glyph] ⇐ Related to Thamudic [glyph] ?
x [glyph]	ī [glyph] ⇐ Perhaps *mutated* from ñ (*ng*)?
r [glyph]	ẽ [glyph]
s [glyph]	λ [glyph]
t [glyph]	v [glyph] ⇐ Suggests Celtic motif (or F)!
ī [glyph] ⇐ Cf. *late* (Anglo-Saxon) runic *ea*, [glyph].	↑ [glyph] ⇐ Suggests runic T, [glyph] (table 8).
a [glyph] ⇐ Tops of pine?	] [glyph] ⇐ Suggests runic P, [glyph] (” ”).
ė [glyph] ⇐ Tops of fir?	
h [glyph]	
k [glyph]	

Boxed inset (Lycian column):

> ***Ogam consaine (Bronze Age):***
>
> b l f s n | h d t k q | m g ng z r

Brace note (pointing to *c* and *q*):

> Note *q* is mirrored *k*, as in tree-alphabet, where C (K) is 9 and Q (Kk) is 18.

Brace note (pointing to *x*):

> Like Sabean *p* and runic *ng* (*ogam consaine* Ng is Greek *xi*, Hebrew *samekh*). Odd.

Brace note (pointing to *h* and *k*):

> Here are *both* forms of Greek chi, 'eastern' *and* 'western'

Brace note (Lydian column, pointing to *ı*):

> Interesting, considering zeta (zayin) is hardened bardic I via erosion of D as in *Zeus*.

Brace note (Lydian column, pointing to *ẽ* and *λ*):

> These two also in Lycian, with slightly altered sound.

TABLE 11: THE BARDIC TAROT OF MARSEILLES

LETTER	TRUMP	DESCRIPTION + SYMBOLIC LINK TO TREE

B-birch — V Pope—*arm* of mother presents her twins, Pope raises hand to bless them: white bark = blessing, clean slate; digits of each limb *counted* at birth.

L-rowan — XIIII Temperance—dressed up as angel, she pours aquarius (♒) between vessels; rowan whip *tames* bewitched horses; learning = temperance.

N-ash — XIII (Death)—Grim Reaper reaps limbs, heads (of king, queen) with scythe held like oar; axe-handle is forest's Grim Reaper; negation, newness.

F-alder — VIII Justice—enthroned, *not* blind, head outlined in yellow, with sword and scales: resists moisture; chief; balances 2 objects of 4 elements each.

S-willow — XVI La Maison Dieu—cannonball upsets crown from tower while twins tumble: S = ϟ = lightning; dots = pollen, cascading boughs; Babel, Babylon, exile.

Ss-blackthorn — XX Judgment—smoke emits pikes + angel w/ trumpet over couple, child, coffin: Judgment Day, *ultimate* strife; 10+10 digits = *fair* combat (see **R**, below).

H-hawthorn — Fool—capped vagrant, bag on pole over mantled shoulder, dog nipping at purse: hedge excludes vagrants; no-number = space traversed, or what *divides*.

D-oak — XII Hanged Man—*dances jig* hung by foot, thus *inverted image on back of eye*: oak's spread makes it the hangman's tree; hero *sacrificed;* horizon *seen*.

T-holly — XI Force—woman in thorny headband grasps a lion's jaws, limiting their spread: holly's *law of phalanx* magnifies many small pricks' *force* by *cohesion*.

K-hazel — VIIII Hermit or Old Man—bearded sage wrapped in cloak wields staff + lantern: *concentrated* wisdom or light (rune **kenaz*, 'torch'), what is *in a nutshell*.

Kk(Q)-apple — XVIII Moon—crustacean in pool, dogs bark between towers under face of one who has taken *refuge* in moon (in *Book of Ballymote*, 'shelter of a hind').

M-vine — VI Lover—stands between cleric and beloved, Cupid aims from cloud on high: *interconnectedness* ('heard it through the *grapevine*'); *sweetness* of life.

G-ivy — X Wheel of Fortune—on stand w/ crank, crowned sphinx on top, beasts ride up & down: to *turn* crank is to *seek* one's fortune; desire wanders, clings.

P-water elder *or* **Ng-reed?** — VII Chariot—roofed, two-horse, driver crowned, mask on each shoulder: Work of the Chariot; symbolizes self-control (Arjuna's charioteer = Kršna).

R-elder — XV Devil—hominid couple chained under winged, deer-horned 'little devil': to burn elder *brings devil into house;* 10 vs. 5 digits = *unfair* combat.

TABLE 11 (Cont.): The Bardic Vowels

LETTER	TRUMP	DESCRIPTION + SYMBOLIC LINK TO TREE
Aa-palm[teyt]	XXI World	nude dancer within wreath surrounded by angel-bull-lion-eagle: celebration; *or* hamlet seen through porthole: location-location-location.
A-fir/pine	I Magician	mountebank, wand raised, stands at table with cups, dice, and such: stage magician *levitates* to *hold attention* (*unite* crowd), like tall fir/pine.
O-furze	IIII Emperor	vigor, bearded profile, sits in field w/ globed scepter, legs crossed: obviously campaigning in *spring*; he rules, & spring, enriches 4 elements.
U-heather	XVII Star	buxom nude empties jugs in pond; 7 stars surround big star like cup: bed of trysts, night fluid-mixing; Boibel Loth's Urania 'Queen of Heaven'.
E-aspen	II Papess	reading; hangings suggest couple, one w/ erection, about to copulate: *heh* in Abraham means *circumcision; quivering* aspen = organ of pleasure.
I-yew	III Empress	eagle on her shield extends tail to embrace her about *base of spine*; *female* pagans weaned under full-waning-or-*old* moon: last *reigns*, limits.
Ii-mistletoe, *the Golden Bough...*	XVIIII Sun	twin gods of year wrestle at play by wall, sun shining, sweat flies: at *Yule*, *dark of moon* (leaving *only* the sun), waxing *overcomes* waning.

TABLE 12: TAROT TRUMPS AND ATOM-TYPES

. . . as if some *seer* peered at the modern world's *atomic numbers* from the High Middle Ages.

ATOM-TYPE & TRUMP	CONNECTION BETWEEN THEM
no-thing (Space)	Fool . . . **Space** *separates*, as does hawthorn when excluding the vagabond shown here, who also by the way *traverses* space (hurrying along chased by dog).
hydrogen H ± 1	I Magician . . . Mountebank pretends power over *physical matter*, most of which is **H**, which *levitates* (zeppelins), as do magicians, and the lofty fir or pine.
helium He ± 0	II Papess . . . The only way for a Pope to be taken for female is by imbibing **He**, which is inert ('she' ignores sexual encounter pictured by the hangings).
lithium Li $+1$	III Empress . . . Shield-eagle (1st slot in atom's 2nd orbit) embraces her about the middle reassuringly; **Li** treats *bipolar*, hence equilibrium? moderation?
beryllium Be $+2$	IIII Emperor . . . Shield-eagle (representing 2nd slot in atom's 2nd orbit) is *content*, does *not* embrace other; **Be** is in *pendent*, a *beryl* (emerald or aquamarine).
boron B $+3$	V Pope . . . Blesses, cleanses (spiritually) with raised hand, beard white like birch bark; **B**'s *ore* is borax, a natural *cleanser* as well as a bleach or *whitener.*
carbon C ± 4	VI Lover . . . **C**, so enamored of its kind it joins in interconnected chains or vines, at the same time attracting enough **H, O**, and **N** to constitute living tissue.
nitrogen N -3	VII Chariot . . . Riding an *open* vehicle, what blows against the face is *four-fifths* **N** and *one*-fifth **O**; thus it is the main material constituting *speech* as well.
oxygen O -2	VIII Justice . . . Scales mean balance, **O** being the only atom-type *indispensible* to it (aries being *up*); alder is the tree of the spirit of *vegetation* that *makes* **O**.
fluorine Fl -1	VIIII Hermit . . . This we *want* set apart, off by itself: hydrofluoric acid, **Fl+H**— strongest chemical reaction known—seeps through flesh, dissolves bone.
neon Ne ± 0	X Wheel of Fortune . . . **Ne** in *neon lights* attracts desire as we seek our fortunes, ivy-like, typically set on a *diurnal* cycle, the swiftest of all cosmic wheels.

TABLE 12 (Cont.)

. . . as if some *seer* peered at the modern world's *atomic numbers* from the High Middle Ages.

ATOM-TYPE & TRUMP	CONNECTION BETWEEN THEM
sodium Na +1	XI Force . . . Controls lion's jaws, roar, word: salt's crystal purity (**Na+Cl**) binds oaths (your mark or bond); affects *heart;* holds water in *intercellular* fluid.
magnesium Mg +2	XII Hanged Man . . . **Mg** burns w/ highly actinic light, in (maritime) *signal* lamps; inverted image on back of eye; utilized in *nerve* signals (to *dance* his jig).
aluminum Al +3	XIII (Death) . . . The skeleton represents strength, lightness, and give in *nature*, as does **Al** but only after it has been separated out, smelted down, and cast.
silicon Si ±4	XIIII Temperance . . . Commonest atom besides **O** in earth's crust or in tempered glass; seismic pressure on (**Si+O**) quartz-bearing rock generates *UFOs*.
phosphorus Ph −3	XV Devil . . . Phosphorus (name) = Lucifer (glows in dark); **Ph** is pivotal atom in chromosomes/heredity, confirming reysh's physiological station (gonads).
sulfur S −2	XVI La Maison Dieu . . . **S** is a prime ingredient in *gunpowder*, or what propels cannonball that is striking the tower; found chiefly in skin, hair, and nails.
chlorine Cl −1	XVII Star . . . Obviously she is pouring some **Cl** in her pool; star pattern has large star (for completed 'neon shell') + 7 other stars, the 7 steps **Cl** is *past* **Ne**.
argon Ar ±0	XVIII Moon . . . **Ar** puts pressure without air's combustion in *light-bulbs*; street lamps *mimic* the moon, lure one's eye to it thinking it may *be* the moon.
potassium K +1	XVIIII Sun . . . What sun ripens is our vege foods, richer in **K** than in the **Na** meat is rich in; wall represents **K**'s being what holds water *within* cells.
calcium Ca +2	XX Judgment . . . Angel holds trumpet up to throat *taurus*, where the parathyroids are that rule **Ca** in the body; and *bone* is what Judgment Day *resurrects*.
scandium Sc +3	XXI World . . . **Sc** is first of the *rare earth* metals, so rare they are often named for wherever man has managed to locate some (Scandinavia, in this case).

CHART 1: ALEF-BEYT LETTER ORDER

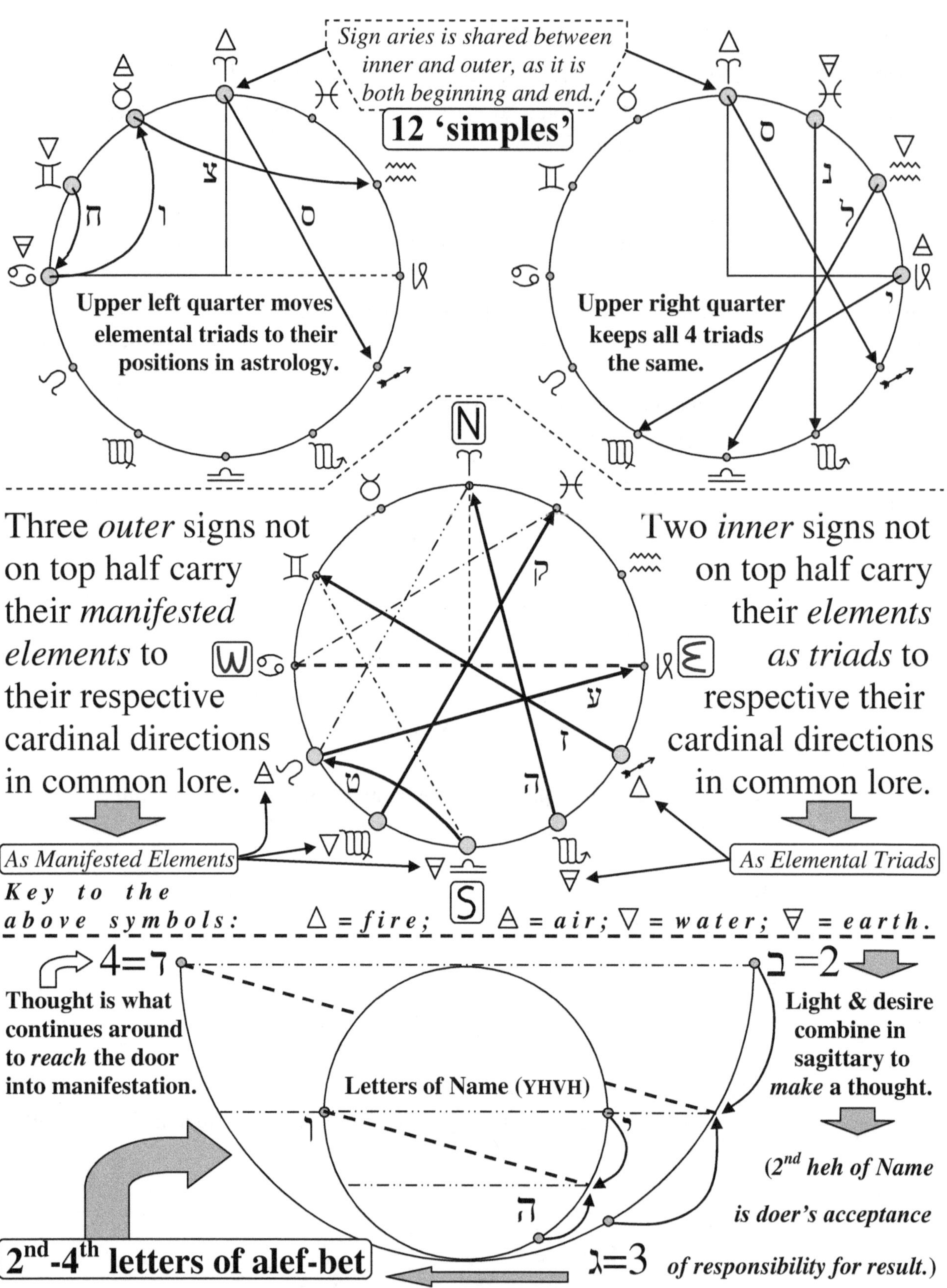

CHART 2: UGARITIC LONG ORDER, SOME COMMENTS
[Listed with their Sabean equivalents, to show the symmetrical pattern of switched shapes.]

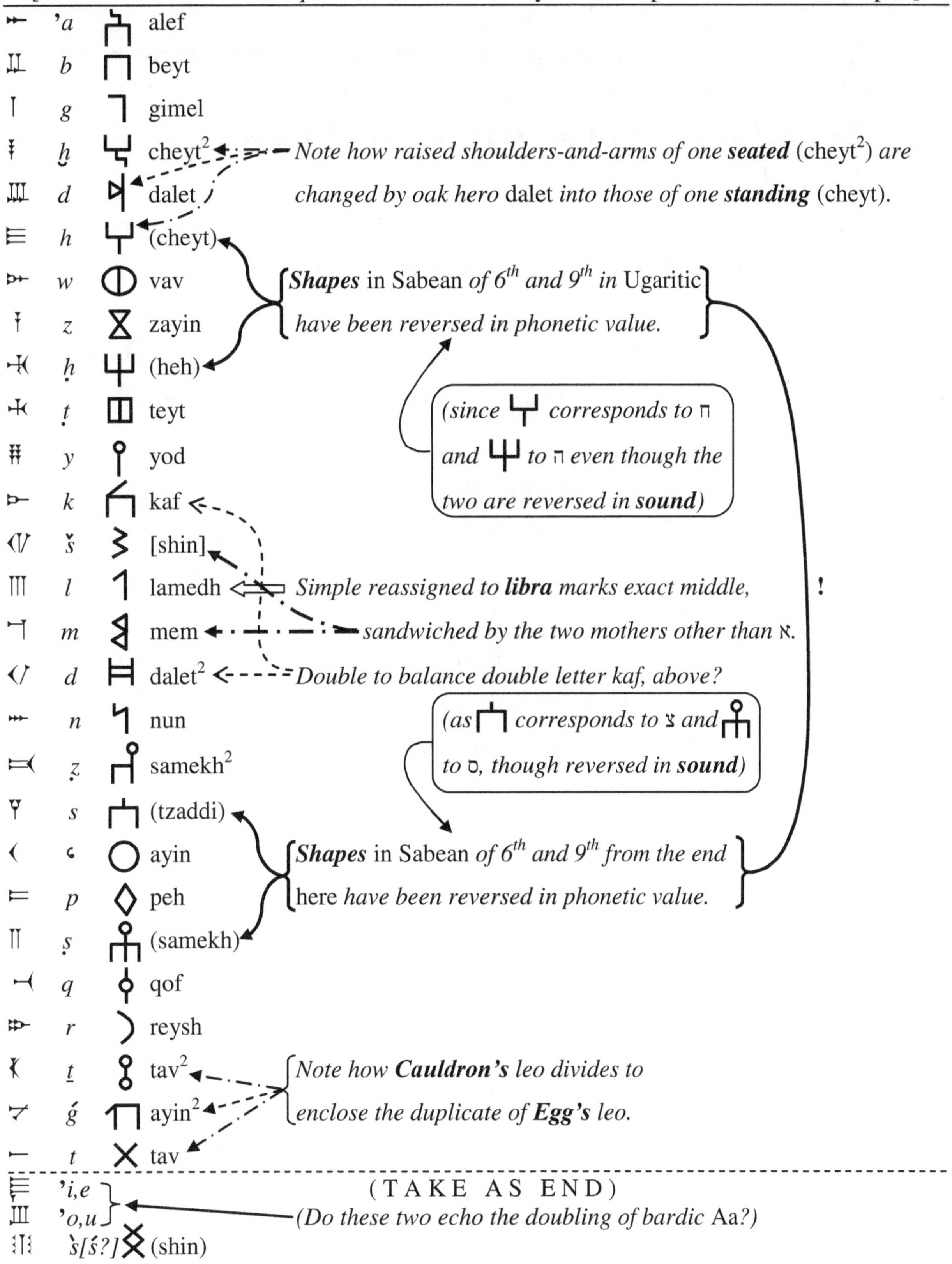

	'a		alef
	b		beyt
	g		gimel
	ḫ		cheyt[2] ← *Note how raised shoulders-and-arms of one **seated** (cheyt[2]) are*
	d		dalet *changed by oak hero dalet into those of one **standing** (cheyt).*
	h		(cheyt)
	w		vav
	z		zayin
	ḥ		(heh)
	ṭ		teyt
	y		yod
	k		kaf
	š		[shin]
	l		lamedh ← *Simple reassigned to **libra** marks exact middle,*
	m		mem ← *sandwiched by the two mothers other than א.*
	d		dalet[2] ← *Double to balance double letter kaf, above?*
	n		nun
	ẓ		samekh[2]
	s		(tzaddi)
	ʿ		ayin
	p		peh
	ṣ		(samekh)
	q		qof
	r		reysh
	ṯ		tav[2] ← *Note how **Cauldron's** leo divides to*
	ġ		ayin[2] ← *enclose the duplicate of **Egg's** leo.*
	t		tav

Shapes in Sabean of 6th and 9th in Ugaritic have been reversed in phonetic value.

*(since ⊔ corresponds to ה and ⊔ to ח even though the two are reversed in **sound**)*

*(as ⊓ corresponds to צ and ⊓ to ס, though reversed in **sound**)*

Shapes in Sabean of 6th and 9th from the end here have been reversed in phonetic value.

!

- -

	'i,e		(TAKE AS END)
	'o,u		*(Do these two echo the doubling of bardic Aa?)*
	ś[ŝ?]		(shin)

CHART 3: SOUTH SEMITIC LETTER ORDER

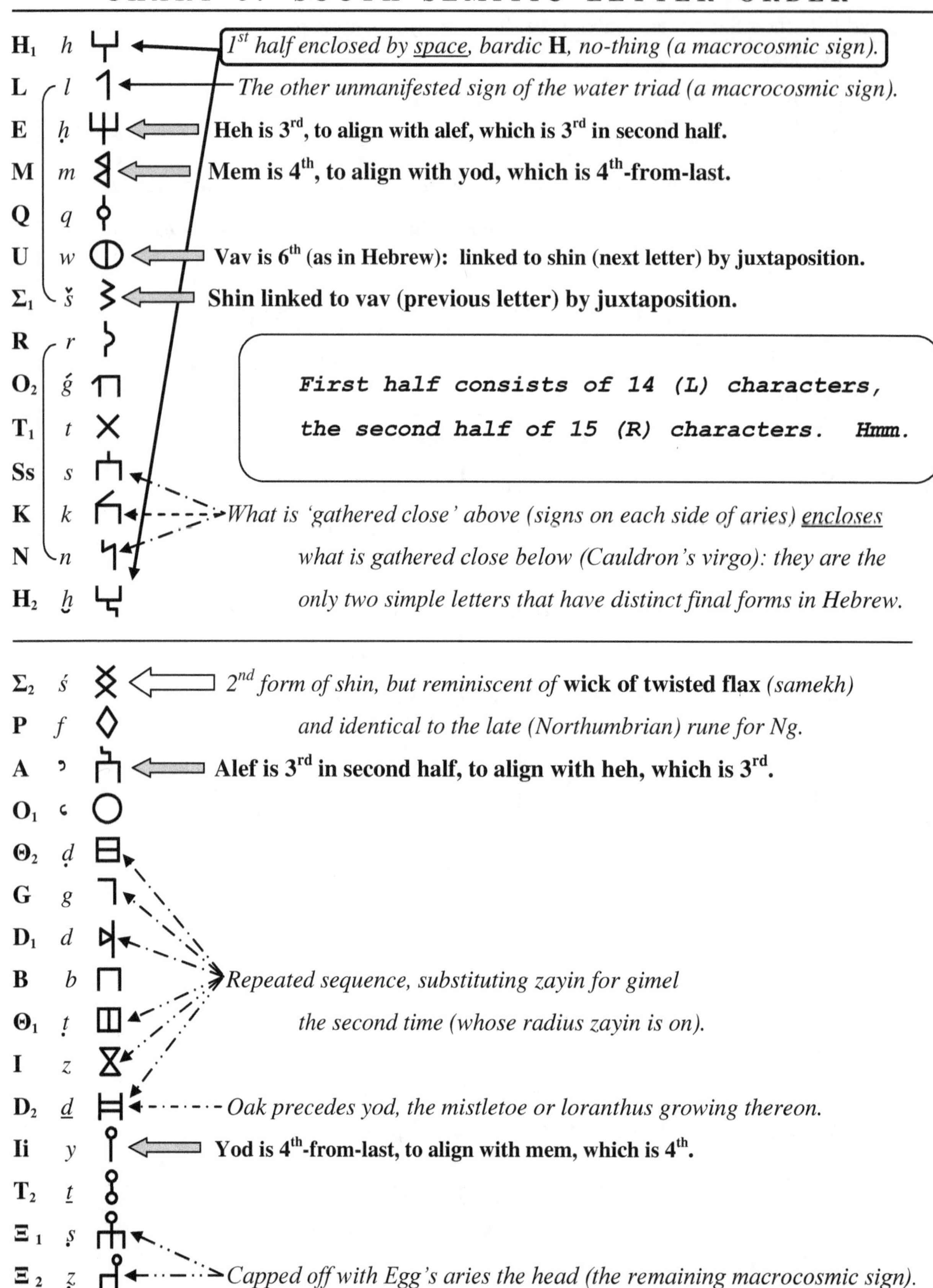

CHART 4: ALTERNATE SOUTH SEMITIC ORDER

[This time with the two samekhs at the end coalesced into a single place.]

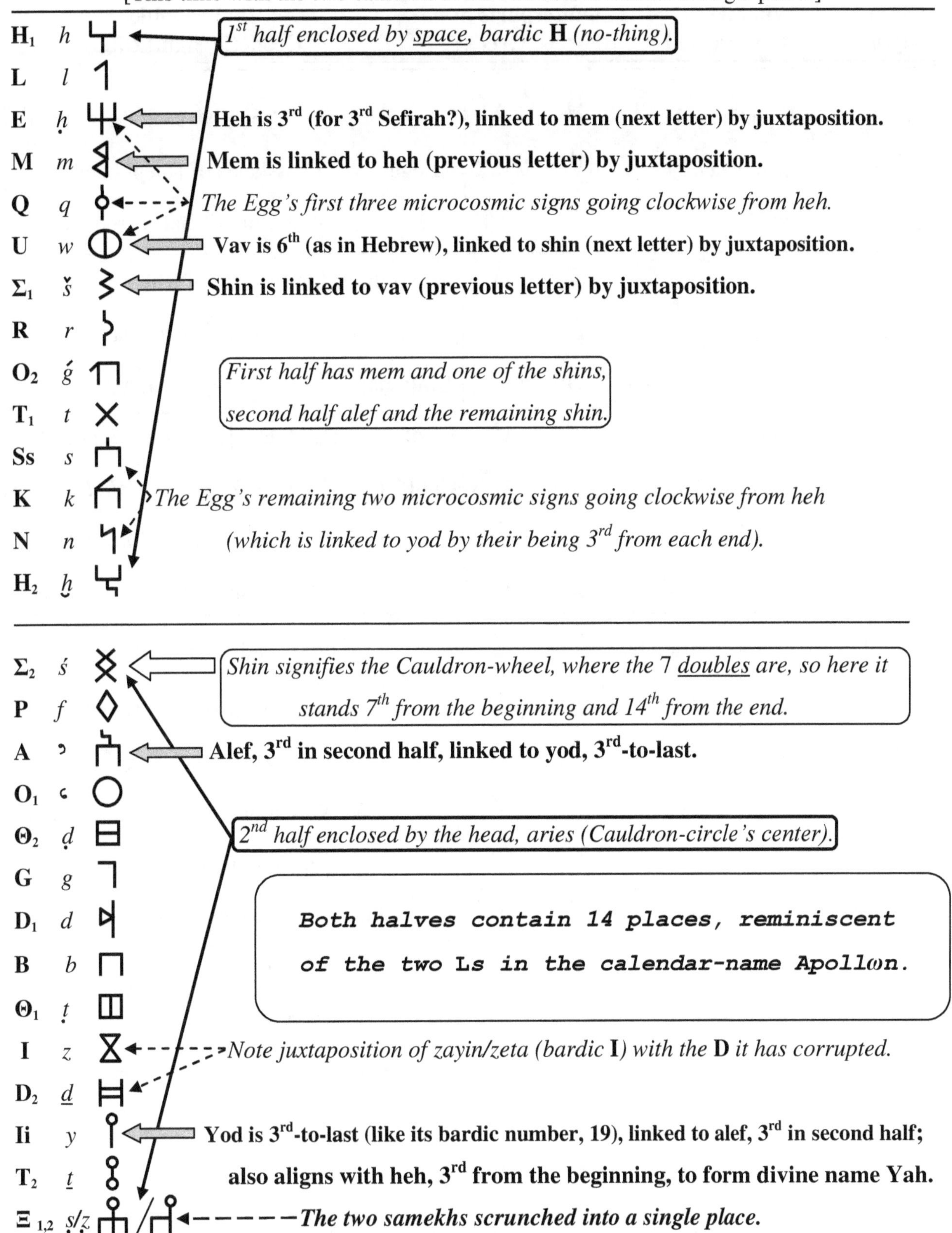

185

CHART 5: POSSIBLE GEODETIC INTERPRETATION

Hiero-glyph	What it Represented	(Counterparts in Hebrew, Greek)		Its Probable Geodetic Signification
ꜣ (ʾ)	Egyptian vulture	א	A	Center of Anatolia
w	quail chick	[שׁ→Σ] Ω		**Logos** · Grasslands of Dnepr bend
m	owl	מ	M	Eastern limit of Baltic (roughly)
d	hand	ד	Δ	Northern Alps, source of Rhine & Danube
ṯ	tongs	ת	T	Tyrrhenian Sea
k	basket with handle	כ	K	**Stations** · Libyan coast
r	mouth	ר	P	**of** · *UPPER* [Giza] *EGYPT*
g	alchemical oven	ג	ΓΧ	**Cauldron** ∪ Syrian Desert; Ϟ *Nafud Desert*
p	reed stool	פ	Π	∪ Southern Azerbaijan; Ϟ *Central Arabia*
b	foot and ankle	ב	B	∪ Kirghiz-Kazak steppe; Ϟ *Gulf of Aden*
ḥ	wick of twisted flax	ס	Ξ	Grasslands within Dnepr bend
s	folded cloth	צ	[Ψ]	Mouths (*throat*) of Danube
ḫ	sieve	ח	H	Mountains of northern Greece
f	horned viper	ו	Y	West coast of Greece, Ulysses' home
ʿ	forearm	ע	O	Straits 'twixt Greece and Crete
q	hill slope	ק	[Φ]	**Zodiac** · Kyrene (Cyrenaica)
ṯ	round loaf	ט	Θ	**Signs** *LOWER* [Giza] *EGYPT*
h	reed shelter in field	ה	E	○ Moab; Ϛ ~ *Gulf of Aqaba*
ꜣ	flowering reed	ז	Z	○ Upper Mesopotamia; Ϛ *The Hejaz*
y	two reed-flowers	י	I	○ Source of Tigris and Euphrates; Ϛ *Mecca*
rw	recumbent lion	ל	Λ	○ Caucasus at Black Sea; Ϛ *N. tip of Eritrea*
n	surface of water	נ	N	○ Sea of Azov; Ϛ *Eastern Sudanese desert*

REFERENCES FOR ALPHABETIC TABLES & CHARTS

Letters (except square Hebrew, Classical Greek, and Ugaritic), all hieroglyphs and their hieratic forms, drawn by me, these last copied (mostly) from Isaac Taylor's *The Alphabet: An Account of the Origin and Development of Letters* (London: Kegan Paul, Trench, & Co., 1883).

Table Zero uses Graves's spellings for tree-letters, for easy reference. Note: some letter-names may not be names of trees in Irish, yet refer to them (as is clear from the *Book of Ballymote* and from O'Flaherty). For example, *úr,* heather, means 'earth': compare English *heath.*

Egyptian Hieroglyphics: primary source, Gardiner, and for Ptolemaic use (in table 7), Budge.

Sabean, Thamudic, and early Ethiopic: primary source, Bernal (table 9, p. 60).

Nordic Tifinag (tables 5 & 6): Fell, *Bronze Age America* (table 2, p. 103).

Berber Tifinag (tables 5 & 6): Fell, op.cit. (p. 14), and Bernal (table 8, p. 50).

Numidian/Libyan (tables 5 & 6): Bernal (table 8, p. 50, from H. Jensen, *Sign, Symbol, and Script: An Account of Man's Efforts to Write*, third edition, fig. 118, p. 155).

Meroitic (table 7): various online sites (they come and go), and Peter T. Daniels and William Bright, ed., *The World's Writing Systems*, p. 85.

Runes (table 8): I have been unable to identify title or author of the source of my original notes!

Italic alphabets (table 9): Etruscan and Latin, *Encyclopedia Britannica* (early 50s ed.); Messapic, Bernal (table 5, p. 39).

Greek alphabets (table 9): Chalcidic and Attica, *Encyclopedia Britannica* (early 50s ed.); Samos, Bernal (table 1, p. 13); Formello, Bernal (same) and the inscriptions themselves.

Anatolian alphabets (table 10): Bernal (table 3, p. 34; *his* source, J. Friedrich, *Extinct Languages* [New York: Philosophical Library, 1957], fig. 49, p. 103).

Both Ugaritic long order (chart 2) and South Semitic (chart 3) are given in Bernal (p. 69): it was my choice, in the former to take *t* as the last *formal* letter, in the latter to decide between *ǧ* and *b* in 9th and 22nd positions (based on Beth Shemesh short abecedarium) and to place *w* 6th, which Bernal accidently omitted (as I discovered on looking up the Beth Shemesh abecedarium online).

Chart 5 was extrapolated from Stecchini's appendix to Tompkins' *Secrets of the Great Pyramid* and from Gnosticism's 'Hymn of the Pearl' (in Jonas, *The Gnostic Religion*, pp. 113*f*, 116*ff*).

References

[1] Robert Graves, *The White Goddess: A historical grammar of poetic myth* (New York: Farrar, Straus & Giroux, 1948)—hereafter referred to as *tWG*.

[2] Aryeh Kaplan, *Sefer Yetzirah: The Book of Creation* (York Beach, ME: Samuel Weiser, 1990), pp. 150*f*—hereafter this work will be referred to as 'Kaplan, *SY*'.

[3] *tWG*, pp. 165, 174, 183, 190.

[4] Kaplan, *SY*, p. 159.

[5] *tWG*, p. 236.

[6] Gershom Scholem: *Major Trends in Jewish Mysticism* (N.Y.: Schocken Books, 1974 [orig. 1946]), pp. 119*ff*; *Origins of the Kabbalah* (Jewish Publication Society Princeton University Press, 1987 [orig. German 1962]), pp. 46, 83, 200, 202; and *Kabbalah* (N.Y.: Meridian, 1978), pp. 4*f*.

[7] Harold W. Percival, *Thinking and Destiny* (Dallas: The Word Foundation, Inc., 1974 [orig. 1946]), pp. 943, 950, 954*f* [pp. 859, 866, 871*f*], hereafter referred to as *T&D*. A recent edition was altered to include the small book *Masonry and Its Symbols* as a chapter, which changed the page numbers; so page numbers for that later (eleventh) edition you will find in brackets after each citation.

[8] Kaplan, *SY*, pp. 42, 43, 79.

[9] Mircea Eliade, *Shamanism: Archaic Techniques of Ecstasy* (Princeton: Princeton University Press, 1964), pp. 99, 133, 493.

[10] Jacob Grimm, *Teutonic Mythology* (in four volumes), translated with notes and appendix by James Steven Stallybrass (New York: Dover Publications, 1966), vol. 1, pp. 210*f*.

[11] *tWG*, chapters 2 and 3.

[12] Barry Fell, *Bronze Age America* (Boston: Little, Brown & Company, 1982).

[13] Betty Jo Teeter Dobbs, *The Foundations of Newton's Alchemy, or "The Hunting of the Greene Lyon"* (New York: Cambridge University Press, 1975).

[14] *T&D*, pp. 773*ff* [pp. 711*ff*].

[15] *T&D*, pp. 793*f* [p. 729].

[16] Raphael Patai, *The Jewish Alchemists: A History and Source Book* (Princeton: Princeton University Press, 1994), p. 162*f*, and Gershom Scholem, *Alchemy and Kabbalah* (Putnam, CT: Spring Publications, 2006), p. 29.

[17] Aryeh Kaplan, *Meditation and Kabbalah* (York Beach, ME: Samuel Weiser, 1982), p. 1.

[18] Kieren Barry, *The Greek Qabalah: Alphabetic Mysticism and Numerology in the Ancient World* (York Beach, ME: Samuel Weiser, 1999).

[19] Gershom Scholem, *Major Trends in Jewish Mysticism* (New York: Schocken Books, 1974), p. 100.

[20] Ibid.

[21] J. Williams ab Ithel, ed., *The Barddas of Iolo Morganwg: A Collection of Original Documents, Illustrative of the Theology, Wisdom, and Usages of the Bardo-Druidic System of the Isle of Britain* (Boston: WeiserBooks, 2004).

[22] Ian Rutherford, "Apollo in Ivy: The Tragic Paean" (p. 120), in *Arion: A Journal of Humanities and the Classics*, Third series, vol. 3, no. 1 (Boston: Boston University, 1995); and of course the opening of *The Bacchae* by Euripides.

[23] *Barddas*, pp. 75, 79.

[24] Martin Bernal, *Cadmean Letters: The Transmission of the Alphabet to the Aegean and Further West before 1400 B.C.* (Winona Lake: Eisenbrauns, 1990), pp. 121*f*.

[25] Harold Waldwin Percival, *Masonry and Its Symbols: In the Light of Thinking and Destiny* (New York: The Word Publishing Company, 1952), p. 36 [*T&D*, later edition, p. 686].

[26] Henry Charles Lea, *The Inquisition of the Middle Ages*, an abridgment by Margaret Nicholson (New York: The Macmillan company, 1961), chapters 3, 4, 6, and 10.

[27] *tWG*, p. 190.

[28] *tWG*, pp. 125, 249*f*.

[29] *tWG*, p. 236.

[30] Ibid.

[31] *T&D*, p. 674 [p. 592].

[32] *Clement of Alexandria*, G. W. Butterworth, tr. (New York: G. P. Putnam's Sons, 1919), p. 45.

---

33 Aryeh Kaplan, tr., intro., and commentary, *The Bahir: Illumination* (York Beach, ME: Samuel Weiser, 1979), p. 31.

34 Gershom Scholem, *Kabbalah* (N.Y.: Meridian, 1978), p. 42.

35 Loeb Classical Library, Plato vol. V, *The Republic, vol. 1* (Cambridge: Harvard University Press, 1982), pp. 521*ff*.

36 *T&D*, pp. 333, 336*f*, 885 [pp. 292, 295*f*, 808].

37 *T&D*, p. 336 [p. 294].

38 Ralph J. Fessenden and Joan S. Fessenden, *The Basis of Organic Chemistry* (Boston: Allyn & Bacon, 1971), p. 326.

39 Kaplan, *SY*, pp. 174*ff*, and the table on pp. 178*f*.

40 C. G. Jung, *Alchemical Studies* (Princeton: Princeton University Press, 1967), p. 185.

41 Percival, *Masonry and Its Symbols*, p. 29 [*T&D*, later edition, p. 682]

42 *T&D*, p. 419 [p. 367].

43 S. Mahdihassan, *Indian Alchemy or Rasayana: In the Light of Asceticism and Geriatrics* (Delhi: Motilal Banarsidass Publishers, 1991), pp. 81, 96.

44 *The Epigraphic Society Occasional Publications and Papers* (Arlington, MA: [archives of the] Dawson Library, 1975*ff*)—hereafter called *ESOP*—vols. 1*f*, and Barry Fell, *America B.C.: Ancient Settlers in the New World* (N.Y.: Pocket Books, Wallaby, 1978), pp. 176, 178, 180, 187.

45 Fell, *America B.C.*, pp. 176, 268; and *Bronze Age America*, pp. 278*ff*.

46 Fell, *America B.C.*, pp. 182, 269*ff*.

47 Barry Fell, *Saga America* (New York: Times Books, 1983), pp. 17, 230, 243, 246*ff*, 250*ff*.

48 Fell, *America B.C.*, chapter 12.

49 Max Freedom Long, *The Huna Code in Religions: The Influence of the Huna Tradition on Modern Faith* (Marina del Rey, CA: DeVorss & Co., 1965), pp. 33*f*.

50 Discussed in the works of Max Freedom Long, as well as in Dr. Erika S. Nau, *Self Awareness through Huna* (Virginia Beach, VA.: Donning Co., Unilaw, 1981).

51 Long, *Huna Code*, pp. 30, 48, 68*ff* (see also Hawaiian dictionary at the end).

---

[52] Long, op.cit., pp. 47, 49.

[53] Long, op.cit., pp. 76*f.*

[54] *T&D*, p. 420 [p. 368].

[55] See for instance *tWG*, p. 70.

[56] C. G. Jung, *Psychology and Alchemy* (Princeton: Princeton University Press, 1968), p. 229.

[57] See, for example, *The World's Writing Systems*, Peter T. Daniels and William Bright, editors (New York: Oxford University Press, 1996), pp. 25, 29, 82, 90.

[58] Isaac Taylor, *The Alphabet: An Account of the Origin and Development of Letters* (London: K. Paul, Trench & Company, 1883), chapter 2; also, tables found in many old Bibles.

[59] Hans Jonas, *The Gnostic Religion: The Message of the Alien God and the Beginnings of Christianity* (Boston: Beacon Press, 1971), pp. 77, 93, 108n, 109, 187*f.*

[60] *T&D*, pp. 810*ff*, 967 [pp. 743*ff*, 884]

[61] *T&D*, pp. 842*f* [pp. 771*f*].

[62] *T&D*, p. 401 [p. 351].

[63] *T&D*, pp. 499, 459 [pp. 438, 403].

[64] Carl B. Boyer, *The History of the Calculus and its Conceptual Development* (New York: Dover Publications, 1959), esp. pp. 48*ff*.

[65] A. J. Arberry, *Sufism: An Account of the Mystics of Islam* (New York: Harper & Row, 1970), p. 98.

[66] *T&D*, pp. 855*ff*, 970 [pp. 782*ff*, 887].

[67] *T&D*, pp. 860*f*, 972 [pp. 787, 889].

[68] *T&D*, pp. 522, 198 [pp. 458, 175].

[69] *T&D*, pp. 845*f* [p. 774].

[70] Fell, *Bronze Age America.*

[71] Fell, *America B.C.*, pp. 262*ff*, 268.

[72] Giorgio de Santillana & Hertha von Dechend, *Hamlet's Mill: An Essay Investigating the Origins of Human Knowledge and its Transmission through Myth* (Boston: David R. Godine, 1992), p. 306.

[73] Peter Berresford Ellis, *The Druids* (Grand Rapids, MI: William B. Eerdmans, 1994), p. 224.

[74] Jacqueline Memory Paterson, *Tree Wisdom* (San Francisco: Thorsons [*An Imprint of* Harper Collins], 1996), pp. 225*f*.

[75] *T&D*, pp. 14, 80*f* [pp. 12, 71*f*].

[76] Alwyn Rees and Brinley Rees, *Celtic Heritage: Ancient Tradition in Ireland and Wales* (New York: Thames & Hudson, 1961), p. 198.

[77] Ellis, op.cit., p. 234.

[78] Kaplan, *SY*, pp. 197, 219.

[79] Kaplan, *SY*, pp. 139, 263.

[80] *Book of Formation (Sepher Yetzirah): The Letters of Our Father Abraham* (Los Angeles: Work of the Chariot, 1970), p. 1.

[81] See, for instance, Ellen Evert Hopman, *A Druid's Herbal of Sacred Tree Medicine* (Rochester, VT: Destiny Books, 2008), p. 74.

[82] Ellis, op.cit., p. 248.

[83] *McGraw-Hill Encyclopedia of Physics,* Sybil P. Parker, editor in chief (San Francisco: McGraw-Hill Book Company, 1983), p. 898.

[84] Rupert Sheldrake, *A New Science of Life: The Hypothesis of Formative Causation* (Los Angeles: J. P. Tarcher, 1981), and *The Presence of the Past: Morphic Resonance and the Habits of Nature* (New York: Times Books, 1988).

[85] Sheldrake, *A New Science of Life*, pp. 114, 119n4.

[86] Percival, *Masonry and its Symbols*, pp. 18*f, 35* [*T&D*, later edition, pp. 676, 685].

[87] Michael A. Cremo and Richard L. Thompson, *Forbidden Archeology: The Hidden History of the Human Race* (Los Angeles: Bhaktivedanta Book Publishing, 1996), especially pp. 454-8, 297-9, 805-814 (summarized 815*f*).

[88] Ellis, op.cit., p. 180.

[89] From Bertrand Russell's *A History of Western Philosophy* (1946), in Ellis, op.cit., p. 188.

[90] Percival, *Masonry and its Symbols*, p. 32 [*T&D*, later edition, p. 683].

[91] Patai, *The Jewish Alchemists*, pp. 162*f.*

[92] Percival, *Masonry and its Symbols*, pp. 39*ff* [*T&D*, later edition, pp. 686*ff*].

[93] C. Scott Littleton, *The New Comparative Mythology: An Anthropological Assessment of the Theories of Georges Dumézil* (Berkeley: University of California Press, 1973), its main theme.

[94] Raphael Patai, *The Hebrew Goddess*, third enlarged ed. (Detroit: Wayne State University, 1990), p. 162.
[95] Lewis Spence, *The Mysteries of Britain: The Secret Rites and Traditions of Ancient Britain Restored* (Van Nuys, CA: Newcastle Publishing, 1993), pp. 86*ff.*

[96] *Barddas*, p. 79.

[97] *Barddas*, p. 75.

[98] *tWG*, p. 123.

[99] *Barddas*, pp. 59, 63, 80, 89, 99, 141.

[100] *Barddas*, p. 59.

[101] Spence, *Mysteries of Britain*, p. 98.

[102] Scholem, *Kabbalah*, p. 107; Kaplan, *SY*, pp. 44*ff*, 71; Kaplan, *Bahir* (commentary), p. 175.

[103] Scholem, *Alchemy and Kabbalah* (Putnam, CT: Spring Publications, 2006), p. 74; Aryeh, *SY*, p. 184; Patai, *The Jewish Alchemists*, p. 123.

[104] Kaplan, *SY*, p. 271.

[105] Dr. Erich Bischoff, *The Kabbalah: An Introduction to Judaic Mysticism and Its Secret Doctrine* (York Beach, ME: Weiser, 1988 [orig. 1910]), p. 34.

[106] *T&D*, pp. 814*f*, 831*f* [pp. 747, 762].

[107] *T&D*, p.832 [p. 762].

[108] *T&D*, p. 973 [p. 892].

[109] *T&D*, p. 838 [p. 768].

[110] *T&D*, pp. 942*ff* [p. 858*ff*].

[111] *T&D*, p. 48 [p. 41*f*].

[112] *T&D*, p. 40 [p. 34*f*].

[113] *T&D*, p. 41 [p. 36].

[114] *T&D*, pp. 950*f* [pp. 866*f*].

[115] *T&D*, pp. 48*f* [pp. 42*f*].

[116] Scholem, *Kabbalah*, p. 130.

[117] Scholem, op.cit., p. 136.

[118] Scholem, op.cit., p. 137.

[119] Sanford L. Drob, *Symbols of the Kabbalah: Philosophical and Psychological Perspectives* (Northvale, NJ: Jason Aronson, 2000), p. 128.

[120] *tWG*, pp. 92, 158.

[121] Kaplan, *Bahir*, p.52.

[122] J.E. Cirlot, *A Dictionary of Symbols* (New York: Barnes & Noble, 1995), p. 281; and Scholem, *Kabbalah*, p. 367.

[123] *The Zohar*, tr. Harry Sperling and Maurice Simon (London: Soncino Press, 1934), vol. 1, p. 53; and Kaplan, *Bahir* (commentary), p. 92.

[124] Gershom Scholem, *Origins of the Kabbalah* (Princeton?: Jewish Publication Society, Princeton University Press, 1987), p. 313.

[125125] Kaplan, *Bahir* (commentary), p. 178.

[126] Scholem, *Kabbalah*, p. 110.

[127] Ibid.

[128] Ibid.

[129] Kaplan, *Bahir*, p. 57.

---

[130] Moshe Idel, *Ascensions on High in Jewish Mysticism: Pillars, Lines, Ladders* (New York: Central European University Press, 2005), chapters 2 and 3, esp. the quotes on pp. 80, 85.

[131] Kaplan, *Bahir*, p. 64.

[132] Scholem, *Kabbalah*, p. 107.

[133] Paraphrased in Spence, *Mysteries of Britain*, pp. 98*ff.*

[134] *Barddas*, p. 170, n. 1.

[135] Spence, op.cit., pp. 98*f.*

[136] Kaplan, *SY*, p. 71.

[137] Kaplan, *SY*, pp. 68, 71, 73.

[138] Kaplan, *SY*, p. 73.

[139] Kaplan, *SY*, p. 83.

[140] Kaplan, *SY*, pp. 88, 163.

[141] Kaplan, *SY*, p. 71.

[142] Kaplan, *SY*, p. 73.

[143] Kaplan, *SY*, p. 77.

[144] Kaplan, *SY*, p. 79.

[145] Quoted in Caitlín and John Matthews, *The Encyclopedia of Celtic Wisdom: The Celtic Shaman's Sourcebook* (Rockport, MA: Element, 1994), p. 52.

[146] Kaplan, *SY*, pp. 145, 148, 150.

[147] Kaplan, *SY*, p. 80.

[148] Kaplan, *SY*, p. 163.

[149] *T&D*, pp. 48, 315[pp. 42, 276*f*].

[150] *T&D*, pp. 316, 317 [pp. 277, 278].

[151] *T&D*, p. 317 [p. 278].

152 Yule custom has 'holly boys' and 'ivy girls' contending in game or satirical song (*tWG*, p. 184); there is even a Christmas carol entitled "The Holly and the Ivy."

153 Grimm, *Teutonic Mythology*, Vol. II, p. 651. He says: "According to the Ostgota-lag (bygdab. 30), any one may in a common wood hew with impunity, all but *oaks* and *hazels*, these have peace, *i.e.* immunity. In Superst. I, 972 we are told that oak and hazel dislike one another, and cannot agree, any more than haw and sloe (white and black thorn; see Suppl.)."

154 *Bulfinch's Mythology* (New York: Modern Library, Random House, no date), p. 263 (in chapter XXXVIII's initial section, called "Northern Mythology"); G. A. Gaskell, *Dictionary of All Scriptures and Myths* (New York: Gramercy Books, 1981), p. 75 (identified as symbols of desire-nature and instinct-nature); also Marijane Osborn and Stella Longland, *Rune Games* (Boston: Routledge & Kegan Paul, 1982), identifies Embla (the first woman) with alder, p. 88.

155 *tWG*, p. 168.

156 Kaplan, *SY*, p. 184, says most versions of *SY* list the planets in the order in which they were created Saturn-Jupiter-Mars-sun-Venus-Mercury-moon—but is unclear whether they attribute them to 3 through 9, or 4 through 10. I was sure I had seen a listing of various schemes Jewish scholars put forth, including the correct one, but I am unable to locate the source.

157 George de Bothezat, *Back to Newton: A Challenge to Einstein's Theory of Relativity* (New York: G. E. Stechert & Co., 1936), pp. 106*f.*

158 Andrew Tomas, *We Are Not the First* (London: Souvineer Press, 1971), pp. 93*f* (batteries, light bulbs); and you yourself can look up the *aeolipile* of Hero of Alexandria (a radial steam turbine).

159 Betty Jo Teeter Dobbs, op.cit., pp. 14, 16*f*, 20, 90 ("'The Dragon kild by Cadmus [in founding Thebes] is ye subject of our work, & his teeth are the matter purified'," Cadmus the one reputed to have brought Greeks letters), 106ff (esp. ¶ on 106*f*), 154, 175, 192.

160 C. Kerényi, *The Gods of the Greeks* (London: Thames & Hudson, 1951), p. 143.

161 *T&D*, pp. 581, 628 [pp. 510, 552].

162 *T&D*, p. 520 [pp. 456*f*].

163 Joseph Dan, ed., Ronald C. Kiener, trans. (of texts), *The Early Kabbalah* (New York: Paulist Press, 1986), pp. 128, 132n.

164 Fletcher G. Watson, *Between the Planets* (Philadelphia: Blakiston Co., 1941), pp. 19*ff.*

165 See Cremo and Thompson, *Forbidden Archeology.*

[166] Hilton Ratcliffe, *The Static Universe: Exploding the myth of Cosmic Expansion* (Montreal: Apeiron, 2010), pp. 84*f*.

[167] See Halton Arp, *Seeing Red: Redshifts, Cosmology and Academic Science* (Montreal: Apeiron, 1998).

[168] *T&D*, p. 704 [p. 619].

[169] Kaplan, *SY*, p. 80.

[170] *T&D*, p. 658 [p. 577].

[171] Drob, *Symbols*, p. 181.

[172] Kaplan, *SY*, p. 81.

[173] Patai, *The Hebrew Goddess*, pp. 166*f* (from a popular short version of Luria's own formula), p. 172 (from Nathan of Hannover, sixteenth to seventeenth century), pp. 189*f* ("to unify the Name—yud-kei with vav-kei," from modern Hasidic-American *Complete Art Scroll Siddur*, pp. 4*f*), and p. 191 (from the modern Sephardic *Siddur Bet Yosef v'Ohel Avraham*, p. 129).

[174] *T&D*

[175] Patai, *The Hebrew Goddess*, p. 52.

[176] Patai, *The Hebrew Goddess*, p. 171.

[177] Kaplan, *SY*, p. 81.

[178] *T&D*, p. 658 [p. 578].

[179] Kaplan, *SY*, p. 81.

[180] See, for instance, the Soncino *Zohar*, vol. 1, pp. 158*f*.

[181] *T&D*, pp. 480*f* [p. 421*f*].

[182] *T&D*, p. 846*f* [pp. 774*f*].

[183] *T&D*, p. 468 [p. 410].

[184] E. V. Gordon, *An Introduction to Old Norse* (Oxford: Clarendon Press, 1957), p. xxxii.

185 *Book of Formation (Sepher Yetzirah): The Letters of Our Father Abraham* (Los Angeles: Work of the Chariot, 1970), p. 6.

186 Discussed in Bothezat, *Back to Newton*, pp. 96*ff*.

187 Sheldrake, *A New Science of Life* and *The Presence of the Past*.

188 *Zohar: The Book of Splendor (Basic Readings from the Kabbalah)*, selected and edited by Gershom Scholem (New York: Schocken Books, 1949), p. 40.

189 *T&D*, p. 579*f* [p. 508].

190 Arthur M. Young, *The Reflexive Universe: Evolution of Consciousness* (Lake Oswego, OR: Robert Briggs Associates, 1976).

191 Arthur M. Young, *Mathematics, Physics & Reality: Two Essays* (Portland, OR: Robert Briggs Associates, 1990), pp. 92*ff*.

192 Kaplan, *SY*, pp. 80, 82.

193 Kaplan, *SY*, p. 83.

194 E. A. Wallis Budge, *The Gods of the Egyptians, or Studies in Egyptian Mythology* (N.Y.: Dover Publications, Inc., 1969) [orig. Chicago: The Open Court Publishing Co., 1904], vol. II, pp. 296-299.

195 Taylor, *The Alphabet*, p. 67.

196 Sir Alan Gardiner, *Egyptian Grammar: Being an Introduction to the Study of Hieroglyphs*, third edition (Oxford: Griffith Institute, Ashmolean Museum, 1957), p. 27.

197 Mircea Eliade, *The Forge and the Crucible: The Origin and Structures of Alchemy* (New York: Harper & Row, 1962) shows the extreme antiquity of the metallurgical traditions that *led* to alchemy.

198 Gardiner, *Egyptian Grammar*, p. 525.

199 Giorgio de Santillana & Hertha von Dechend, op.cit., pp. 322*f*.

200 Professor Livio Catullo Stecchini's appendix (pp. 287-382) to Peter Tompkins' *Secrets of the Great Pyramid* (New York: Harper Collophon Books, 1978) called 'Notes on the Relation of Ancient Measures to the Great Pyramid', pp. 327-331.

201 Stecchini, op.cit., pp. 348*ff*.

[202] Stecchini, op.cit., p. 346.

[203] Jonas, *The Gnostic Religion*, pp. 113*f*, 116*ff*.

[204] John Gardner and John Maier, tr., *Gilgamesh: Translated from the Sîn-leqi-unninnī version* (New York: Vintage Books, a division of Random House, 1984).

[205] Gardner and Maier, op.cit., pp. 26*ff*.

[206] Gardner and Maier, op.cit., Tablet I, column ii (p. 67).

[207] *T&D*, pp. 35*f* [p. 31].

[208] Gardner and Maier, op.cit., Tablet IX, column ii (p. 198).

[209] Gardner and Maier, op.cit., Tablet X, column ii (p. 213).

[210] Gardner and Maier, op.cit., Tablet X, column iii (p. 217) and p. 218.

[211] Gardner and Maier, op.cit., Tablet XI, column i (p. 226).

[212] Ibid.

[213] Arberry, *Sufism*, p. 111.

[214] Giorgio de Santillana & Hertha von Dechend, op.cit., p. 438*n*.

[215] Gardiner, *Egyptian Grammar*, p. 482.

[216] Giorgio de Santillana & Hertha von Dechend, op.cit., p. 448*n*.

[217] Bernal, *Cadmean Letters*, pp. 78, 101.

[218] *tWG*, p. 211.

[219] Expounded upon in Fell's *Bronze Age America*.

[220] Grimm, *Teutonic Mythology*, vol. 1, p. 131.

[221] Paterson, *Tree Wisdom*, p. 255.

[222] C. Kerényi, op.cit., p. 114.

[223] *The Kalevala: An Epic Poem After Oral Tradition by Elias Lönnrot*, tr. from the Finnish with an Introduction and Notes by Keith Bosley (U.K.: Oxford University Press, 1989), p. xxiii.

---

[224] Bernal, *Cadmean Letters*, pp. 92f.

[225] Ben Edwin Perry, tr. and ed., *Babrius and Phaedrus* (Cambridge, MA: Harvard University Press, 1984).

[226] Fell, *Bronze Age America*, p. 127.

[227] Fell, op.cit., p. 128.

[228] See Eric J. Lerner, *The Big Bang Never Happened* (New York: Vintage Books, 1992), as well as the work of Anthony Peratt (on a more technical level).

[229] See Petr Beckmann, *Einstein Plus Two* (Boulder, CO: The Golem Press, 1987).

[230] This is the main theme of Halton Arp's *Seeing Red*.

[231] Brian Greene, *The Elegant Universe: Superstrings, Hidden Dimensions, and the Quest for the Ultimate Theory* (New York: W. W. Norton & Company, 2010).

[232] See Bernard Aschner, Md., *Arthritis Can Be Cured* (New York: Arco Publishing Inc., 1979).